Bangalore
4/2014

MARVELS & MYSTERIES
OF THE
MAHABHARATA

PROBING THE FOLDS OF INDIA'S EPOCHAL TRAGEDY

ABHIJIT BASU

PLATINUM PRESS

ISBN 978-93-81836-78-1
© Abhijit Basu, 2013
Cover   Brand Masala
Layouts   Chandravadan R. Shiroorkar, Leadstart Design
Editing   Suchita Vemuri
Printing   Manipal Technologies Ltd

Published in India 2013 by
PLATINUM PRESS
An imprint of
LEADSTART PUBLISHING PVT LTD
Trade Centre, Level 1, Bandra Kurla Complex
Bandra (E), Mumbai 400 051, INDIA
T + 91 22 40700804   **F** +91 22 40700800
E info@leadstartcorp.com **W** www.leadstartcorp.com
US Office Axis Corp, 7845 E Oakbrook Circle, Madison, WI 53717, USA

To
Ratna, Manu, Urmi & Vihit

ABOUT THE AUTHOR

ABHIJIT BASU, one-time research scientist and former administrator of government finances, is presently engaged as part-time independent director in the corporate sector. An avowed admirer of the ideal of the Renaissance Man, Basu has also been a life-long follower of the liberal arts, especially Sanskrit, English and Bengali literature, and history, apart from his keen interest in the sciences.

Of late, Basu has been busy as an author and polymath editor, covering a broad spectrum of topics and ideas. His first book, 'a collection of critical, scholarly and absorbing essays,' titled *Prophets, Poets and Philosopher-Kings: Sketches on India's Spiritual & Literary Heritage* (Celestial Books 2012), was well received: *Versatile scholar Abhijit Basu's analytical and interdisciplinary research into the eternal and transnational relevance of the overwhelming ancient India, enriched with lucid prose and current bibliography, is invaluable for aspiring researchers and students of literature and cultural studies.* (The Tribune, 20 May 2012.)

Basu hails from an old Kolkata-based house of civil servants, professionals and academics. He considers himself blessed in having had gentle exemplars as parents, and now an attached family to shower affections upon. Abhijit Basu can be reached at: a_basu5@yahoo.com

CONTENTS

INTRODUCTION

THE *MAHABHARATA* ~ SOME NUANCES, SOME FACTS

Vyasa's *Mahabharata*, with its enormous spread and depth, has engaged readers and writers through the ages in search of ever-newer insights. The introductory words of Sauti – that while some can memorise the epic, others are inspired to comment upon it – are as true today as on the occasion of its pristine narration in the old *Naimisha* grove. The Great Epic of India is a narrative apart. It is unique in its multiplicity of facets: as literature in the form of poetic drama; as a chronicle comprising a core of history overlaid with legend and myth; and as an encyclopaedia of ancient philosophy (with the *Bhagavad-Gita* as an eternal bequest to mankind), secular knowledge and thought. The grand appeal of the *Mahabharata* lies in this plurality of characteristics – something not found matched by any other epic of the world.

The *Mahabharata* is more regaling to those who look at it with a macro-vision rather than with a narrow tunnel-view. Admittedly, it has a good deal of 'mythical' content. But its value as great literature sinks in only when there is a 'willing suspension of disbelief'. After all, supernatural episodes like Yudhishthira's exchanges with the crane-guard (*baka-yaksha*), or his last great journey to heaven, are quintessential to the *Mahabharata*'s timeless charm. Then again, is Yudhishthira himself fact or fiction? Vedic literature makes no reference to him, though his (or rather his brother Arjuna's,) descendants – Pareekshit and Janamejaya – find mention therein. Panini, of the late Vedic age, does however illustrate the grammatical significance of his name.[i] Similarly, for all the perceived layers of didactic deposits on the Krshna story, there plausibly was a towering personality at the core of those abiding legends. True, the battle of Kurukshetra was not quite as calamitous as some modern wars the world has seen, yet it is hard to discount the age-old civilisational memory of a great tribal conflict that sucked into its implosive vortex warriors from practically the entire Indian subcontinent and its neighbourhood.

Today's general stance on the *Mahabharata* story seems to lie somewhere between the two extremes of diehard scepticism and rigid faith, with regard to its historical core. Now, if one accepts the authenticity of the *Mahabharata* war, the next logical question is: when did it happen? After sifting the available collateral indications, three dates emerge – 3100 BC (derived from an Aryabhata reference); 1500 BC (Bronze Age); and 1000 BC (Iron Age). Taking a median-conservative reckoning and the broad time-band of the two later dates (1500-1000 BC), this is what was happening in India and the world at around the time of the Kurukshetra battle.[ii]

In the Indian subcontinent, the Indus Valley Civilisation had vanished and Indo-Aryans were spreading across its northern plains, heralding the initial transition from a pastoral-farming-warrior culture to a proto-urban farming-warrior one. There was also some shift in the nuances of India's spiritual continuum. The early Vedic elemental gods – Indra, Agni, and Surya – were gradually being overshadowed by the triad of Brahma, Vishnu, and Rudra-Shiva, with the third absorbing much of the so-called pre-Aryan faith. There was also a parallel intellectual movement towards Vedantic monism.

China, in those 500 years, was laying its own milestones of an advanced literate civilisation, expanding progressively from the initial Shang to the later Zhou dynasties, with rice-farming continuing to spread into Southeast Asia and the Korean peninsula. Around the same time, in West Asia, the powerful Bronze Age empires of the Hittites (Asia Minor), and Babylonia, as well as the Mediterranean Egyptian Empire, waxed and waned, alongside newer developments such as the use of iron, invention of the alphabet, and the rise of monotheistic Israel. Europe too, was experiencing upheavals, with the Greek (Mycenaean) and Cretan (Minoan) civilisations initially flourishing and then sinking into oblivion, to the accompaniment of large population movements.

Coming to the description of the *Mahabharata* war, if one discounts such arguable exaggerations as use of 'celestial' missiles, the rest contains interesting leads to the organisation and conduct of war in those days. The basic army formation was built round Divisions (*Akshauhini*) comprising four parts (*Caturanga*): elephants, cavalry, chariots and infantry. War elephants were first employed in India, the practice extending to the Greeks, Persians, and the Mediterranean. To ancient soldiers and their horses, a rampaging elephant with its humongous bulk and destructive power, presented a potently intimidating spectacle. Alexander himself was so impressed by the war elephants of Porus and the Nanda Empire that he established an elephant force to guard his palace at Babylon, and created the post of Elephantarch, to lead his pachyderm units.[iii] Later, the Carthaginians, under Hannibal, with their elephant units, wrought havoc in the Roman ranks in the early Punic War, till the genius of Scipio Africanus devised a strategy to trap or goad away those formidable beasts in the final Roman victory at the Battle of Zama (202 BC).[iv]

It is in the matter of war ethics that the Kurukshetra battle stands out by virtue of its civilised norms. The rules for the conduct of war, mutually agreed upon by the opposing sides, are described at some length in the very first chapter of the *Bheeshma-parva* (see Supplementary Notes), and are no less chivalrous than the modern international protocols laid down in The Hague and Geneva Conventions of 1907 and 1949 respectively. After sunset, there was to be a break in hostilities (but there were occasions when engagements spilled into the night). One who resorted to a war of words (to galvanise oneself or intimidate the opponent), was to be countered with words – weapons were to be used only with due notice. An unready or otherwise overwhelmed opponent was not to be struck. Nor was harm to be directed at one who was unarmed, bereft of his carrier, seeking mercy, or without protective armour. Soldiers leaving their formation were not to be killed. Fighting was to be between equals – charioteers with charioteers; cavalry with cavalry; elephant-riders with elephant-riders; and infantry with infantry. Under no circumstances were non-combatant helpers to be attacked. Engagements were to be on the battlefield only, at agreed hours. This rule was, however, breached by Ashvatthama in the *Sauptika-parva*. There were other interesting facets to the war. The main protagonists had chariots with four horses. The flag-staff rose from within the chariot; when injured, the warrior would hold onto it for support. Famous chariot-warriors were surrounded by guards, and had vehicles laden with shafts and other missiles. There were also brothel-camps near the battlefield.

No less interesting is the picture of contemporary social mores the *Mahabharata* presents. It was not an overly intolerant society. The caste (or rather 'class') system, was in its early stages, with more emphasis on division of duties than on iron-clad stratification of society. Even in the matter of duties, honourable exceptions were allowed, but more in regard to the *Brahmanas*. Vishvaamitra of pre-*Mahabharata* days was an exception, where a *Kshatriya* achieved Brahminical status. Leading *Brahmanas*, such as Drona and Krpa, were revered for their mastery of the art of war, which was regarded as a major discipline of study. But Drona's action in destroying thousands of ordinary soldiers with his 'celestial' weapon was denounced by sages as contrary to righteous war, and Bheema chastised him for grossly violating his Brahminical *dharma*. In fact, from the *Drona-parva* onwards, there was a definite degeneration in the ethics of war by both armies, seemingly symptomatic of the imminence of the amoral *Kali* epoch. It was not uncommon to assimilate in society worthy barbarians and vanquished aborigines as *Kshatriya*s and *Dasa*s respectively. The admixture of *varnas* (classes) was generally feared, but in the *Anushaasana-parva*, Bheeshma mentions umpteen examples of it. Untouchability was not generally prevalent and highborn were served food by slaves.

Some *Brahmanas* and practically all *Kshatriya*s ate meat. Imbibing sacrificial wine (*soma*), was the prerogative of the *Brahmanas* and *Kshatriyas*, while the consumption of other liquor (*suraa*), was common among all sections. There are references to beef-eating and cattle-sacrifices, but such practices were generally abhorred at the time the *Mahabharata* was composed. Horse sacrifices, a Proto-Indo-European practice, involved gruesome rituals. Human sacrifices were denigrated; although Jarasandha planned many of those. Gambling was a popular sport, especially among the *Kshatriyas*, who looked upon dice-play as a way of life.

A son was considered a passport to heaven, leading to the practice of *kshetraja* births. Women were usually respected and protected, but at times were bought, sold, and put up as stakes in games of dice. There was also the custom of presenting beautiful maids as slaves to kings and dignitaries, again suggesting a certain tendency to look upon women as property. However, there seems to have been no gender discrimination, since male slaves too were staked in dice and presented as gifts. Kings often had several wives and concubines; but a man with a single wife was considered eminently virtuous. There are instances of widows dying with their husbands. But many, such as Satyavati, Kunti, Subhadraa and Uttaraa, lived on with their sons and families.[v]

These are some of the nuances and period pictures a discerning reader may elicit from the *Mahabharata*. But India's great epochal tragedy has much more to offer by way of the marvels and mysteries that characterise its *dramatis personae* on the one hand and its historicity on the other. This book is an attempt to unravel some of those intriguing characteristics that make the epic so very enthralling in its totality.

NOTES & REFERENCES

i. Panini, a Sanskrit grammarian from Pushkalavati in ancient Gandhara, belonged to the 6th century BC. His great book of Sanskrit grammar, *Ashtaadhyaayee* (Eight Chapters), is the world's earliest known treatise on descriptive linguistics. For Panini's illustration of the grammatical basis of the name 'Yudhishthira', see Note 6.2 under Chapter 6.

ii. Some global civilisational milestones during the period 1500-1000 BC, are crisply depicted in *Time Map of World History*, http://www.timemaps.com/history/world-1000bc

iii. Among the ancient historical records of the campaigns of Alexander, mention may be made of two Roman works: Plutarch's *The Life of Alexander the Great*, Random House Publishing, 2004 (where Plutarch mentions, *inter alia*, that the army of the Magadha-based Nanda Empire had 6,000 war elephants); and also, *Life of Alexander the Great, Book-VIII* by Quintus Curtius Rufus, available at: http://penelope. uchicago.edu/Thayer/E/Roman/Texts/Curtius/home.html As regards modern studies on war elephants and Alexander establishing his own elephant force in Babylon, the following may be referred to: Konstantin Nossov, *War Elephants*, Osprey Publishing, Oxford/New York, 2008, p.19.

iv. James Lacey, *Rome's Craftiest General: Scipio Africanus*, Military History Magazine, 8 June 2007: http://www.historynet.com/ romes-craftiest-general-scipio-africanus.htm Here is a relevant extract: *After some initial skirmishing, Hannibal sent his 80 war elephants forward. But this was a different Roman army than the one he had faced at Cannae—tougher and more disciplined, led by men accustomed to Hannibal's tactics. Faced with the choice of smashing into the heavily armed legionnaires or running unimpeded through the gaps in their formations, most of the elephants took the path of least resistance and passed harmlessly through the Roman army. Others, frightened by the blasts of massed Roman trumpeters, ran down their own cavalry.*

v. Several such period practices are mentioned in the introductory chapter of Rajshekhar Basu's *Mahabharat Saranuvad* (Bengali), M.C. Sarkar & Sons, Calcutta, 1949 (Bengali calendar: 1356), 10th reprint: 1987.

PART I

~~~~~~~~~~~~~~~~~~~~~~~~

THE STORY

~~~~~~

PART I: THE STORY

1 The Enigmatic Saint-Chronicler

Is Vyasa mere myth, or a legend central to the *itihaasa* of the *Mahabharata*? Unlike Homer, about whose life and personality 'antiquity knew nothing definite', Vyasa, with his illustrious family lineage, and outstanding corpus of Vedic-Puranic works, stands out as a figure of commanding presence and rare versatility. An enigma personified, he is the elusive narrator who prefers to let others narrate for him, and still has the penchant of appearing from nowhere as an insider-outsider, to impact the lives of seven generations of the Kuru dynasty. Born of a fisherwoman and an illustrious *Brahmana* sage, his mixed birth and elevating tutelage (under his sage-father), add to his enigmatic status as the scholar-saint who is called, through the practice of *niyoga*, to procreate Kuru heirs.

Pandu, Vyasa's crowned offspring; and Vidura, his half-breed son, are enigmas in their own right. The former, with his unusually pale complexion; his supposed impotency; his wandering asceticism; his *kshetraja* sons, and his mystery-laden death, has been the subject of unending speculations. Vidura, endowed with qualities of mind and body, and hence better suited to rule than either of his two brothers, was disqualified on account of his mixed birth. As Pandu's younger brother, he could have been the natural choice, according to the system of *niyoga*, to father the childless king's *kshetraja* sons. Some commentators do support that hypothesis. We cannot be sure, but the special attachment and temperamental similarities between Vidura and Yudhishthira (as personifications of *dharma*), whose bodies and souls reportedly merge at Vidura's hair-raising scene of death, do keep us guessing.

Duryodhana and the Kauravas were Vyasa's direct descendants; the Pandavas, with their *kshetraja* origin, were not. Still, the great sage did his best to secure a fair peace for the latter by appealing to Dhrtarashtra's sense of duty. He is the *Mahabharata*'s self-effacing voice of conscience, who supported the righteous cause of the Pandavas against the unrighteous inheritors of his bloodline.

2 Pilgrim's Progress

Yudhishthira fascinates us in a cerebral sense. He is the *Mahabharata*'s *jnana yogi*, perfectly complementing Arjuna, the epic's *karma yogi*.

Also fascinating are his contrarieties as a *Kshatriya* prince with the disposition of a true *Brahmana*, ever conflicted by his natural inclination for peace and pure pursuits, and his perceived class duty to fight to win, not always by the purest of means, as the leader of his wronged royal line. He is also subject to bouts of indecision and depression. But, unlike Hamlet, *to be or not to be...*is never a question with Yudhishthira, who continues 'being' from this world to the beyond. He overcomes indecision with the keen pupil's knack of listening to wise counsel, until he himself graduates to the rarefied level of the true *jnani*, a philosopher-king who predated Plato's time by many centuries.

Yudhishthira and Arjuna: the one difference that sets them apart is in imbibing wisdom from experiences. While Yudhishthira seeks to learn from events, the all-conquering Arjuna, with his amazing wanderlust, seeks only to dominate and teach events a lesson. Significantly however, the fratricide in Kurukshetra, which leaves Yudhishthira with a burden of guilt, does not impact similarly on Arjuna, 'released from all sin' by the blessings of Shri Krshna.

Yudhishthira's feet of clay become evident in his inadequacy in weapon skills and his strange obsession with dice, despite all the hardship the game caused his family. But his disguise as a dice-playing Brahmin in king Viraata's court is amenable to the subtle explanation that he found the way out of his ethical dilemma (of adopting a false identity) in the disclosure inherent in his subtle choice of the *Mleccha* appellation – *Kanka*, meaning 'pretended Brahman'.

The forest-bound 12 years of the *Vana-parva* saw the flowering of the philosopher in Yudhishthira. To begin with, he had ethical debates with his two reproachful family members, patiently contending with the logical arguments of Draupadi on the one hand, and the specious sophistry of Bheema on the other. Second, the forest was a school of learning for him, where he elicited valuable lessons from great sages in contra-distinction to the illustrious Rama, who, also exiled to the forest and with all his superior qualities of leadership, valour, romantic charisma and poetic sensitivity to nature, did not quite match up to the eldest Pandava in harvesting wisdom from the forester sages.

That wisdom and knowledge is critical to Yudhishthira's pivotal role in twice saving his brothers from death — first in rescuing Bheema from the reptilian clutches of accursed Nahusha, and then in bringing back to life all his four siblings by answering unerringly a long string of questions posed by Lord Dharma, the enigmatic god-parent, in his guise as the crane guard (*baka-yaksha*). This catechism does represent the quintessential *Mahabharata*, involving 126 pairs of questions and answers, in diverse fields of knowledge. The adage of the whole (knowable) world being left-overs of Vyasa (*vyaasocchishto jagat-sarvam*), is strikingly validated in this eclectic repository of knowledge-turned-into-wisdom.

Having scaled such heights of wisdom in the forest, Yudhishthira's involvement in a fratricidal war after returning to the mainstream of life, may seem paradoxical. However, to be fair to him, the war is thrust upon the Pandavas despite Krshna's best efforts for an amicable settlement in the failed negotiations of the *Udyoga-parva*. But once on the warpath, a strange contrariety seems to afflict Yudhishthira, to whom expediency of battle now seems to be more important than ethical scruples. These atypical wartime aberrations could, however, be attributed to the inner conflict between his peaceable nature and his class duty as a war leader. At the end of the battle, we see the re-emergence of the pilgrim Yudhishthira, now overwhelmed with grief. In acute penitence, he twice wishes to return to the forest, but is persuaded to desist and discharge his royal functions by Bheeshma and Vyasa.

His repentance, endless thirst for knowledge and purity of conduct, led him to the exalting end of the *Mahaaprasthaanika-parva* and *Svargaarohanika-parva*, where Yudhishthira lifted himself to the highest peak of human greatness, succeeded in his ultimate test, and earned the right to ascend to heaven in his bodily self.

3 Legends Interpreted

Irawati Karve's *Yuganta* makes interesting reading, more so for its ironically irreverent objectivity and clinical analysis of some of the important *Mahabharata* characters and episodes. In particular, her interpretations of two intriguing *Mahabharata* legends deserve fresh review: (i) burning of the great Khandava forest; and (ii) the legend of Krshna-Vaasudeva. The episode of fiery destruction of the once sylvan Khandava, purportedly by the Krshna-Arjuna combine at the behest of the god Agni, obviously intrigued the anthropologist in Karve. Why were all denizens of the forest — birds, animals and the *Nagas* — so thoroughly destroyed? How could Arjuna, who took pride in his excess-abhorring epithet *Beebhatsu*, indulge in the abominable massacre? A plausible clue lies in the instinct of *lebensraum* (land hunger), that characterised the early Aryan migrants.

According to Karve, the Pandavas, who wanted the forest land to be cleared to augment their modest kingdom, usurped it after a massacre, cloaked as a sanctified deed. The prevailing *Kshatriya* ethics were not technically infringed, because the hapless victims were not Aryans. Still, as additional fig-leaves to cover the gory act, the epic plays down the human qualities of the *Nagas* and describes the other inhabitants of the forest as birds and animals. Indeed, the anthropology of Khandava does have a few angles susceptible to radical interpretation.

As regards Krshna, he surprises us as the linchpin of several seemingly controversial turns in the epic drama. His ruthless yet contrasting roles in the exterminations of Jarasandha and Shishupala, offer an interesting study. Apart from Krshna's kinship with Kunti, his friendship with Arjuna, and his conviction regarding the righteousness of the Pandava cause, there was also the strategic Yadava motive of joining force with the Pandava-Pancala combine in the struggle against the arch enemy – Jarasandha. Given the odds posed by Jarasandha's formidable military might and boon of immunity against all weapons, Krshna resorted to deceit — so manoeuvring things that Bheema killed him after 27 days of one-to-one wrestling by tearing his body in two. There was no deceit, however, in Krshna's summary beheading of Shishupala, whose vitriolic defiance against the ceremonial honouring of Krshna grossly transgressed propriety and threatened to ruin Yudhishthira's *Rajasooya* sacrifice. These interventions by Krshna were made to serve the common interests of his Yadava clan, his *Kshatriya* class, and his Pandava friends. But there was probably a deeper personal ambition as well — to become the unchallenged *Vaasudeva*, with demigod status.

Indeed, Krshna, the *Mahabharata*'s greatest enigma, apart from being discovered in ever newer lights by his own and later generations, was apparently evolving and discovering himself throughout his exceptionally eventful life. History shows that true greatness becomes more evident later, mostly in posthumous light. In the case of Shri Krshna, it is no wonder that his deification, causing all those didactic and devotional accretions on the epic, was the work of later generations. He himself perhaps felt the inner urge towards self-actualisation by claiming the modest title of *Vaasudeva*, with occasional displays of the refulgence of divinity. And the syncretistic philosophy uttered by him in the *Bhagavad-Gita*, is surely the one shining beacon of universal truth to sustain mankind on the course of harmonious living and spiritual quest, for generations to come.

4 Heroine Nonpareil

There are several facets to Draupadi that account for her pre-eminence as the leading lady of the *Mahabharata*. Her holy 'birth' from the fire of a sacrifice consecrated to secure revenge was heralded by a sinister oracle. The divine forecast was later validated through an internecine war that had, as one of its causes, her humiliation in the Kaurava court. She bore the marks of that fateful humiliation as symbols of an all-consuming spirit of gender-nuanced protest — fretting, fuming, and forcefully chiding her husbands to avenge the insults suffered by her.

But for all her vengeful wrath, she was also the epitome of conscientiousness as a dutiful wife, a punctilious daughter-in-law, ever-hospitable hostess, and compassionate family member, caring for others in distress. An epitome of grace and dignity in her personal conduct, flippancy was foreign to her noble nature. The apocryphal story of her raucous mirth at Duryodhana's watery plunge in the Indraprastha palace is far removed from the original narrator's description in the *Sabhaa-parva*.

Her atypical polyandry provided grist to the mill of her detractors, who denigrated her as a woman of easy virtue, until they were silenced by the miracle that thwarted Duhshasana's attempt to disrobe her in open court. Venerated as one of the *pancakanyaa*, she had, in fact, more dimensions to her remarkable personality than even the illustrious Sita. Her ravishing beauty cast a powerful spell on her suitors in the *svayamvara* hall. All five Pandava brothers felt her spell, and their shared matrimony and rotational cohabitation were the means to preserve fraternal unity. Draupadi, on her part, discharged her demanding marital role as common wife to five virile husbands with remarkable success, while also excelling as a homemaker, loved by all her five husbands, and loving them back in her own way.

Draupadi's age-defying attractiveness caused a younger Jayadratha and a lustful Keecaka to try to seize her by force; but with characteristic fortitude she managed to push them to the ground. A lady of great intellectual attributes, her laments and reproaches that adorn the *Vana-parva*, *Udyoga-parva*, and *Shaanti-parva*, are priceless rhetorical gems, comparable to the best in world literature. She confronted Yudhishthira and the Kuru elders with a subtle conundrum of right and wrong during her humiliation in the dice hall. Of Yudhishthira, she asked whom he had lost first, himself or her? Of the elders, she enquired what was to be her righteous duty in the circumstances. The questions were not amenable to satisfactory answers, given the socio-cultural idiom of the age. Even today, commentators are divided on the issue.

First, there are analysts like Irawati Karve, who contend that posing the questions was 'folly' on Draupadi's part, because irrespective of the answer, her position would have been desperate, since there was no precedent in Vedic times of a woman denying her husband. The *Mahabharata* vividly portrays her pitiable plight in the dice hall with an evocative turn of phrase — *naathavateem anaathavat* (helpless, despite having powerful protectors). Karve is also critical of Draupadi 'standing there arguing about legal technicalities like a lady pundit when ... she should only have cried out for decency and pity in the name of the *Kshatriya* code'. Interestingly, the line of reasoning is similar to the chauvinistic words of Shakuni to Karna in Pratibha Ray's adaptation of the dice hall scene.

But what Draupadi did must also be seen from a larger societal perspective. She was that rare entity — a woman dissenter against social injustice victimising women and patrilocal custom. Her protest is viewed by many as progressive assertion of civilisational dissent against the reactionary cultural machismo of the Vedic age. Hence, being judgemental about Draupadi's dissent solely from the viewpoint of her personal safety, would mean missing out on the larger socio-cultural message encapsulated in her attitude and conduct. Draupadi was the trail-blazing dissident, who symbolised and presaged vengeance against the injustice of the prevailing social order. An ever-fascinating figure in our traditional ballads and rituals, Draupadi has emerged as a powerful exemplar of feminist aspirations through the vibrant works of several modern artistes, dramatists and authors.

5 Exalting Tragedy

The *Mahabharata*'s finale is in itself a marvel. Its last three Books are the shortest cantos in this magnum opus. The brevity of the last Acts is perhaps suggestive of their unadulterated purity. Their tautness also helps in enhancing the dramatic effect of the epic's conclusion.

A case in point is the stark *Maushala-parva*, which begins with the jolt of a dramatic flashback. The accursed destruction of the Yadava clan is tersely announced in Vaishampayana's prefatory words to Janamejaya. Curses indeed play a key role in the *Mahabharata* drama — much more than they do in the *Ramayana* story, which is more an epic of human effort (*purushakaara*), whereas in the *Mahabharata*, Fate and Time (*niyati* and *kaala*), are the primary drivers. At least six curses have their telling impact on the *Mahabharata* storyline.

Comparisons with the Greek epics and tragic drama are also relevant. The deaths of Agamemnon and Achilles, the sufferings of Oedipus and Orestes, were results of curses — but there they reveal a leitmotif of divine unfairness, which is more pronounced in Greek and Biblical literature than in Indian traditions. The Old Testament story of cruel punishments inflicted by God on the pious Job has little or no parallel in ancient Indian literature, where the causality of poetic justice is generally more at play.

In the *Mahabharata*, by far the weirdest curse is the one regarding Shamva giving birth to the deadly iron bolt that forms the backdrop of the *Maushala-parva*. The episode, symptomatic of Yadava hubris, does seem too mind-boggling not to have some grain of ancient veracity. The epic-Puranic lore of annihilation of the Yadavas also seems to have a trans-national parallel in the Semitic Biblical account of the destruction of Sodom and Gomorrah, in the Book of Genesis. The similarities are significant: the sages came to visit Krshna, whereas angels came to visit Abraham and Lot; the Yadavas had turned arrogant, cruel and dissolute, whereas the Sodomites became overweening, selfishly inhospitable and blatantly sinful; at Prabhasa, iron bolts were the instruments of sudden death, whereas in the Biblical cities, fire and brimstone caused abrupt annihilation.

But the two silent 'deaths' that follow the Prabhasa mayhem aptly prove the *Mahabharata*'s power to amaze readers with its dramatic contrasts. Nothing can match the eerie grandeur of Balarama sitting in yogic posture and a thousand-hooded white serpent emerging from his mouth to enter the ocean. In the *Mahabharata*'s dramatic context, the tranquil-yet-awesome end of Balarama represents the turning point where the epic of myriad moods enters its last phase of *shaanta rasa*. And then Krshna, for all his cosmic glory, amazes us with the subtle commonness of his own forlorn end, in line with the dark prophecies of Gandhari and the sages. The epochal significance of Krshna's passing needs to be viewed in the context of his fascinating role in the *Mahabharata*, with all its bewildering but essentially credible 'contradictions' inherent in Krshna's own credibility as a towering demigod-god with a human side.

One such contradiction is the seeming gap between what Krshna promised and what he did, in relation to the Kurukshetra war. Initially, he professes equal relationship with the Kauravas and the Pandavas; but when both Duryodhana and Arjuna approach him for help, his 'feigned slumber' betrays a latent bias for the latter. Once the war begins, Krshna reveals himself as the foremost facilitator and protector of the Pandavas, especially Arjuna; and the foremost nemesis of the Kauravas. What is even more baffling is the lack of all normal ethical compunctions in most of the Krshna-driven tactics of war. None other than Krshna could have suggested that the method of killing the invincible Bheeshma be elicited from

Bheeshma himself. The disarming and killing of a rampaging Drona through Yudhishthira's half-lie regarding the purported death of Ashvatthama — perhaps the most sordid act in the supposedly 'just war' — is again the direct result of Krshna's counsel. But it is in meeting the threat posed to Arjuna by the valiant Karna, that Krshna amazes us by the core consistency of his adroitly planned battle strategy, which is to evade any direct encounter between the two great heroes until Karna is reduced to a lesser force having expended his main weapon elsewhere. Karna's end is arguably one of the most glorious deaths depicted in all the world's epics, steeped as it is in the pathos of a true hero's *purushakaara* valiantly fighting a losing battle against the cruel forces of destiny. Its sheer marvel is heightened when juxtaposed with the unscrupulous manner in which he is felled by Arjuna under Krshna's overt guidance.

Ultimately, in consonance with the ringing last words of the *Gita*, the Krshna-Arjuna combine did bring fortune, victory, welfare, and morality to the Pandavas. But all these came in shades of grey, leading to, as predicted by the dying Duryodhana, 'a disheartened and mournful existence' for them. How can one possibly justify Krshna's seeming lack of ethical scruples in destroying the great Kaurava generals? The answer is to be explored in the nuance-laden verses of the *Bhagavad-Gita*, relating to the Lord's manifestation in every age to establish righteousness and sustain the eternal law (*dharma*). It is this ultimate law that becomes the dominant principle in a *dharma-yuddha*, requiring the subordination of other principles to attain its end. The *Ramayana* too, illustrates the point in the variant responses of Ravana's two conscientious brothers (Vibheeshana and Kumbhakarna), when faced with the choice between *bhraatr-dharma* (brotherly duty) and the ultimate *dharma* (aiding the righteous). This 'significant trait of Krishnaism' involves a 'new ethical code' that emphasises the desirability and urgency of attaining the right end by any expedient means, even though some of those means may not seem right. There is indeed a certain universal quality to this 'code', an apt example of which is the celebrated farewell speech of General MacArthur, stressing that once war becomes unavoidable, *there is no substitute for victory*.

In the final analysis, the *Mahabharata* is much more than a war story – just as it is much more than a morality play. The only appropriate descriptor for it is tragedy, an epic tragedy to be precise. Indeed, in the global trans-cultural context, Edith Hamilton's characterisation of the tragedy of Aeschylus as having 'the strange power to exalt and not depress', sounds much like the quintessence of the *Mahabharata*.

Death is the one certain truth in life; and so stories depicting the totality of lives have necessarily to end in bereavements. The other eternal truth about life is its mixed baggage of pleasure and pain; therefore, a great epic must also depict that reality. The *Mahabharata* sensitises us to accept, in a spirit of tranquil detachment, this home truth of the ephemerality of life's pleasures and pains, while pursuing our individual ends of righteousness, wealth, pleasure or salvation. We hear this message in Vidura's stoical words to the bereaved and grieving Dhrtarashtra: *All accumulations end in decay; worldly ascendances end in decline; all unions culminate in separation; and all lives end in death.*

1
THE ENIGMATIC SAINT-CHRONICLER

THE CHARISMATIC DUO

One of the reasons the *Mahabharata* has so profound an impact on the reader is due to two key players, who combine in their towering personalities, backgrounds, conduct, and stupendous achievements, the twin characteristics of venerable image and subtle enigma. One of them is, of course, Krshna, of whom much will be said in the pages to follow. The other, equally certainly, is Vyasa, variously called the poet, editor, or distributor, of the great epic, who himself plays a pivotal role in many of the turning points of the drama. Between them, these two personages share a rare charisma that enables them to move, with equally fluid facility, across all levels of society and exert their mystical and magnetic influence on king and commoner alike. This profound charisma is, in turn, the outward manifestation of a supremely endowed personality raised to colossal greatness by self-driven efforts and attainments. No wonder then that their presence among the *dramatis personae* should add a dimension of uniquely captivating enigma to the storyline of the *Mahabharata*.

THE VYASA LEGEND

Is Vyasa just a mythical figure as has been suggested by some analysts of the Western school? One might be persuaded to answer in the negative if one attaches some credence to the collateral references that abound in various ancient works, as also *in situ* in the *Mahabharata* itself, in regard to its biographical elements and the corpus of works attributed to him. However, academic objectivity requires mention of at least one allegorical construction regarding the great sage that has been termed by some knowledgeable circles as a 'reasonable suggestion'. The suggestion in question is that of Bruce Sullivan, who makes the case that Vyasa *'represents Brahma (sharing with him the symbolising of brahmanical orthodoxy, the creation and dissemination of the Veda, and being frequently called pitamaha, 'grandfather').* Sullivan examines the portrayal of Vyasa within the *Mahabharata* as seer, priest, ascetic and spiritual preceptor, and highlights three episodes where Vyasa intervenes in the plot.... Sullivan also supplies a plausible reason for the lack of subsequent recognition of the identity proposed in the decline in Brahma's religious significance'.[1.1]

But notwithstanding the reasonableness or otherwise of such constructions, our key concern in this protohistorical-philosophical-dramatic analysis is that Vyasa, like Krshna, is too central to the *itihaasa* (history, or chronicle) of the *Mahabharata* to be relegated to the blurry status of myth or allegory. One must agree Vyasa is a legend; but then legends are the staple of ancient history, as illustrated in the works of Herodotus and other ancient Greco-Roman historians.

VYASA'S ROLE IN THE *MAHABHARATA*

There is an intriguing singularity in the part played by Vyasa in the entire *Mahabharata* saga. As TRS Sharma points out in an incisive analysis[1.2], he is perhaps the most elusive of narrators in that he does not narrate anything himself. He sits there at Janamejaya's sacrifice, listening in on his own story, told by Vaishampayana and others. When it comes to expatiating endlessly on *Raajadharma*, *Daanadharma* and *Mokshadharma*, he lets Bheeshma take over the narration. His gift of celestial vision to Sanjaya turns the latter into a war correspondent for Dhrtarashtra, and for us all — a correspondent whose despatches to posterity cover much deeper matters than just a war. The entire philosophy of the *Bhagavad-Gita* comes 'home to us through *Sanjaya Uvaaca*'. There are other narrators too – especially visiting sages like Narada, Brhadashva, Lomasha and Markandeya – who tell stories to whet the philosophical and epistemic appetite of Yudhishthira during his wonderfully instructive years in the forest. And Yudhishthira himself strikes the thinking reader as an able spokesman for Vyasa. The wisdom which elevates his replies to the *Yaksha-prashna*, to the level of distilled universal philosophy, is surely the worldview of Vyasa. Nowhere is this philosophy, this liberated worldview, more tellingly expounded than in dealing with the question that seems the *leitmotif* of the Vyasa-Yudhishthira insight: how to define a true *Brahmana*? Does one become a *Brahmana* by birth, or by one's nature, or by one's action? The obsessive search for a satisfactory answer to this question of identity is perhaps only to be expected from Vyasa, born (as we shall discuss), to a fisherwoman and a leading *Brahmana* sage; as also from Yudhishthira, with his *Kshatriya* birth and *Brahmana* nature being ever in conflict.

Sharma, in his intriguing analysis, suggests that Vyasa has a unique 'negative capability' – a quality famously attributed by Keats to Shakespeare and other literary greats – 'of being in uncertainties, mysteries, doubts without any irritable reaching after fact and reason'.[13] The suggestion seems validated by several dichotomies in Vyasa. We see him as an insider-outsider, and also as a contemporary impacting the lives of seven generations of the Bharata dynasty: from Shantanu (Queen Satyavati being his mother), through Bheeshma-Vicitraveerya (his half-brothers, not to mention the short-lived Citrangada), to Dhrtarashtra-Pandu (his *kshetraja* sons, along with Vidura), further down the genealogy to the Kaurava-Pandava brothers and cousins (all his grandsons), through Abhimanyu, Pareekshit, and finally to Janamejaya. He is obviously deeply implicated in the fortunes of these protagonists, all of whom are his descendants, yet he manages to remain detached as the 'begetter of the epic' itself.

Again, his intrusions into his own narrative tend to suggest that he favours a Pandava victory against the Kauravas. At the same time, he has obvious doubts and reservations about the unfair means used by his favourites, Arjuna and Bheema, in defeating Drona, Karna, and Duryodhana. As we have already seen, he is the prime narrator but delegates the actual narration to others. Yet, this aloofness, this avoidance of the limelight, appears quite contrary to his penchant for appearing out of nowhere in times of crisis, like a *deus ex machina*[14] of Greco-Roman plays, to solve problems as the family's friend, philosopher and guide. We shall come to these appearances and their impact on the course of events, but before that we must necessarily discuss the antecedents of this amazing personality.

MIXED YET EXALTED PEDIGREE & ELEVATING NURTURE
Vyasa was the son of Satyavati, the daughter of a *Dasa* (non-Aryan) chieftain of fisherfolk and ferrymen residing in a hamlet on the banks of the Ganges. Satyavati's looks were fetching, but she also had the not-so-fetching characteristic of fishy body odour. Her pious father had assigned her the sacred task of

ferrying sages and pilgrims in her boat. One day, the itinerant sage-teacher Parashara (grandson of the *Brahmarshi* Vashishta), felt drawn to her. To screen the bashful maiden from public view, the great sage used a mystic spell to create a thick mist around them, and behind its cover took her to a solitary riverine island for cohabitation. The ascetic's blessing caused her foul smell to change to the finest fragrance. In due course a son was born to her. Being of dark (*Krshna*) complexion and having been born on an island (*dveepa*), he came to be called Krshna-Dvaipayana. Parashara took the child with him, but before leaving, granted Satyavati another boon, whereby she regained her lost virginity. In due course she married the enamoured King Shantanu, but only after her father extracted the severe (*bheeshana*) pledge of renunciation from Shantanu's son and heir apparent Devavrata Bheeshma, that secured the line of royal succession to her children.

Thus, Dvaipayana was the son of Parashara, and great-grandson of Vashishta – two of the greatest names in the annals of Indian spiritualism and scholarship. Nurtured by the tutelage and inspiration of his phenomenally endowed father, and propelled in equal measure by his own prodigious talent, he soon proved himself worthy of this hallowed family tradition. His intellect and scholarship earned him the sobriquet *Vishaalabuddhi* (one of vast intellect). But he earned another sobriquet by which he was destined to be venerated by all Indians. Hindus traditionally believe that Krshna-Dvaipayana categorised the original single *Veda* into four, so as to make the divine knowledge intelligible to the masses. Hence he is called *Veda*-Vyasa (Splitter of the *Vedas*), or simply Vyasa, who followed his presentation to the people of the *Vedas*, with the other great popular gift of the *Mahabharata*.

Vyasa's exalted pedigree and phenomenal personal achievements prompt a global comparison with Homer – the only other creator of comparable epics. But, outside his perceived identity as the composer of the two great Greek epics, not much else is known of Homer. We know very little about his background, genealogy, and other works. The view of the renowned classicist Geoffrey Kirk, that 'antiquity knew nothing definite about the life and personality of Homer' seems to be the general consensus on the Homeric question.[1.5] In contrast, Vyasa, with his illustrious family lineage, and the outstanding and voluminous corpus of works attributed to him (classification of the *Vedas*, composition of the *Puranas*, commentaries on *Vedanta*, etc.), stands out as a figure of commanding presence and rare versatility.

THE VYASA INTERVENTIONS

Regarding Vyasa's intermittent appearances in the course of the unfolding *Mahabharata* drama, Alf Hiltebeitel has tracked Vyasa through the epic and says he appears 41 times, the interventions being often crucial to the fortunes of the protagonists.[1.6] Here we shall limit ourselves to discussing only seven of the more important interventions. Two of them happen in the *Aadi-parva*; one in the *Vana-parva*; and one each in the *Bheeshma-parva*, *Drona-parva*, *Aashvamedhika*, and *Aashramavaasika-parva*. These are in addition to the two initial instances in the *Aadi-parva's Anukramanikaa* and *Amshaavatarana* sub-chapters, where Vyasa figures as the epic's composer – the former relating to the legend of his finding a scribe in Ganesha, to record his great story; and the latter regarding his visit to Janamejaya's serpent sacrifice, where, on the request of the king, he asks Vaishampayana to narrate the story.

As regards Vyasa's own participative role in shaping that eventful story, the first appearance is perhaps the most influential. The mighty and selfless Bheeshma had won the two princesses from Kashi – Ambika and Ambalika – as brides for his step-brother Vicitraveerya. But the latter, after seven years of unrestrained pleasure with his two young wives, was afflicted with tuberculosis and died. What made the tragedy worse for the royal house was that the young king, for all his carnal excesses, failed to have sons to carry on the lineage.

NIYOGA: SATYAVATI 'ASSIGNS' VYASA A FAMILIAL JOB

It is at this juncture in the *Mahabharata* that we come across the mention of *niyoga*, or surrogate fatherhood, for the first time. This obviously prevalent practice would play an important role in the future course of the epic drama. A sorrowful Satyavati, after consoling the young widows, calls upon her stepson Bheeshma to discharge his *kulaacaara* (familial duty) of propagating the family tree by impregnating his sisters-in-law:

Ime mahishyou bhraatuste kaashiraja sute shubhe /

Roopayauvana-sampanne putrakaame ca bhaarata //
Tayor-utpaadayaapatyan santaanaaya kulasya nah /
Man-niyogaan-mahaabaaho dharman kartumiharhasi //
~ Aadi; 103.9-10[1.7]
O Bharata, these two daughters of the king of Kashi are endowed
with beauty and youth, and are also desirous for sons. O the
one of mighty arms, on my express order (*niyoga*) you procreate
offspring in both of them for the sake of saving our family.

The ever-righteous Bheeshma then tells the queen: 'O mother,
I can sacrifice everything, but cannot be untrue to my pledge
of celibacy and renunciation. But let me tell you a way that is
in conformity with *Kshatriya* traditions whereby Shantanu's
line can be saved. In ancient times, when the redoubtable
Parashurama had exterminated all the *Kshatriyas* from the world,
Kshatriya women produced children by cohabiting with *Veda*-
trained *Brahmanas*, because, according to the *Veda*, a *kshetraja*
son is deemed to be the wedded husband's son. So, mother, you
may employ, on appropriate payment, a qualified *Brahmana* to
produce children from the widows of Vicitraveerya'.

Seeing a way out of the problem, Satyavati overcomes her
reluctance to confide her own past history, and finally tells
Bheeshma: 'The son I had during my maidenhood is a great
sage and yogi named Krshna-Dvaipayana, who has earned the
honorific 'Vyasa' for his accomplishment of dividing the *Vedas*.
After his birth, he left with his father Parashara, but assured
me that whenever I remember him in times of need, he would
come to help. O Bheeshma, if you approve, then on my request,
that great ascetic would produce sons in the *kshetra* (field) of
Vicitraveerya:
Tava hyanumate Bheeshma! niyatan sa mahaatapaah /
Vicitraveerya-kshetreshu putraan-utpaadayishyati //
~ Aadi; 104.19

Bheeshma indicates his support, and Satyavati meditates on
Vyasa. The telepathy works, as the *Veda*-chanting Vyasa appears
in no time. After a mutual exchange of cordial greetings, he asks
his mother what she wishes him to do. When Satyavati conveys
her request, the great sage replies:
Tathaa tava mahaapraajne dharma pranihitaa matih /

Tasmaad-aham tan-niyogaad dharmam-uddishya kaaranam //
Eepsitan te karishyaami drshtan hiyetat sanaatanam /
Bhraatuhputraan pradaasyami mitraa-varunayoh samaan //
~ Aadi; 104.40-41

O the greatly wise one, your mind is dedicated to *dharma*. Therefore, obeying your desire and addressing the cause of eternal *dharma*, I shall carry out your assignment. I shall present my brother with sons equal to Mitra (Surya) and Varuna.

VYASA'S CAUTIONARY WORDS IGNORED

Vyasa then gives special operating instructions since it is not easy for ordinary mortals to come into close proximity with the *yogic* aura of a great ascetic: 'Let the two queens purify themselves by observing year-long austerities; then can they come near me.'

But Satyavati is not prepared to wait that long. She says: 'A kingdom without a king is reduced to a land of orphans, having no rains and forsaken by gods. Therefore, arrange things in such manner that the queens become pregnant forthwith; Bheeshma will nurture the babies'. Vyasa then has to agree, but still cautions his mother: 'If I have to beget sons right now, then the queens should prepare themselves to withstand my ugly looks, loathsome odour, and uncouth garb.'

Vyasa the poet does not say it in so many words, but it is a fair assumption that Satyavati's sudden call had pulled him out of some deep austerity. At the best of times he was far from good-looking; but the effect of his austerities would have taken their toll on his looks, body odour and ascetic's garb – over and above the spiritual emanation that others would find hard to bear when close to him. No wonder he advised caution, which, if heeded, could have changed the whole story. But returning to the scenario proper, a determined Satyavati persuades Ambika to go into the bedchamber, telling her in a confidential tone:

Kaushalye devaraste'sti so'dya tvaanupravekshyati /
Apramatta prateeksheynan nisheethe hyagamishyati //
~ Aadi; 105.2

O Kaushalya (Ambika)! Your elder brother-in-law will come to you tonight. Lie in wait for him in a calm and composed manner.

Perhaps Ambika expected Bheeshma to be the appointed agent. In any case, the record says she lay down on the fine bed, thinking of Bheeshma and the other Kuru heroes. After a while, Vyasa enters the lamp-lit chamber. Seeing his dark complexion, glowing eyes, yellow-brown matted hair and flowing beard, Ambika closes her eyes in the grip of terror. After exiting the chamber, Vyasa tells Satyavati: 'The son will be as strong as a hundred elephants, will be learned, intelligent, and will father a hundred sons; but will be blind due to his mother's lapse'. Satyavati protests: 'A blind person cannot be a suitable king for the great Kuru dynasty; give us one more son'. On the Queen-Mother's persuasion, Ambalika goes to the bedchamber and keeps her eyes open. But seeing Vyasa's formidable looks, turns pale in fear. A sad Vyasa tells Satyavati, 'This son will be valorous, famous, and will father five sons; but will be of a pale complexion due to his mother's fault'.

In due course, Ambika gives birth to a blind son and Ambalika to a pallid one. They are named Dhrtarashtra and Pandu, respectively. But a persistent Satyavati again asks Ambika to lie with Vyasa. Driven by her revulsion, this time Ambika sends a maid, bedecked in her own jewellery, as a replacement. The *Maharshi* is pleased at the reception and ministration by the maid, and blesses her saying, 'You will no longer remain a servant girl; a profoundly virtuous son will be born to you; he will be the epitome of righteousness and lucid wisdom'. This son is duly born and given the name Vidura.

Such is Vyasa's first intervention in the story told by him. It was an episode laden with portents for the future. By disregarding Vyasa's words of caution, Satyavati not only brought sinister misfortunes upon the very dynasty she sought to preserve, but exposed the entire order of kings and warriors to a collective tragedy that would sap the vitality of India for generations to come. Dhrtarashtra and Pandu – both bearing congenital burdens of their mothers' aversion to ordained union with the holiest of holies – were destined to suffer handicaps that could only bode ill for the future. The former lived long, but could not effectively rule due to his blindness, living on as a helpless and latently partial witness to his sons' evil doings. The latter did rule with valorous distinction for some time, but (for all the stories about hunting expeditions and the adoption of *pravrajyaa* [wandering asceticism], following a curse that ruled out sexual acts), was perhaps compelled by personal inadequacies to retire with his two wives to the hills. There he met with an untimely and mystery-laden death, ostensibly caused by his breaking sixteen years of celibacy and attempting coitus with his younger wife.

THE PANDU MYSTERY

At this point, a little digression is needed to make some modern sense (to the extent one can), of the mystery that was Pandu. Recorded history does not make any mention of him or the Pandavas, who are central to the epic drama. There are two aspects to the Pandu mystery: one relating to his unusual complexion, and the other about his sexuality.

Regarding the first, there could be several angles of speculation. Was he an albino, or one with sub-optimal body pigmentation? Or, as has been tentatively suggested by some Western scholars, were the Pandavas of Mongoloid or non-Aryan tribal stock? The polyandrous sharing of one wife by the five brothers being a pointer to that? Then there are the other intriguing clues: the literal significance of the word *Pandu* (pale); the mysterious birth of the five brothers in the Himalayan outer reaches inhabited by *Kirata* and other hill tribes; Yudhishthira's cryptic words to Drupada: *We follow the practice of our ancestors* (Aadi; 194.29), in the context of the fraternal sharing of one wife; or even Bheema's lack of facial hair. But, in line with the well-argued stand of a noted Bengali essayist,[1.8] we cannot carry these speculations beyond a point, as they would deflect us from our larger goal of exploring a meeting point between truth, legend and human drama, between effort and destiny, between heroic action and visionary thought. In the *Mahabharata* and the *Puranas*, the Pandavas have been presented as an illustrious branch of the Kuru genealogy; they reveal themselves as exemplars of the attitudes and faiths of the Aryan *Kshatriya* nobility; and, above all, they have been so accepted and regarded in the millennial traditions of their own land.

Coming now to the second aspect of the Pandu riddle: was he really the victim of a curse that barred him from practising sex, or was he actually impotent? Or was he unable to procreate due to a hormonal deficiency or low sperm count? The last possibility seems the most likely, and could also be the reason for removing himself from the public gaze, so that he could get his wives to produce *kshetraja* sons without people knowing who actually fathered them. The *Mahabharata* tells us that he was keen to have *kshetraja* sons as his passport to heaven, believed to be barred to one dying without issue. The epic also says he did this through the agency of Kunti's *abhicaara-mantra* (incantation of spell to make anyone do her bidding).[1.9]

The story of Kunti using her powers to produce one pre-marital son (the heroic Karna), and then three of the five glorious Pandava brothers, makes fascinating reading. The problem is in making a non-mythical interpretation of it. So far as Karna's birth is concerned, the real father could be anybody distinguished enough to be an idol for the young Kunti. Irawati Karve seems to suggest that the sage Durvasa fits the bill[1.10], as does SL Bhyrappa in his magnum opus, *Parva*, a remarkable modern effort at conjectural reconstruction of the great epic sans its mythological elements.[1.11] But we do not have much by way of plausible clues to make a definitive, non-mythical interpretation of the biological fatherhood of the five Pandavas, except in the case of Yudhishthira. There are indeed some speculative theories (again, Karve being one such theorist[1.12]), that Vidura could have been Yudhishthira's surrogate father.

THE ENIGMA THAT WAS VIDURA

Vidura presents another enigma. Endowed with fine qualities of mind and body, and for those reasons eminently better suited than his two brothers to rule the kingdom, he was nevertheless disqualified from kingship on account of his mixed birth. He remained all through his life the friend, philosopher and guide to the Hastinapura court, the epitome of steadfast virtue, great wisdom, and unwavering loyalty, qualities he must have inherited from his saint progenitor (Vyasa). As Pandu's younger brother, he could have been a natural choice, according to the system of *niyoga*, for fathering the childless king's *kshetraja* sons, and Karve does suggest that was the case. But the question is: why should the truth have been hidden by Pandu, when there were clear precedents of such *niyoga* in his own lineage? One possible reason could be that Vidura's low-born mother could have put a question mark on Yudhishthira's succession.

The epic itself is silent on the issue, which may be significant as a contrary indicator, since the narrative is otherwise quite transparent about Karna's birth and about the *kshetraja* sons fathered by Parashara and Vyasa. We cannot reach a definitive conclusion, though the special bond of affection and temperamental similarities between Vidura and Yudhishthira (both regarded as personifications of *dharma*; whose bodies and souls seemingly merged at the time of Vidura's hair-raising scene of death in the *Aashramavasika-parva*), do keep us guessing. But such affection could merely signify they were similar by nature. We have, therefore, to leave the matter as one more of the intriguing mysteries of the *Mahabharata*.

VIDURA'S EERIE END

But before we move on, it would be pertinent to flash forward to the passing away of Vidura, which seems to have some profound mystical significance attached to it. As mentioned above, the episode happens near the end of the story, in the *Aashramavasika-parva*. Fifteen years have passed after the tragic battle of Kurukshetra. Despite all the regard and courtesy he receives from King Yudhishthira, a typically insensitive comment from Bheema makes Dhrtarashtra realise and resolve that it is time for him to retire to the forest. Gandhari, Kunti, and Vidura, accompany him.

The dutiful Yudhishthira would make periodical visits to check on their welfare. When he does not see Vidura on one such visit, he asks, 'O King, why do I not see *kshattaa* Vidura?' The old king replies: 'He is performing hard penance, subsisting on nothing but air; his emaciated body is covered with veins. Occasionally people report having seen him in some solitary corners of this forest.'

Right then, Yudhishthira sights Vidura, a mass of matted hair on a naked, dust-covered bag of skin and bones, holding a piece of wood in his mouth to signal the ascetic's abnegation of speech and food. Casting a disinterested glance at the cottage, the apparition is about to move away when Yudhishthira runs after him crying, 'O Vidura, I am your dear Yudhishthira. I have come to see you.' They keep running till they are deep inside the forest, when Vidura stops. There, the strange ascetic leans against a tree and locking his eyes on Yudhishthira's eyes, and pressing their bodies, limbs and organs together in a tight hold, he enters through yogic transference into Yudhishthira's being. The latter suddenly feels his strength and lucidity of mind increase greatly. Seeing Vidura's lifeless form resting against the tree, he remembers Vyasa's words, that both he and Vidura are parts of the god Dharma. He decides to perform the last rites, but is prevented by an oracular voice: 'O King, do not cremate Vidura's body. Let it be where it is; he has attained the celestial refuge of holy ascetics; grieve not for him'.

The next morning, the clairvoyant Vyasa visits the cottage and clarifies things to a mourning Dhrtarashtra: 'O King of Kuru, you have heard of the destiny of Vidura. Dharma himself took human form as Vidura under the curse of Mandavya. Under Brahma's instruction, I had produced him in the *kshetra* of Vicitraveerya. Yudhishthira too, has been born from Dharma. Dharma is Vidura, and Vidura is Yudhishthira. Look again at Yudhishthira, who is ever-obedient to you; Vidura by his yogic power has entered the body of this eldest of Pandavas'. Vidura's last action does indeed look like a father bequeathing all to his son, in accordance with certain Vedic and Upanishadic traditions.[1.13] Even if made in the context of a symbolic father-son relationship, it was no doubt a strong enabling factor that sustained Yudhishthira in his final heaven-bound mission.

OTHER VYASA INTERVENTIONS
Reverting to the topic of Vyasa's sudden appearances at the drama's turning points, the second such occasion arises in the *Vaivaahika* sub-chapter of the *Aadi-parva*, when, during his debate with King Drupada (in the presence of Kunti, Dhrshtadyumna, and others), Yudhishthira sticks to his resolve to abide by their mother's utterance (notwithstanding its unwitting nature), that all five Pandavas enter into a polyandrous marriage with Draupadi. The two sides cannot come to any agreement. Then Vyasa decides to arrive on the scene.

Apprising him of the problem, Drupada reasons, 'In my view, it is against both scriptures and customs for one woman to have several husbands'. Dhrshtadyumna adds, 'How can a virtuous elder brother have physical relations with his younger brother's wife?' Yudhishthira replies, 'The *Puranas* provide instances of highly virtuous daughters of sages entering into matrimonial relations with many husbands. My mind is my best guide, and my mind wants to redeem my mother's word as the right duty' because:

Gurorhi vacanan praahurdharmyan dharmajnasattama /
Guroonan caiva sarveshaan maataa paramako guruh //
~ Aadi; 195.16

[O foremost of the righteous, Guru's word is held as the supreme duty, and one's mother is held as the greatest of all Gurus.]

My mother has said, 'All of you enjoy what has been earned like a gift of alms'; hence, I consider that to be our bounden duty.'

Kunti voices her support: 'I fully agree with my righteous son. I greatly fear any recourse to falsehood; tell me how we can be saved from it'. Vyasa assures them saying: 'My good Lady, you shall be relieved of any falsehood. King of Pancala, what Yudhishthira proposes is the eternal *dharma*, though not for all; you alone come, I shall tell you the significance behind it'. So saying, he takes Drupada by the hand and they retire to the king's inner chamber. There the sage recounts to the king an ancient story to the effect that the five Pandavas are human incarnations of five Indras sentenced to earthly lives by Mahadeva, who also sent Lakshmi in the form of Draupadi to be their consort. Vyasa provides Drupada with transcendental vision, whereby the king sees the five Pandava brothers in their celestial splendour. The awestruck monarch then gives his consent and Draupadi marries the five brothers on five consecutive days. The marriage cements the Pandava-Pancala alliance, and Draupadi herself is destined to play a major role in future developments. In this way, Vyasa, the player-playwright, makes a telling impact at a crucial turning point of the great drama. One might say that he carries the day for polyandry by spinning a farfetched yarn invoking divinities to a gullible king; but another way to look at it would be to ascribe his forceful intervention to an inner urge (clairvoyance perhaps), to pave the way for *niyati* (destiny).

Vyasa's third appearance happens early in the *Vana-parva*, this time to counsel Dhrtarashtra about his duty as king and family elder. The Pandavas have been consigned to the forest through the machinations of Duryodhana and his scheming coterie, comprising Shakuni, Karna, and Duhshasana. Not content with that, the coterie plan to actually kill them, to pre-empt any possibility of Dhrtarashtra changing his mind under Vidura's influence. The omniscient Vyasa then appears before his vacillating son, saying: 'The fact that the Pandavas have been exiled to the forest as a result of unfair means with dice is not at all to my liking. They will return after thirteen years to extract their revenge. You should caution your evil-minded and foolish son that he would only bring death upon himself if he persists in his plans to eliminate his cousins. King, I warn you, if you ignore this hatred of the Pandavas that is being nursed by Duryodhana, your inaction would only lead to grave danger'.

When Dhrtarashtra admits that parental love makes him unable to control his son despite knowing his evil tendencies, the saint, in a 'frame-tale' characteristic of the epic structure, tells him a fable regarding a parent's duty to take special care of children who are weak and virtuous. He then advises his son: 'Dhrtarashtra, regard all your sons with equal affection, but be more merciful to the weaker among them. My son, you yourself, Pandu, and Vidura are all equal to me. You have a hundred sons; there are only five of Pandu's in your care, and they are afflicted by adversity and misery. I am worried how they will survive and prosper. If you want to save the Kauravas then do your utmost to ensure that Duryodhana lives in peace with the Pandavas.'

Dhrtarashtra replies, 'O wisest of sages, what you say is all true. Please do me the favour of yourself advising the wicked Duryodhana'. But Vyasa does not do that; he leaves, saying, 'The sage Maitreya is coming here after visiting the Pandavas. He would advise Duryodhana'. This was the great sage's penultimate attempt to arouse Dhrtarashtra's *purushakaara* (human effort), in a bid to change the course of destiny. Vyasa obviously knew the futility of any outsider's advice to one bent on taking the evil course; but he had come, counting on the slim hope of exhorting Dhrtarashtra to use his royal authority to control his errant son, which did not prove successful. Nor was Maitreya successful in reforming Duryodhana, who treated the sage's wise counsel with dismissive contempt, prompting the holy man to leave after sternly warning Duryodhana of an accursed doom unless he mended his ways.

Far from mending his ways, Duryodhana rejects even the minimum demand of the forest-returned Pandavas for five villages as their token share of the kingdom, and so precipitates the fateful Kurukshetra war. This is the portentous juncture at the very beginning of the *Bheeshma-parva*, when Vyasa, now almost resigned to the inevitability of fate, revisits his son, telling him: 'The last hour of your sons and many other kings is now near — they would soon kill one another in mutually destructive battle. But do not grieve, because all that is destiny. My son, if you wish to see the battle, I shall bless you with divine vision'. Dhrtarashtra replies, 'O greatest of *Brahmarshis*, I have no inclination to see the decimation of my kinsfolk; but with your blessing I would like to hear the full concurrent narration of this battle'. Vyasa says, 'I bless your aide, the virtuous Sanjaya, with transcendental vision and omniscience, by which he would directly witness all events in this war and narrate the same to you. I, on my part, would tell the world about the heroic Kuru-Pandava story. Grieve not, what will happen is destiny; victory will smile on the just and the righteous. In this war there will be tremendous loss of lives, I can see many terrible omens of it with my mind's eye. Dhrtarashtra, time is running out; you alone are still capable of averting this war; take charge, and show the right way to your relatives and friends. Fratricidal killing is an abominable act and is abhorrent to me; do not let that happen. What use to you is a kingdom that smears you with sin? Let the Pandavas have their just share and let the Kauravas live in peace.'

But a pusillanimous Dhrtarashtra expresses his helplessness: 'My father, I am only human, and cannot rise above normal frailty. I am not inclined to do wrong, but my sons are not under my control. Please have mercy on me'. A saddened Vyasa finally says, 'King, victory achieved on the basis of the principles of peace and generosity is the best; success earned through division or dissension is the second best; but the spoils of war are the worst. Victory is not assured by just superior forces; it is subject to uncertainty and is finally caused by destiny. Those who win first may well be losers in the end'. These were the prophetic last words uttered by Vyasa to signal the end of his personal efforts to avert the war.

There will be occasion for us to discuss the fifth intervention of Vyasa in the final chapter, in the context of the connection between the *Mahabharata* and the Rama story. (Briefly, it happens in the *Drona-parva*, when the sage consoles Yudhishthira, who is grief-stricken after Abhimanyu's death, with tales of death as the inevitable end of even the most virtuous of kings.) And we have already discussed the seventh appearance of Vyasa in the *Aashramavaasika-parva*, after Vidura passes away. In between, the sage makes his only other appearance, again to console a penitent Yudhishthira after the death of Bheeshma, during the *Aashvamedhika-parva*. After the sacramental offering of Ganga water to the departed elder, Yudhishthira collapses in a paroxysm of heart-rending grief. Bheema, Dhrtarashtra, even Krshna – all try to revive his spirits, but without success. Yudhishthira expresses the firm desire to retire to the forest, as he feels inconsolable at the deaths of the beloved Bheeshma and valiant Karna (whose true identity he is now aware of).

Finally, Vyasa's sharp reprimand restores the woe-begotten king to his senses: 'My dear one, you seem to be suffering from juvenile delusion, and we all are trying in vain to console you. You are well aware of the duties of a *Kshatriya*, as also those of salvation, governance, and charity. Despite knowing the precepts of all scriptures, why are you still afflicted by the delusion of ignorance? If you think of yourself as a sinner, let me tell you the way for expiation. One can be freed of sin through austerity, sacrifice and charity; therefore, like Daasharathee Rama and like your own ancestor Bharata, perform the *Ashvamedha Yajna* (Horse Sacrifice) and then dispense a lot of charity.' Yudhishthira abides by this wise counsel and somewhat regains his composure.

THE *MAHABHARATA*'S VOICE OF CONSCIENCE

We have now reviewed all seven interventions by Vyasa in the amazing narrative of which he himself is the original chronicler. The first two of these episodes, viz. the birth of

Vicitraveerya's *kshetraja* sons, and the marriage of Draupadi, involve the germination of the seeds of the future drama. The third and fourth occasions see Vyasa driving himself against destiny to counsel a vacillating Dhrtarashtra on his duty as king and family's guardian. The fifth and sixth ones involve consoling and advising Yudhishthira when the righteous elder Pandava needed advice to regain his calm. And the seventh occasion was to hold the hand of the forest-bound Dhrtarashtra and apprise him of the subtle significance of the wise Vidura's death.

If one tries to analyse the cause and effect of the sage's role in the *Mahabharata* drama, some striking conclusions emerge. Talking of effect, the end result of it all was the actual wiping out of the *kshetraja* line fathered by Vyasa himself. Indeed, it was the family branch of the *Dhaartarashtra*s (Duryodhana and the other Kauravas), and not that of the Pandavas (who themselves were *kshetraja*s of unknown origin, if one ignores the speculation that Vidura might have fathered Yudhishthira), that were the true inheritors of the sage's progeny. None of the Kauravas survived the tragedy. The only one of the Pandu line to continue the dynasty was Pareekshit, son of Abhimanyu and Uttaraa. Abhimanyu, himself the son of Arjuna and Subhadra, had a pronounced Yadava heredity (through his mother and grandmother, Kunti), and Uttaraa brought in a share of the Viraata blood. Thus, Pareekshit and Janamejaya had arguably little or no biological connection with either Vyasa or the original Kuru line, of which Vyasa was the officially assigned propagator.

Viewed in the above context, Vyasa's role seems all the more self-effacing – if one can use such an adjective to qualify a personality who, by all accounts, was the epitome of a liberated soul, far above the sense of self. But what else can one say, considering the consistent support the saint gives to the cause of justice and righteousness, even against the interests of those to whom he was a direct ancestor? After all, Duryodhana was Dhrtarashtra's son and Vyasa's grandson; but Vyasa never uttered a word in support or encouragement of the eldest Kaurava. For all his fabled omniscience, he still tried to avert the family tragedy by arousing King Dhrtarashtra's sense of duty. But in doing so, he steadfastly supported the Pandavas as the just cause. If Krshna was the *Mahabharata*'s man of destiny, and if Bheeshma was its embodiment of sacrifice, Vyasa (together with son Vidura), was the great epic's voice of conscience.

NOTES & REFERENCES

1.1 John Brockington. The Sanskrit Epics, Leiden, Boston, (1998). p.24.

1.2 TRS Sharma, *Introduction* to *Reflections and Variations on the Mahabharata*, Sahitya Academy, New Delhi, pp. 15-18.

1.3 The quotation on 'negative capability' appears in a letter (Dec 1817), written by John Keats to his brothers, George and Thomas. The context was Keats' criticism of Coleridge, whom he thought sought knowledge over beauty. Keats meant that poets should not confine themselves to a position of supposed certitude, but be receptive to life or nature with all its mysteries and uncertainties. John Keats, *The Complete Poetical Works and Letters of John Keats*, *Cambridge Edition*, p. 277.

1.4 Rajshekhar Basu, *Mahabharat Saranuvad* (Bengali). The apt simile appears in the introductory chapter.

1.5 GS Kirk, *The Iliad: a Commentary* (Cambridge 1985), v.1.

1.6 TRS Sharma, p.17.

1.7 *Maharshi Vedavyasa-racitam Mahabharatam*, Aryashastra Publications, Kolkata. Unless otherwise stated, the *Mahabharata shlokas* referred to in this work are from the above publiction.

1.8 Buddhadev Basu, *Mahabharater Katha*, (Bengali), M.C. Sarkar & Sons, Kolkata 73, pp.164-165. The analysis of the Pandavas' origin and its implications, is largely based on the details given against Note 87 of the commentary.

1.9 The *Aadi-Parva* (Ch.110), tells us that Kunti, in her maidenhood, so pleased the sage Durvasa by her ministrations that he taught her an occult *abhicaara* incantation, which would bind men, including divinities, in her spell, to father sons as she wished. In her youthful curiosity, she tried out the *mantra* on Surya (we need 'wilful suspension of disbelief' to appreciate such supernaturalisms), when the Sun-God appeared and produced a son with in-born signs of an invincible hero; the deity then restored Kunti's virginity to save her from social stigma. The son, who was set adrift, was found and brought up by the *soota* Adhiratha, and grew up to be Karna, the formidable warrior – the valorous Hector of the *Mahabharata*. When Pandu, anxious to have *kshetraja* sons, comes to know of Kunti's occult powers, he persuades her to summon Dharma, Vaayu, and Indra, to produce Yudhishthira, Bheema, and Arjuna, respectively.

On Madri's entreaty, Pandu asks Kunti to use the *mantra* on her co-wife's behalf. Madri calls on the Ashvinees, to produce Nakula and Sahadeva. This is viewed by Kunti as a numerical breach of faith, and she stops further procreations.

1.10 Irawati Karve, *Yuganta* (English), Orient Blackswan Pvt. Ltd., Hyderabad, 2008, Reprint 2011, p.42. The following extract is relevant: *Kunti was serving a Brahmin for a year and that she should bear him a son was not such an extraordinary occurrence.[1] [[1]There is a record in the Mahabharata of another woman, Satyavati, Kunti's grandmother-in-law, having had a child before marriage by a Brahmin.]*

1.11 SL Bhyrappa, *Parva*, Sahitya Academy, New Delhi, pp. 73-108. Bhyrappa suggests the reason Pandu retired to the hills was to seek a cure for his impotency, using medicinal herbs known to the Himalayan sages – which seems a plausible speculation. He further suggests the 'treatment' was taking time, and so the gods who fathered the Pandavas (Dharma, Indra, Maruta and the Ashvinees), all came from the northern *Deva* mountain to perform *niyoga* at Pandu's request.

1.12 Karve, pp. 70-72.

1.13 The relevant precepts appear in a short hymn in the *Brhadaaranyaka Upanishad* (1.5.17). A graphic description of the tradition is contained in the following extract of the *Kousheetaki Braahmana* (2.15), translated by Max Muller, pp.291-92: *Next follows the father's tradition to the son, and thus they explain it. The father, when going to depart, calls his son, after having strewn the house with fresh grass, and having laid the sacrificial fire, and having placed near it a pot of water with a jug (full of rice), himself covered with a new cloth, and dressed in white. He places himself above his son, touching his organs with his own organs, or he may deliver the tradition to him while he sits before him. Then he delivers it to him. The father says: 'Let me place my speech in thee.' The son says: 'I take thy speech in me.' The father says: 'Let me place my scent (prâna) in thee.' The son says: 'I take thy scent in me.' The father says: 'Let me place my eye in thee.' The son says: 'I take thy eye in me.' The father says: 'Let me place my ear in thee.' The son says: 'I take thy ear in me.' The father says: 'Let me place my tastes of food in thee.' The son says: 'I take thy tastes of food in me.' The father says: 'Let me place my actions in thee! The son says: 'I take thy actions in me.' The father says: 'Let me place my pleasure and pain in thee.' The son says: 'I take thy pleasure and pain in me.' The father says: 'Let me place happiness, joy, and offspring in thee.' The son says: 'I take thy happiness, joy, and offspring in me.' The father says: 'Let me place my walking in thee.' The son says: 'I take thy walking in me 1.' The father says: 'Let me place my mind in thee.' The son says: 'I take thy* mind in me.' The father says: 'Let me place my knowledge (pragnâ) in thee.' The son says: 'I take thy knowledge in me.' But if the father is very ill, he may say shortly: 'Let me place my spirits (prânas) in thee,' and the son: 'I take thy spirits in me.' Then the son walks round his father keeping his right side towards him, and goes away. The father calls after him: 'May fame, glory of countenance, and honour always follow thee.' Then the other looks back over his left shoulder, covering himself with his hand or the hem of his garment, saying: 'Obtain the heavenly worlds (svarga) and all desires.' If the father recovers, let him be under the authority of his son, or let him wander about (as an ascetic). But if he departs, then let them despatch him, as he ought to be despatched, yea, as he ought to be despatched. Web: http://www.sacred-texts.com/hin/sbe01/sbe01240.htm

2
PILGRIM'S PROGRESS

THE *MAHABHARATA*'S PHILOSOPHER-KING

We left the previous chapter with an allusion to the *Mahabharata*'s three epitomes: of destiny, sacrifice, and conscience. The epic's rich canvas includes two more striking role models – Yudhishthira and Arjuna – the former being the man of thought, and the latter the man of action. Here we look primarily into the gradual flowering of the thinker in Yudhishthira, with some comparative sidelights on the characteristics of Arjuna, and to a lesser extent, of Rama. This would aid our investigation about how an action-packed 'warrior story' was turned into a drama with deepest philosophical insights of timeless human significance.

The triumvirate who determined the course of that subtle philosophical drama were Krshna, Vyasa, and Yudhishthira. Of Vyasa, we have already had some glimpses. Krshna's pervasive role we shall keep citing as a core refrain. As for Yudhishthira, his is a fascinating character in a purely cerebral sense – all the more in context of the apparent contradictions he has to contend with and overcome in his own life. He is a *Kshatriya* prince with the disposition of a true *Brahmana*, ever conflicted by his natural inclination (*svabhaava dharma*) for peace and pure (*saattvika*) pursuits, and his perceived class duty (*kula dharma*), to fight to win, not always by the purest of means, as the leader of his wronged royal line.

If the younger Arjuna strikes us as the epic's *karma yogi*, the elder Pandava is his perfect foil as its *jnana yogi* par excellence. Till the prime of his life he consciously exerts himself to discharge all the duties of an ideal householder (*grhi*) – as a devoted husband with only one-fifth marital rights[2.1] and a conscientious elder ever vigilant in preserving and protecting his family. But as the years pass and he makes compromises with his own principles in the interests of that very family, his guilt-laden mind repeatedly seeks solace in the role of an ascetic (*sannyaasi*). He is subject to bouts of benumbing indecision and depression at crucial points of the drama. But, unlike Hamlet, his depression is in the nature of soul-cleansing penitence rather than suicidal escapism. After all, *to be or not to be...* is never a question with Yudhishthira, who continues 'being' from this world to the beyond. Unlike Hamlet again, his indecision is not a source of tragic weakness. Quite the contrary, Yudhishthira's vacillations almost always lead either to a stronger resolve or a better decision, because he has the keen pupil's knack of listening to the best minds for wise counsel – until he himself graduates to the rarefied level of the true *jnani*, walking alone and unaided to the goal of transcendental salvation in the great epic's incomparably sublime climax. He is indeed the scholar extraordinaire – the philosopher-king who predated Plato by many centuries.

A CHEQUERED BIOGRAPHY
Among all the star cast of the *Mahabharata*'s principal characters, Yudhishthira is perhaps the most variegated. As Buddhadev Basu, the noted Bengali poet-critic cogently brings out in his scholarly commentaries,[2.2] Yudhishthira, after dazzling us with his philosophical brilliance in the *Vana-parva* (more on which later), seems suddenly to slip into an idiosyncratic pattern of being perennially conflicted by the opposing pulls of his inclinations and his circumstances. This phase of inner conflict and deeply intrinsic oscillation stretches over the greater part of the narrative – from the war preparations in the *Udyoga-parva*, right up to his final expiatory acts in the *Aashvamedhika-parva*. And for that very reason – because he is so busy ratiocinating on his intellectual, ethical, and spiritual uncertainties, while constantly changing within himself – he keeps growing in stature. Through all his slippages, penitence, and contradictions, we discern the lone pilgrim, trudging slowly but surely along the path of gradual evolution and enlightenment.

YUDHISHTHIRA AND ARJUNA
We cannot help but compare the thinker Yudhishthira and the doer Arjuna. Against the apparent inconsistencies of the former, the latter is the epitome of consistency, cast in the shining stereotype of the heroes' hero – a noble prince, an adorable lover, an incessantly travelling landbound Odysseus; and above all, an all-conquering Achilles, ever prepared to dominate adversaries with his own valour (aided at times by his divine charioteer).

Even his rare doubts or uncertainties seem to add to his aura of consistent nobility – as is the case with his humane despondency just before the fratricidal battle, or with his uncharacteristic diatribe against his eldest brother for the deceitful half-truth the latter uttered to overcome Drona.[2.3, 2.4]

Arjuna stands out among all the other *dramatis personae* of both the Indian epics for the variety of the many events that constitute his life story. Twice he spends twelve-year-long banishments in the forest;[2.5] twice he sets out on extensive conquests; thrice he 'dies', only to be restored to life.[2.6] All through his 24 forest-bound years, we see him continually on the move. Unlike Yudhishthira's peregrinations, his are not confined within the limits of Aryavarta; he travels far and wide – from the far-northern Himalayas to the southern seas, from Manipur in the far east to the westernmost extremity of Dvaraka. He seems to have seen all the mountains, bathed in all the rivers, visited all the holy sites of the wonder that was ancient India. His conquests would have done Alexander proud – Kashmir, Sind, and Chedi (Central India); Gandhara (modern Afghanistan); and Pragjyotishapura (Assam); and even as far north as Uttarakuruvarsha and Kimpurushavarsha (Tibet and Central Asia). Indeed, his amazing wanderlust is not confined to terra firma; he descends (or rather, is dragged by the adoring Uloopi), to the netherworld of the *Nagas*; and his quest for divine arms takes him to Indra's heaven.

En route to that celestial mission, he does something no mortal, not even the great Rama, has ever done. He engages in one-to-one combat with none less than the god Shiva himself, who tests him in the guise of a *Kirata* hunter. Even in that unparalleled encounter, he proves to be no pushover. He assails his unflinching antagonist with arrows, with sword, with body punches, and finally with stones and trees, before the latter reveals himself and blesses Arjuna with Shiva's equivalent of the formidable *Brahmashira* weapon, the *Paashupataastra*. While in heaven, his spurning of Urvashi's amorous advances brings on him a curse, whereby he has to spend a year as a dancing eunuch in King Viraata's palace. But even there he wields arms to defeat the Kauravas in their marauding raid on Viraata's cattle.

In the sheer number and variety of his circumstances, in the glamour and charisma of his conquests in love and war, Arjuna is indeed nonpareil; but for all that, there is hardly any noticeable change in his mindset or his behaviour. He is like the proverbial rolling stone, in whom multifarious happenings do not get converted into incremental experience. He remains an unchanging, merry youth, who counts all adversaries as killable; the whole world as a pleasure-ground; and dominance as the goal of action. There is rarely a gap between his resolve and action, hardly a shadow of doubt to cloud his handsome countenance – except for the one instance of touching melancholy at a climactic point in India's distant antiquity.

Yudhishthira and Arjuna, seen in juxtaposition, present a case study of perfect complementarity. Whatever qualities one lacks, are more than made up by the other: one is the thinker, the other the doer; one excels in the realm of knowledge, the other on the field of battle; one is subdued and contemplative, the other dominating and decisive. Such perfect dovetailing of qualities makes the two brothers an ideal pair for any joint enterprise, especially given their sibling bonding as the affectionate elder and the adoring and loyal junior. But the one difference that sets them apart as individuals, is in imbibing wisdom from experiences. While Yudhishthira seeks to learn from events, Arjuna seeks only to teach events a lesson. As a result, the former matures into a true philosopher, whereas the latter's mind mostly stays cocooned in the mould of an irrepressible action hero – at least till Krshna shows him, and through him the world at large, the light of eternal truth. But Arjuna's intellect proves incapable of retaining for long even the transcendental vision of the *Gita* (which enabled him to rise above his 'petty faint-heartedness' before the 'just' war); and he later requests Krshna (in the *Anu-Gita* sub-chapter of *Aashvamedhika-parva*), to recount to him that forgotten wisdom.[2.7]

Significantly, the great battle of Kurukshetra itself leaves different imprints in the minds of the two brothers. Yudhishthira spends his after-years carrying a heavy burden of guilt. But, strangely enough, no such guilt bothers Arjuna. Just before the battle, a despondent Arjuna shrinks at the very thought of killing his mentors:

Guroon-ahatvaa hi mahaanubhaavaan
shreyo bhoktoom bhaikshyam-apeeha loke /
Hatvaartha-kaamaams-tu guroon-ihai-va
bhunjeeya bhogaan rudhirapradigdhaan //
~ Gita: 2.05

It is better to live in this world by begging than to slay these venerable teachers. By killing these elders, we shall only be enjoying here the pleasures that are smeared in blood.

Ultimately, in those 18 blood-drenched days, Arjuna does become a party to the slaying of those elders. Why then do we not see the kind of remorse that burdens the soul of Yudhishthira? Is there, after all, a paradox here? But no, the genius of Vyasa does not leave such loose ends. The answer to Arjuna's lack of guilt can be found in the blessing of personal exoneration he received from Krshna near the end of the *Bhagavad-Gita*:

Sarvadharmaan parityajya maam-ekam sharanam vraja /
Aham tvaa sarvapaapebhyo mokshayishyaami maa shucah //
~ Gita; 18.66

Abandoning all duties, come to Me alone for shelter. I shall release you from all sins; do not lament.

YUDHISHTHIRA'S VICISSITUDES

Yudhishthira, in his own way, is also an enigma through a large part of the story. From his younger days in the *Aadi-parva* till the end of the Bhaarata war in the *Sauptika-parva*, he baffles us with his human frailty, but for one long interlude of shining glory during his forest-bound years in the *Vana-parva*. Thereafter, the 36-odd post-Kurukshetra years, from the *Stree-parva* to the *Mahaaprasthaanika-parva*, see the emergence of a new Yudhishthira, a character rendered pure and sublime by the soul-cleansing combination of sincere penitence and subtle wisdom.[28]

We get the first glimpse of the ordinary Yudhishthira in his early days at Drona's academy. The Acarya points to a stuffed bird placed as target on a tree, and asks the eldest Pandava, 'What do you see?' The model answer from a promising marksman should have been that he saw only the target – an answer that later comes from Arjuna. But Yudhishthira, inept as he is in weapon skills, replies that he sees the bird, the tree, the Acarya, and his brothers. The annoyed teacher dismisses him, saying he is just not fit for such tests.

STRANGE OBSESSION WITH DICE
Then, in the *Sabhaa-parva*'s fateful game of dice, we come across a seemingly clear instance of Yudhishthira's feet of clay. Had he not agreed to play, there would have been no loss engineered by Shakuni with his loaded dice, no humiliation of Draupadi, and no banishment (*vana-vaasa*) of the Pandavas. His infamous act of putting Draupadi at stake is worse even than Rama subjecting Sita to the fire test to prove her chastity. Rama's action had the rationale of perceived royal duty, of satisfying popular misgivings. Yudhishthira deserved the reproach he faced from both Draupadi and Bheema, for this impetuos act.

But the addiction to dice still did not leave him for some time, making it perhaps the sole exception where our model learner did not learn enough from experience. Indeed, one cannot help being surprised at the insouciance with which, at the beginning of the Pandavas' year of living incognito in the *Viraata-parva*, he declares, 'King Viraata is fond of dice-play; hence I shall take the guise of a Brahmin named Kanka, and entertain the king as his like-minded courtier, engaging him at play on an ornate bloodstone board, with dice made of cat's eye, gold or ivory, and with red and black pawns'. Quite evidently, he relishes the idea of having a go at his favourite hobby. Of course, by then he had learnt the subtle secrets of dice (*aksha-hrdaya*) from the sage Brhadashva (Vana; 79).[2.9] Interestingly, thereafter Yudhishthira spent a whole year playing with Viraata and never losing. But after *Viraata-parva*, we do not see him playing his favourite sport ever again. Perhaps, the year-long vindication of his skill was enough for him; or perhaps Draupadi's laments and his own ratiocination of the deceitful impact of gambling[2.10] finally made him renounce the habit.

Indeed, the game of *dyoota*, like the practice of *niyoga*, is a significant theme of the epic, central to several of its intriguing turning points. The former, much like the latter, seems to have a deeper sociological significance attached to it. As we shall see later (Chapter 7), Yudhishthira's action in never refusing a game of dice could possibly be legitimised if one accepts Gerrit Jan

Held's ethnological thesis that the dice game was the traditional means of circulating tribal wealth – something that Yudhishthira, as *Dharmaraja* and acclaimed upholder of traditions, was obliged to foster. Ethnographically again, it is well established that a *Kshatriya* of yore never refused a call to battle or a game of dice. That brings us to a possible explanation for Yudhishthira's choice of profession while in disguise. He assumed the guise of a *Brahmana* to escape identification for a year; but how could he escape violating his higher *dharma* of never departing from the truth? Would such a violation not have grounded his levitating chariot much before it actually became surface-bound after his half-truth regarding the purported death of Ashvatthama, causing Drona to drop his arms? It is unusual of Vyasa to leave such an elementary incongruence in his narration.

THE NAME MATTERED

The mystery gets resolved if we consider that Yudhishthira found a way out of his ethical dilemma by his choice of appellation. *Kanka* means 'heron' or some such fish-eating bird. The name seems appropriate for one visiting the habitat of fish or *Matsya*, the name of Viraata's kingdom. But according to Monier William's Dictionary, *Kanka* also means a 'false or pretended Brahman in native lexicons'. Now, we know that Yudhishthira, like Vidura, knew the *Mleccha* language (as is seen in their conversation when Vidura warned his favoured nephew about Duryodhana's plot to kill the Pandavas at Varanavata). We also know that the territories beyond the Himalayas were regarded as *Mleccha* or 'Barbarian land'. Hence, Yudhishthira could plausibly say, *Kanko'ham* (I am Kanka), to conceal his identity while not telling a lie as the name itself signified 'a pretended *Brahmana*'. Besides, even the passion for dice and the straightforward signification of carnivorous heron imply atypical tendencies for a *Brahmana*. Yudhishthira thus seems to have made abundant semantic disclosures to keep on the right side of truth.

EVOLUTION OF A TRUE *JNANI*

In the foregoing section, the topic of dice took us from the second to the fourth book of the *Mahabharata* – from the *Sabhaa-parva* to the *Viraata-parva* – skipping the eventful *Vana-parva* between. We must now fill that gap, because those 12 forest-bound years actually saw the gradual flowering of the brilliantly promising philosopher in Yudhishthira. Thematically, it is appropriate to structure the discussion into three parts. To start with, we may review the ethical debates Yudhishthira had with Draupadi and Bheema. Secondly, in the larger context of comparing the forest-banishments of Yudhishthira and Rama, we can consider the valuable lessons the elder Pandava elicited from great sages; and finally, we can take up the deeper issue of the nature of his relationship and interactions with his parent deity, *Dharma*, and the several tests in the *Vana-parva* and afterwards that he was subjected to during those mysterious interactions.

DEBATE WITH DRAUPADI

Draupadi was perhaps the one member of the Pandava household who could engage in logical argument with Yudhishthira on almost equal terms. If Yudhishthira of the *Vana-parva* is a Yajnavalkya in the making, then Draupadi brings out the best in him as the in-house, everyday Gargi. One cannot help being impressed by the qualities of sheer fortitude, sense of duty, and practical wisdom, that suffuse the actions and words of this uniquely endowed lady, all through her trials and tribulations. A *Mahabharata* 'marvel' in her own right, much will be said of her in a later chapter. Without pre-empting those analyses, we can discuss some of her intellectual arguments with Yudhishthira in the present context.

Indeed, her spirited words of reproach to Yudhishthira convey, with the cogency of an accomplished logician, all that can be said against the elder Pandava's perceived limitations: 'They say that there is no *Kshatriya* who cannot be roused to anger; but you seem to be an exception to the rule. A *Kshatriya*, who does not display vigour when required, but only forbears and forgives, is despised and exploited by all. O King, Dhrtarashtra's sons are evil and rapacious; they are not worthy of forgiveness; it is your duty to confront them with vigour and spirit.'

Yudhishthira replies: 'My dear, you are blessed with great knowledge; so you should understand that anger can cause both good and evil. Control over anger is always beneficial. Enraged people are prone to commit sinful acts; that is why I keep my anger in check. One who is not driven to counter anger with more anger saves not only himself, but others too from grave danger. One who can check rising anger with the strength of intuitive reason is hailed by the wise to be truly vigorous. And that strength, that vigour, comes from the ability to forgive, which alone holds the world together.'

Kshamaa brahma kshamaa satyam
kshamaa bhootanca bhaavi ca /
Kshamaa tapah kshamaa shoucam
kshamayedam dhrtam jagat //
~ Vana; 29.37

Forgiveness is *Brahman*; forgiveness is Truth; forgiveness is the past and the future too; forgiveness is worship; forgiveness is purity, and it is forgiveness that sustains the world.

Draupadi is still not convinced: 'I salute our Maker and Providence, who has created this delusion in you, causing your mind to deviate from your ancestors' line of duty. None in this world can achieve success just through righteousness, non-violence, forgiveness, innocence and charity. You have performed many great *yajnas*; still contrary judgement has led you to lose your kingdom, your wealth, your brothers, and even me, through the game of dice. Despite being upright, gentle, generous, modest, and truthful, why did you succumb to the temptation of gambling? Men are but puppets in god's hand. Seeing your misery and Duryodhana's prosperity, I only blame god for having ordained an unfair dispensation in which a sinner does not suffer for his sin, because he is powerful. I feel pity for the weak, because god does not look after them.'

Yudhishthira reasons: 'O Yajnaseni, what you say sounds wonderfully attractive, but betrays a sad lack of faith. I do not hanker after any returns for righteousness; I engage in charity because it is right; I perform *yajnas* because it is my duty. I do my best to discharge my work as a householder without expecting any rewards. A person who seeks reward for doing his duty, and one who is driven by the atheist's calculation to worry about such reward, can never derive the benefits of *dharma*. O Draupadi, you are arguing beyond limits. Do not blame god; and do not doubt *dharma*, the path of virtue, which has been extolled by omniscient seers, and which has been followed by all good people.'

Draupadi indicates agreement, but adds a caveat: 'I should blame neither god nor *dharma*; my distress has caused me to say what I should not. But please listen, I have something else to say. O King, you do your work without giving in to weariness. An individual who depends solely on providence or on sudden divine dispensation only misleads himself. Success comes from three possible causes — destiny, past deeds, and human effort (*purushakaara*). The grave adversity that confronts us will certainly be alleviated once you decide to act with *purushakaara*.'

BHEEMA ADDS HIS SPECIOUS LOGIC

With characteristic impatience Bheema next takes up the thread of the argument: 'Why at all should we suffer this life in a grove, abnegating duty, wealth and worldly pleasure? Duryodhana has stolen our kingdom like a leftover-eating fox steals meat from a powerful lion. O King, you are redeeming your pledge by sacrificing your kingdom; subjecting yourself and us to misery for the sake of small virtue. We, who are under your control, are making our foes happy by inflicting sorrow on our friends. We suffer now because, out of obedience to you, we did not kill the *Dhaartaraashtras*. I am afraid that your constant harping on *dharma* has reduced you to the status of a *kleeva* (neutered entity). O King, either you adopt *sanyaasa* (total renunciation) or pursue the course of *dharma*, *artha*, and *kaama*; anything in between can only entail a life of distress. There is nothing superior to *dharma*, but it takes a lot of wealth to accomplish any noble work of *dharma*. A *Kshatriya*'s *dharma* is his might and vigour, not the life of a beggar. No king can win fortune by just clinging to *dharma*. Just as a farmer reaps a load of crops by sowing a small amount of seeds, in the same way a wise person gains higher virtue by sacrificing smaller ones.'

Yudhishthira says: 'I cannot blame you for your strong words, since you all have been so afflicted by my improper action. I had ventured into dice-play in the hope of winning Duryodhana's kingdom, but the cunning Shakuni beat me by exploiting my honesty with his deceit. Duryodhana had made us his slaves; it was Draupadi who had then saved us. But I had agreed to the stakes in the second round of dice; I cannot break that agreement now. You had threatened to burn my dice-throwing arms; Arjuna had then prevented you. You also had flaunted your mace; why did you not put it to use then? Why did you not object when I made the pledge? Having not done anything then, what good do you achieve by scolding me now? Just as people have to wait for the crop after sowing of seeds, likewise you have to wait for happy days to come again.'

Bheema retorts: 'If we are to wait for 13 years, we may be near our death by that time. Your nature is more like a tender-hearted *Brahmana*, why have you been born in the class of *Kshatriyas*? We have just spent 13 months in the forest; imagine how long 13 years will be. Wise ones say that just as *pootikaa* (a variety of spinach) is the surrogate for *somalataa* (herb used in Vedic sacrificial rites), likewise a month can be taken as substitute for a year. Or, if you have any ethical reservations against reckoning thirteen months as 13 years, then you may satisfy a dutifully load-bearing bull with lot of food – that should relieve you of all consequential sin.' (Vana; 53.33-34).

Yudhishthira, as one may expect, is not swayed by such convenient sophistry. Instead, he persuades Bheema, at least for the time being, with practical logic: 'Destiny supports those who exert force after thorough consultation and reflection. It is not advisable to plunge into action by a restless overestimation of one's own power. The Kauravas are no pushovers; and they are supported by all those kings who felt harassed by our conquests; Bheeshma, Drona and Krpa are unbiased, but still bound by their loyalty to Dhrtarashtra; the wrathful and invincible Karna too is inimical to us. You cannot kill Duryodhana without first defeating all these valiant heroes.'

YUDHISHTHIRA AND RAMA
One striking feature that emerges from a probe into Yudhishthira's character is that it does not quite fit into any known stereotype. The only other epic figure whose life story bears some outward resemblance to Yudhishthira's is Rama. The resemblance is on two counts: both are driven by an inner urge to pursue the path of *saattvika* (pure) *dharma*; and more importantly, both spend long years in forest-bound exile along with wife and brother(s). But there are major differences too in the circumstances and attitudes of the two epic protagonists. Each embarks on exile in the forest in order to be true to a pledge; but the difference

lies in the truth being upheld, and in the nature of the pledge being redeemed. Rama is innocent in the causality behind his exile, whereas Yudhishthira's exile is of his own making. Rama voluntarily renounces his throne for no fault of his. Yudhishthira loses his kingdom, not through the machinations of a jealous stepmother, nor by holding himself bound to a henpecked father's words, but due to poor judgement, that causes him to lose, after accepting the challenge to a second round of dice, even after Shakuni's skulduggery became evident in the first round. Rama's travails in forest are caused by external agencies; Yudhishthira's are more intrinsic and psychological, caused by the abiding sense of remorse and guilt (that his imprudence has brought misery upon his dear ones), and aggravated by the words of reproach he has to hear.

Rama of the *Aranya-kaanda* reminds us more of Arjuna than of the forester Yudhishthira. He slays many *rakshasas*, and obtains divine weapons from the sage Agastya. But in all his peregrinations through the groves of piety, he does not discuss any deep philosophical issues with the many great saints with whom he comes into contact. The only knowledge he seems keen on eliciting is which forest is better to camp in.

Rama and Yudhishthira, both are pre-eminent scions of illustrious Kshatriya dynasties, and both are resilient endurers of many vicissitudes. But Rama is by nature what Yudhishthira could never be. The *Ikshvaku* is industrious and a warrior nonpareil. In the *Gita*, while enumerating the one God's dual manifestations, Shri Krshna says: '*Raamah shastrabhrtaam aham*' (of wielders of weapon, I am Rama). He has all the qualities of a leader: understands politics; takes quick and hard decisions at times of crisis; is a great organiser; and brims with self-belief. All these charismatic traits of a great king and general are supplemented by the romantic essence of an equally great lover. The lovelorn Rama of the *Aranya-kaanda* and *Kishkindhyaa-kaanda* portrayed by Valmiki, and the pathos of his estrangement from his beloved Sita, are potent ingredients of great romantic drama. Besides these, Rama also touches the heart with his love for nature. Early in the *Kishkindhyaa-kanda*, the woe-begotten Rama finds an almost sensual solace in the picturesque ambience of the Pampa Lake and its surrounding flora and fauna (Kishkindhyaa; 1.1-21).

Again, when we hear Rama describing the seasonal charms of the rain-drenched and autumnal Kishkindhyaa (Kishkindhyaa; 28, 30), he strikes us as a forerunner to the world's best romantic nature-poets, from Kalidasa to Wordsworth.[2.11]

In all these varied dimensions, Yudhishthira cannot hold a candle to Rama. He is no hero in the conventional sense. Nor is he, by any yardstick, a charismatic leader or decisive politician. He hardly ever shows the ardour of a romantic lover. And, for all his travels across all those great forests, rivers and lakes, he hardly ever displays any affinity to nature. With such disinterests, how then does he spend his 12 years in the forest? Actually, he keeps himself busy in his own area of core competence. He in his turn does something Rama could not. To Yudhishthira, the forest is a great school of learning, and the 12 years in the forest make for a long course of continuous and steady acquisition of knowledge and wisdom.

PILGRIM'S PROGRESS
Yudhishthira of the *Vana-parva* is in a league of his own – an itinerant sage-prince and untiring seeker of truth – a rare combination the world has hardly ever seen. For the most part, in this long third book of the epic, he is a listener. As already mentioned, he has to contend with the reproach of a spirited Draupadi and an impatient Bheema. Their criticisms add to his remorse, but do not sway him from the 'razor-thin' path of righteousness he has charted for himself and his family. What influences him is the subtle wisdom emanating from the lips of great sages. He is an avid listener of enlightening discourses on the *Shastras* and *Puranas* from such eminent *hrshis* as Brhadashva, Narada, Lomasha and Markandeya. He acquires knowledge on philosophy, ethics and the wider cosmic history, with the diligent application of a gifted pupil; in the process, he lifts himself to the highest level of self-realisation and world-vision. He thirsts for knowledge for its own sake. After all, there are no examinations laid out in the curriculum of his forest academy. But the knowledge so acquired he applies to most telling effect by faring brilliantly in several challenging tests in his life. The greatest of these comes at the end, during his final journey to heaven. But before that, twice during the *Vana-parva*, he emerges with flying colours in significant tests when, like a true hero, he saves his brothers from the jaws of death.

DELIVERANCE OF NAHUSHA
The first test is taken by King Nahusha, in his accursed form of a monstrous python. The snake, which has Bheema in its deadly constricting hold, offers to release him only if Yudhishthira can answer its questions correctly.

The python asks: 'Who is a *Brahmana*? And, what is the truth to be known?' Yudhishthira replies:
Satyam daanam kshamaa sheelam-aanrshamsyam tapo dayaa /
Drshyante yatra naagendra sa Brahmana iti smrtah //
Vedyam sarpa param brahma nirduhkhama-sukhanca yat /
Yatra gatvaa na shocanti bhavatah kim vivakshitam //
~ Vana; 180. 21-22
O King of serpents, one who has truthfulness, charity, forgiveness, pure character, non-cruelty, austerity and compassion is called a *Brahmana*; and, the supreme *Brahman*, bereft of joy and sorrow, is the knowable truth, attainment of which dispels all illusion of pain; pray tell me, what is your view?

The python responds: 'But even *Shoodras* (of the fourth *Varna*), could have those qualities; and there is no entity in the world that is beyond pleasure or pain.'

Yudhishthira replies: 'A *Shoodra* who has these attributes is not a *Shoodra*, he is a *Brahmana*; a *Brahmana* who does not possess these is not a true *Brahmana* – he should be called a *Shoodra*. And, whatever may be your opinion, my view is that there is a supreme reality or *Brahman*, which transcends pleasure and pain.'
The serpent persists: 'If being a *Brahmana* is determined by personal qualities, then so long as one is not so qualified, he cannot be regarded as a *Brahmana*; would it not then undo the basic four-fold division of classes?
Yudhishthira answers: 'I believe that there is always some admixture of shades between all *Varna*s, which makes it very difficult to adjudge a person's class (*samkaraat sarva-varnaanaam dushpareekshyeti me matih*).'
Such liberated and unprejudiced philosophy which is not constrained by the *Vedas*, but takes cognisance of the essential differences between individuals based on their qualities, actions and nature (*guna, karma* and *svabhaava*), attributes stressed in the

Bhagavad-Gita, is only indicative of a person of true wisdom.[2.12] Yudhishthira's reply frees Bheema from reptilian bondage. Nahusha too, is released from his curse, under the terms of the redemption clause mercifully provided by the curse-giver, the sage Agastya. But a sterner test awaits Yudhishthira, from Lord Dharma himself, in the guise of a guardian-crane (*baka-yaksha*), at the very end of their forest-bound years, by the side of a beautiful lake, adorned with golden flowers.

QUINTESSENTIAL *MAHABHARATA*: THE *YAKSHA* QUESTIONS
Before Yudhishthira, his four brothers had fallen dead after drinking from the lake against the express prohibition of the avian guard.[2.13] But Yudhishthira is different, he does not wish to trespass, nor is he imprudent by nature. So when the *yaksha* cautions him: 'You may drink only after answering my questions,' he replies: 'I have no desire to have something that belongs to you without your approval; ask your questions, I shall answer to the best of my ability.' The mysterious guard then asks a string of searching questions which, to all intents and purposes, seem to be a passing-out test for Yudhishthira after his 12-year course in the forest.

Such catechism is an ancient Upanishadic device used to bring out or impart subtle knowledge through questions and answers.[2.14] While Upanishadic knowledge of the non-dual *Brahman* is not the central theme of the *Mahabharata*, the great epic is still a veritable encyclopaedia on a broad spectrum of subjects, including philosophy, metaphysics and ethics. Setting aside the dialectical questions raised by Arjuna in the *Bhagavad-Gita*, we come across four remarkable episodes in the *Mahabharata* where the catechistic form is used to good effect to convey knowledge at varying levels of profundity. Interestingly, all four find place in the *Vana-parva*: the arguments won by Ashtaavakra to rescue his father from his watery prison; the Nahusha questions that are addressed with aplomb by Yudhishthira; Savitri's precisely logical answers that win her five great boons, including her husband's life; and the deeply intriguing *yaksha-prashnas* that constitute a fitting finale to the treasure-trove of knowledge that is the third book of the *Mahabharata*.

One can discern a gradual ascendance of the level of polemics from the first to the fourth episode. Much of the exchange between Ashtaavakra and Vandee (King Janaka's court pundit), is like a contest in riddles, albeit riddles to test memorised knowledge and ready wit. Vandee's faltering at number 13, reduces the contest to the level of comical one-upmanship.[2.15] But in the second episode, Yudhishthira's replies to the python reveal a deeper, independent ratiocination. Third, Savitri's discourse with Yama displays reason supported by practical logic. But still one cannot help thinking that, like the serpent Nahusha, Yama too, accedes to his petitioner's appeal a little too readily.

But the test by the crane-guard is much stiffer in its degree of difficulty. It is far more comprehensive in its scope, involving a total philosophy of life, ranging from the practical to the transcendental. The 126 questions[2.16] are compiled from diverse branches of knowledge – philosophy, scriptures, ethics, metaphysics, social and family values, politics, governance and cosmology; even psychology and biology find their place in the syllabus of this curious test. Not all the questions though, are steeped in high wisdom. Some are similar to the Ashtaavakra riddles; some are meant to elicit traditional eulogies of the *Vedas* and *Brahmanas*; or homilies on gods or parents. But taken together, they are the quintessence of the *Mahabharata*, representing an impressive kaleidoscope of ancient thought – an encyclopaedia of traditional beliefs and profoundly independent ideas; a handy digest of scriptural knowledge and secular wisdom, covering almost everything from familial values to natural and social sciences. The adage of the whole (knowable) world being left-overs of Vyasa (*vyaasocchishto jagat-sarvam*), is strikingly validated in this eclectic repository of knowledge-turned-into-wisdom. No less striking is that the philosophical éclat of the *yaksha-prashna*s is not an isolated flash of stand-alone brilliance. A discerning reader can perceive how several of these subtle strands of wisdom are connected by a fine thread of thematic and conceptual integrity with other episodes in this great work of Vyasa.

A broad generic tabulation of a selection of 65 of those 126 pairs of questions and answers should give one some idea of the range of topics covered in the curious test, their inter-linkage with other parts of this perfectly integrated epic, as also the development of thought and views in Vyasa and Yudhishthira's time.

Yaksha's Question	Yudhishthira's Answer	Field of Knowledge	Reference / Remarks
Who causes the sun to rise?	*Brahman* makes the sun rise.	Metaphysics, Cosmology, Spiritual Philosophy	Vana; 313. 45-46.
Who move around the sun?	The gods move around it.		Are not the answers somewhat reminiscent of Savitri's statement to Yama that 'the saints drive the sun with the help of Truth (*santo hi satyena nayanti suryam.* Vana; 297.48)?
Who causes it to set?	*Dharma* causes it to set.		
In which is it established?	It is established in Truth.		

Both Savitri and Yudhishthira seem to echo the Kathopanishad (2:1:9): 'yatashcodeti suryohstam yatra ca gacchati / tam devaah sarve arpitaastadu naatyeti kashcana / etadvai tat // From which the sun rises, and in which it sets, all the gods are immanent in it. None can surpass it. It is He (Brahman)'[2.17].

The source of the ideation can be traced to the Rg-Veda (10: 85): 'Truth it is that holds up the Earth; the sun holds up the heavens; under the influence of Truth the *Aadityas* reside on the firmament, and the moon (*Soma-deva*) is sheltered there.'

In a sense, all these thoughts represent attempts by ancient minds to postulate the 'first principles' of cosmic reality.

By what can one:	Philosophy of life	Vana; 313. 47-48.
Become *shrotriya* (acquire sacred knowledge)?	One becomes *shrotriya* by studying the Vedas.	The Mahabharata's in-built integrity of ideation is evident in the concordance of the last point about the way to become endowed with wisdom, with what Krshna tells Arjuna at a dramatic moment in the *Karna-parva*. Yudhishthira, peeved at being let off by Karna on the battlefield with an earful of insults, chides Arjuna into surrendering his *Gandeeva* to a worthier hero, for having failed to overcome Karna. Arjuna then takes up his scimitar to kill Yudhishthira, and tells Krshna that he is pledged to behead anyone who asks him to surrender *Gandeeva* to another person. Krshna dissuades Arjuna with words that echo Yudhishthira's reply to the *yaksha*: '*Idaaneem paartha jaanaami na vrddhaah sevitaastvayaa / kale na purushavyaaghra samrambham yad bhavaanagaat* – O Partha, I now understand that you have not served elderly (wise) persons. That is why you have become angry at this wrong time' (Karna; 69.16).
Achieve great distinction? Win support of others?	One achieves greatness by *tapasyaa* (austere efforts).	
Become *buddhimaan* (endowed with wisdom/ intelligence)?	One wins support with perseverance. One becomes *buddhimaan* by serving elderly (wise) persons (*dhrtyaa dviteeyavaan bhavati buddhimaan vrddhasevayaa*).	

What imparts divinity to a Brahmana?	Study of the Vedas imparts divinity to a Brahmana.	Scriptures; Philosophy of life; Ethics	Vana; 313. 49-50.
Which habit makes him virtuous?	Austere effort makes him virtuous.		
Which characteristic in him is human?	Mortality is his human characteristic.		
Which conduct makes him false?	Slandering others makes him false.		

What imparts divinity to a *Kshatriya*?	Prowess in arms imparts divinity to a *Kshatriya*.	Scriptures; Philosophy of life; Ethics	Vana; 313. 51-52.
Which habit makes him virtuous?	Sacrifice (*Yajna*) makes him virtuous.		By his own standards, Yudhishthira, with all his contrarieties, should qualify as a conscientious *Kshatriya*, at least on the second
Which characteristic in him is human?	Fear is his human characteristic.		and fourth counts. He was a great believer in *yajnas*. Second, he never refused nor dis- owned a *sharanaagata*,
Which conduct makes him false?	Deserting a seeker of shelter (*sharanaagata*) makes him false.		as is amply attested to by this very episode of his encounter with the *baka-yaksha*, brought about by his decision to send all his brothers in search of a distressed Brahmin's lost flint- wood. In the end, all he wanted (other than his brothers' lives), after passing his test was nothing, not even any subtle spiritual blessing, for himself; just that his *sharanaa- gata* should get back his flintwood.

Which person, despite being intelligent; worshipped by people; honoured by all; engaged in sensual enjoyments and in the act of respiration, is still not actually alive?	One who does not nourish the five entities — viz., gods, guests, servants, ancestors and his own soul — is actually a living dead.	Scriptures; Philosophy of life	Vana; 313. 57-58.
Who is: Weightier than the Earth? Taller than the sky? Faster than wind? More numerous than grass?	Mother is weightier (worthier of worship) than the Earth. Father is taller than the sky. Mind is faster than wind. Thoughts are more numerous than grass.	Traditional values; Psychology	Vana; 313. 59-60. Yudhishthira's veneration of his mother is evident from the fact that he insisted on all five Pandavas marrying Draupadi just to uphold an unwitting remark by Kunti.
Who does not close its eyes even when asleep? What does not throb on being born? What does not have a heart? What gets augmented with speed?	Fish does not close its eyes when asleep. Egg does not throb on being born. Stone has no heart. River gets augmented with speed of flow.	Biology; Natural science	Vana; 313. 61-62. In a significant inter-linkage of episodes, exactly the same questions and answers appear in the Vana-parva, during King Janaka's 'admission test' to Ashtaavakra: Vana; 134. 28-29.

Who is the friend of one living abroad?	One's companion is a friend abroad.	Philosophy of life; Familial and Social values	Vana; 313. 63-64.
Who is the friend at home?	A householder's friend is his wife.		
Who is the friend of a sick person?	A sick person's friend is his physician.		
Who is the friend of a dying person?	A dying person's friend is charity.		
Which quality is the best in a worthy person?	Expertise is the best quality.	Personal philosophy	Vana; 313. 73-74.
What is the greatest wealth?	Knowledge of scriptures is the greatest wealth.		
What is the greatest gain?	Regaining health is the greatest gain.		
Which is the greatest happiness?	Contentment is the greatest happiness.		
Which quality (*dharma*) is the highest?	Non-cruelty (mercy) is the highest *dharma*.	Ethics; Scriptures; Psychology	Vana; 313. 75-76.
Which duty (*dharma*) yields fruits?	Vedic rites are always fruitful.		
By controlling what, does one not repent?	By controlling the mind one never repents.		
Alliance with whom is never broken?	Alliance with a righteous person is never broken.		

Abandoning what makes one popular?	Abandoning pride makes one popular.	Psychology (behavioural science)	Vana; 313. 77-78.

A striking concordance exists between these replies and the human psychological insights of the Bhagavad-Gita: 'Anger, desire and greed are the three doors to hell leading to self-destruction' (Gita; 16.21); |
| Eschewing what saves one from grief? | Eschewing anger saves one from grief. | | |
| Renouncing what makes one rich? | By renouncing desire one becomes (feels) rich. | | and, |
| Abandoning what makes one happy? | Abandoning greed makes one happy. | | 'Ostentation, pride, haughtiness, anger, harshness and ignorance are demoniac proclivities' (Gita; 16.04).

The significant difference, however, is that Krshna teaches this wisdom to Arjuna, whereas the self-learned Yudhishthira articulates it himself. |
| For what reason is donation given:

To the Brahmana?

To the actor and dancer?

To the servant?

To the king? | Donation is given:

To the Brahmana as duty (dharma).

To the actor and dancer for fame.

To the servant for nurture.

To the king from fear. | Sociology; Governance | Vana; 313. 79-80.

Again, the last answer is consistent with Bheeshma's counsel in the Raajadharma chapter of the Shaanti-parva, that a king should extract tax from his subjects by instilling fear of the enemy and loss of wealth. |

Which person is (a living) dead?	People sunk in poverty are (all but) dead.	Economics; Politics/ Governance; Scriptures	Vana; 313. 83-84.
Which state is dead (ruined)?	A state without a firm ruler is a dead (ruined) state.		The *inter se* distinction of types between these four answers is representative of the quintessential Mahabharata. The first two are universal secular enunciations of socio-economic and political truths, valid for all time; whereas the last pair represent traditionally orthodox pronouncements of ritualistic religion.
Which last rites are dead (wasted)?	Last rites without Vedic priests are dead (wasted).		
Which *Yajna* (worship) is dead (undone)?	Worship without the Brahmin's fee is dead (undone).		
Which foe of a person is the most difficult to subdue?	Anger is a person's most indomitable foe.	Ethics; Human psyche; Philosophy of life	Vana; 313. 91-92.
Which disease is endless?	Greed is the endless disease.		
Which person is virtuous?	A benefactor of all beings is virtuous.		
Which one is vicious?	A cruel person is to be considered vicious.		
What, according to the sages, is:	Consistency in one's nature is steadiness.	Human psyche; Personal philosophy; Ethics	Vana; 313. 95-96. One can discern an all-embracing concern for the whole world of creation in this refrain on the welfare of 'all beings' (*sarvabhoota*) – a concern characteristic of the width of ancient Indian vision.
Steadiness? Endurance?	Quelling of the senses is endurance.		
Supreme ablution?	Removing impurities of the mind (*manomala*) is the supreme ablution.		
Greatest charity?			

	Protecting all beings is the greatest charity.		
Dharma (righteous-ness), *artha* (wealth) and *kaama* (desire) are mutually opposed. How can these three ever-opposed goals coexist in harmony?	When a person's *dharma* and his wife remain in mutual accord (*paraspara-vashaanugou*) under his control, then *dharma*, *artha* and *kaama* can co-exist in harmony.	Personal philosophy; Family psyche	Vana; 313. 101-102. In reply to an earlier question (Vana; 313. 72), Yudhishthira had said: '*bhaaryaa daivakrtah sakhaa* – wife is one's divinely caused friend'. Yudhishthira's emphasis on the part played by the wife in guiding family values is consistent with the ringing prayer in Markandeya-Purana (*Candee*):'*bhaaryaam manoramaam dehi manovrtyanusaarineem* – Bless me with a pleasant wife who shares my mental inclinations'. This also is reminiscent of the immortal mournful eulogy of a dear departed wife contained in the *Aja-vilaapa* segment of Kalidasa's Raghuvamsha (8.67): '*grhinee sacivah sakhee mithah priya-shishyaa lalite kalaa-vidhou* – You were the mistress of my home, my counsellor, friend of my intimate moments, and my dear pupil in fine arts'. The importance attached by Yudhishthi ra

			to conjugal accord is further evident in his patient endeavour to persuade Draupadi about the validity of his way of thinking.
Lineage, conduct, studies of the Vedas and scriptures — which of these is required to attain the status of a learned Brahmana?	Those who indulge in dis- solute habits despite being studious, pro- fessorial, and knowledgeable in scriptures, are actually fools. Only those who act according to those studies and precepts are the learned ones (*yah kriyaavaan sa panditah*).	Philosophy; Scriptures	Vana; 313. 107,110. Yudhishthira's emphasis on action being the key determinant of a *Pandita* (learned person), is a distinctly special definition of the term; one does not come across it elsewhere. However, it makes eminent sense as example is always better than precept.[2.18]
Who is happy?	A happy person is one who, without incurring debt, and without living away from home, cooks his vegetables in his own home in the fifth or sixth hour of the day.	Personal philosophy	Vana; 313. 114,115. Yudhishthira sets out the eternal values of the householder (*grhastha*): management of personal finance; domesticity; and frugal self-reliance in living habits. The urge not to live away from home may remind one of the theme of *Nostos* (homecoming) that drove Odysseus through all his travails at sea when all that he desired was to return home after the Trojan War.

What is amazing?	Everyday, living beings are dying (departing for Yama's abode). Yet the rest wish for permanence; what could be more amazing?	Philosophy; Human psychology	Vana; 313. 114,116. The 'amazement' here is that of a *jnani* at the ostrich-like tendency of worldly people to dissociate the mind from personal mortality and to pursue materialism as the driving principle of life.
Which is the (right) path?	Logic (unrelated to scripture) has no basis, Vedas are mutually different. And there are no two sages (*muni*s) who do not differ in opinion. The truth of *dharma* lies hidden in the cave of mystery. Hence the path trodden by eminent men / many people (*mahaajano*) is the path to follow.	Personal philosophy	Vana; 313. 114,117. The significance of *mahaajano* has been interpreted in two different ways: 'a great multitude of men', and 'great or eminent men'. Both meanings appear in the Dictionary of Monier-Williams. The Aryashastra Mahabharata translates the term as *mahaajana-gana*, thereby implying 'great men'. But Neelkantha's annotation says: *bahujana-sammatam-eva maargam-anusaret* — 'Follow the path that is accepted by many people'. Buddhadev Basu suggests that perhaps Yudhishthira kept both meanings open in his subtle answer.

But Yudhishthira's own philosophy seems more inclined to the path followed/enjoined by 'great persons'. For one thing, he seems to place more reliance on the words of sages and wise elders (including Vidura and mother Kunti), than the scriptures, or common practice. Again, his unequivocal choice of polyandry (by no means a practice enjoined by scriptures, or followed by people at large), *vis-à-vis* Draupadi, based on Kunti's words and Vyasa's counsel, is a case in point.

| What is the message? | In this cauldron of great illusion (*asmin mahaa-mohamaye kataahe*); with the sun as fire, day-night as fuel; and using months and seasons as a stirrer, Time is cooking all beings. That is the message. | Philosophy; Metaphysics | Vana; 313. 114,118.

Such categorical affirmation of the ultimate existential truth, with all its starkly metaphysical connotations, is expected only from a seer of exceptional penetration. |
| --- | --- | --- | --- |

So far you have given valid answers to my questions.	The sound in praise of one's good deeds touches both heaven and earth. So long as that sound exists, one is regarded as a *purusha*.	Philosophy of life	Vana; 313. 119-121.
Now, explain: Who is a *purusha* (personage)?			Perhaps Yudhishthira had his own idols in mind while giving these two replies.
Who is the wealthiest person?	One to whom the agreeable and disagreeable, pleasure and pain, the past and future, are all equal, is the wealthiest person.		Bheeshma, with his immortal sacrifices, commitment to truth, and valour, could plausibly have been his ideal of *purusha*. Vyasa or Vidura could be his models of a person with the highest (spiritual) endowments.

The guard-examiner was happy with Yudhishthira's answers. He asked the prince to name one brother he wanted back alive. Yudhishthira promptly named his step-brother Nakula, so that one son of each of his two mothers might live. In further elaboration to the *yaksha*, he says:

Yathaa kuntee tathaa maadree vishesho naasti me tayoh /
Maatribhyaam samam-icchaami nakulo yaksha jeevatu //
~ Vana; 313.132
O *yaksha*, I do not distinguish between Kunti and Madri;
I wish to treat them equally as my mothers, so let Nakula be alive.

His righteous impartiality made the *yaksha* even happier, and he restored all the brothers to life. Then Dharma revealed himself and said: 'O best of kings, *varam vrneeshva*, ask for a boon.' Yudhishthira promptly asked, but not anything for himself. All he sought was that the fire-worshipper (*agnihotree*) Brahmin, who had earlier asked for his help, should get back his lost flintwood. The flintwood, which had been taken by Dharma himself in the guise of a deer, to set up his meeting with Yudhishthira, was duly restored to its owner. The pleased deity then offered another boon to the philosopher-prince.

His duties as brother and protector having been done, we could expect this generous offer to be Yudhishthira's cue to ask for something of deep philosophical significance. Perhaps, like Naciketa, he could have elicited the eternal truth of *Brahman*. Or perhaps, like Maitreyi, he could have said: 'What use to me is that which does not make me immortal?' But, somewhat to our disappointment, we find his feet too entangled in immediate temporal concerns to explore such subtleties. All he asks is that he and his family not be discovered during their year in disguise. It seems, after a brief peregrination into the transcendent realm, he has descended again into the 'cauldron of great illusion'. The boon-giver seems to will him to ask for something deeper than mere earthly needs, for Dharma again says: 'O best of men, ask once more; I am not satisfied enough by granting these wishes of yours'. But obviously Yudhishthira still has some way to go in his evolution as a *jnani*; all he asks for is that he be blessed with the power to overcome greed, illusion and anger, and that his mind remain steadfast in charity, worship and truth. Dharma grants him the boon, but cannot help commenting that Yudhishthira is by nature endowed with these attributes. In hindsight, however, we know he needed these, and that in the next phase of his life, some of these very qualities would be compromised.

ENIGMA OF *DHARMA*, THE 'CRITICAL PARENT'
Before we go into that phase of contrariety, it is pertinent to explore further into the mystery of Yudhishthira's guardian deity and divine *pater* (Dharma), who is so concerned about his son's attitudinal progress that he considers it necessary to meet him thrice in sub-human guise – twice to test him and once to convey a message. The tests are both designed as critical examinations of his gifted son – one 'mid-term' and the other 'final'. The first test is, of course, the episode of the crane-guard in *Vana-parva* (Book 3). The second , which is Yudhishthira's qualifying test for an unparalleled bodily entry into heaven, is at the very end, in the *Mahaaprasthaanika-parva* (Book 17), when Dharma, disguised as a dog following Yudhishthira, finally

grades the scholar-prince when his term on earth (the university of knowledge), draws to a close.

In-between, at the end of King Yudhishthira's fabulous horse-sacrifice and its attendant lavish charity in the *Aashvamedhika-parva* (Book 14), the deity appears as a weird half-golden, blue-eyed mongoose, as if to taunt and shake the victorious king from his regal complacency by announcing that Yudhishthira's prodigious charity is no match for the gift of gram-flour given by an impoverished grain-gleaner Brahmin. The mongoose clarifies that, wallowing in the meagre remnants of that flour caused half its body to turn golden; since then it has been scouring sacrificial sites in the hope of turning the other half golden as well, but to no avail. Its visit to Yudhishthira's sacrifice has been as fruitless, showing that charity by the rich, causing no hardship of austerity to the giver, is of little value. The moot point about this curious episode is: what message does it convey to Yudhishthira? Can one suggest that it is a call to renounce worldly riches and embrace asceticism? Perhaps yes, but post-Kurukshetra, the world at this point is still 'too much with' King Yudhishthira. It would take 36 more years for him to heed Dharma's call and set out on his ultimate mission of renunciation.

But who really is this Dharma, this enigmatic god-parent, ever so affectionate, at the same time ever so judgemental of his pilgrim son? One rarely hears about him outside the *Mahabharata*; and even there, Vyasa seems to have deliberately cloaked him in obscurity. His role as the begetter of Yudhishthira is narrated in just eight verses (Aadi; 122.1-8), which only tell us that he appeared before the meditating Kunti in an aerial vehicle of sun-like brilliance, and by yogic power took human form to unite with her. The prevalent interpretation is that Dharma is another appellation for Yama, the ancient *soma*-drinking god of death, the Rg-Vedic presider of the *pitrs*, who later got transformed as the judge, restrainer, and punisher of the dead, corresponding to the Greek Pluto and Minos.[2.19] Elsewhere in the *Mahabharata* (Savitri episode: Vana; 297.8-9), Yama is described as a dark and terrible (*bhayaavaha*) entity with solar effulgence and red eyes, wearing a crown, dressed in blood-red garments, and holding a noose to bind the thumb-sized spirit after drawing it from the body. One may wonder how to reconcile that fearsome and solemn-but-fair deity of the *Rg-Veda* or of the Naciketa or Savitri stories, with this dissimulating crane-guard, who tests, approves, and then reveals himself to Yudhishthira with these words of paternal affection:

Aham te janakas-taata dharmoh-amrduparaakrama /
Tvaam didrkshur-anupraapto viddhi maam bharatarshabha //
~ Vana: 314.6

My child, I am your father, the severely powerful Dharma. I have come with the desire to see you. Know me, O the best of Bharatas.

Despite the self-description as 'severely powerful', can one see any resemblance between this divinity and the formidable Yama? Indeed, the resemblance is more in nuances than in appearance. For one thing, both are critical examiners and objective judges. More importantly perhaps, Yama or Shamana, as his very names indicate, is the upholder of self-restraint (*samyama*), tranquillity and peace.[2.20] Are those qualities not the essence of Yudhishthira's mission on earth, as exemplified in his answers to the *yaksha*?

THE FAILED NEGOTIATIONS

The encounter with the crane-guard is undoubtedly a high point in the evolution of Yudhishthira as an outstanding scholar. Given such flowering of wisdom in our prince-protagonist, his getting embroiled in an utterly destructive civil war shortly after returning to the mainstream of life, may seem rather anti-climactic. However, to be fair to Yudhishthira, the war was thrust upon him by inexorable destiny, as is borne out by the failed negotiations of the *Udyoga-parva* (Book 4). Sanjaya brings a proposal for peace to the Pandava camp at Upaplavya saying: 'O King, infirm Dhrtarashtra does not support war, and suffers anguish because wise well-wishers are telling him that fratricide is the worst of sins. He has sent me to convey his desire for peace. Victory or defeat in war will bring no good. Both Bheeshma and Dhrtarashtra want you to sue for peace and friendship.'

Yudhishthira replies: 'Sanjaya, I have not expressed any desire for war; so why are you afraid on that count? Peace is surely preferable to war; only a fool would seek war if a fair end can be achieved without such drastic measures. But there is no end to man's desire. Dhrtarashtra has plenty; yet, despite knowing the nature of Duryodhana and his evil coterie, he ignores Vidura's wise counsel and pursues the unrighteous course. You know how we have suffered; still, considering your request, we are ready to forgive all. Let peace prevail; but let Duryodhana return Indraprastha to us.'

Sanjaya then appeals to Yudhishthira's pure conscience: 'O foe-less Yudhishthira, even if the Kauravas do not give you your share of the kingdom, it would still be better for you to subsist by begging than to resort to war. Your nature is to forgive, not to crave pleasure or power. What happiness would you gain by slaying Bheeshma, Drona, and others? If your advisers instigate you to war, then you withdraw yourself, leaving everything to them. Do not deviate from your path to heaven.'

Sanjaya's words obviously strike some deep chord in Yudhishthira's mind. He now lays bare the inner conflict between his peaceable nature (*svabhaava dharma*), and his perceived duty (*kula dharma*), as a warrior prince: 'Sanjaya, at times of crisis the course of *dharma* may change; so wise men decide on their duties by proper application of mind. But, unless one is desperate, it is discreditable to adopt another's *dharma*; in that case only you may blame us. I follow the course taken by my forefathers. If I forsake the path of peace by not agreeing to hold back arms, I would be blamed. But if, even after preparing for battle I abdicate my warrior's duty by desisting from fight, I would still be liable to be faulted. The illustrious Vaasudeva wishes both parties well; let him advise us what should be done.'

Krshna says: 'I counsel peace, since I do wish both sides well. But Sanjaya, you would agree that whereas Yudhishthira, despite his *Kshatriya* duties, has evinced a clear desire for peace, Dhrtarashtra and his sons are rapacious; hence, more strife seems inevitable. You are now counselling restraint to the Pandavas; do you not recollect Duryodhana's thievery and the outrage on Draupadi that happened in the dicing contest? Still, I consider it the righteous course to make efforts for peace without sacrificing the interest of the Pandavas; the question is whether the Kauravas will see reason. You should advise Dhrtarashtra with the clear understanding that the Pandavas seek peace, but are capable for war as well.'

By now Yudhishthira has reached a firm decision, and his parting words to Sanjaya constitute a proposition of rare magnanimity, conclusively vindicating his genuine desire for peace: 'You tell Duryodhana not to covet what belongs to others. We want peace; let him give a province to us. Or at least, let him give the five of us five villages, and we can have an amicable settlement. O Sanjaya, I am ready for both the balm of peace and the astringent of war.'

On Sanjaya's departure, Yudhishthira turns to Krshna, saying: 'You alone can save us from our predicament. Dhrtarashtra seeks peace without returning to us our kingdom; his love for his son makes him oblivious to his duty. We have no friend like you. Tell us a way whereby our interest and our duty are both served.'
Krshna says: 'I shall visit the Kaurava court in an effort to achieve the auspicious object of establishing peace without detriment to your interest.'

Interestingly, the briefings that Krshna receives from the five Pandavas before his departure for Hastinapura, are on somewhat unexpected lines insofar as the uncharacteristic opinions expressed by Bheema and Sahadeva are concerned. Yudhishthira says he trusts Krshna's judgement to speak righteously beneficial words that may be mild or strong to suit the occasion. Arjuna and Nakula opine on similar lines. But Bheema, normally the most truculently disposed towards the Kauravas, seems to out-Yudhishthira Yudhishthira in talking peace, saying: 'Madhu-sudana, you couch your words so that peace is secured; do not threaten war. Duryodhana is prone to anger and impatience; talk sweetly to him. We would rather be miserable, but the Bharata line must not perish. You ask grandsire Bheeshma and other courtiers to make efforts to pacify Duryodhana and establish fraternity between the two sides. I want peace; Dharmaraja too values peace. Even Arjuna is of kindly nature and does not seek war.'

Bheema speaking the language of appeasement! Can anything be more out of character? Whatever be its reason, Krshna views the mood-swing in the most warlike Pandava brother as a cause for concern, given the imminent likelihood of hostilities. He deliberately scoffs at Bheema for his *kleeva*-like softness towards the Kauravas, reminding him of his pledges to the contrary. Krshna's provocation works and Bheema reverts to his usual blustering ways. Quite surprisingly, however, Sahadeva turns out to be the most belligerent among the five brothers and tells Krshna: 'Notwithstanding the scriptural validity of Dharmaraja's words, you should so conduct your mission that war becomes a reality, even if the Kauravas sue for peace. After the humiliation suffered by Pancali in the dice hall, my anger will not subside till Duryodhana is killed. If my brothers are finicky about *dharma*, then I alone shall forsake *dharma* to wage war.'

Expectedly, the most stirring appeal for an armed showdown comes from Draupadi. 'Do not agree to any proposal for peace without a share of the kingdom. Do not be swayed by mercy; an enemy, who is not persuaded by peaceful and generous overtures, has necessarily to be punished. Such an action will be fulfilment of the Pandavas' duty; will be creditable on your part; and will be satisfying to the *Kshatriya amour propre*.' Then she holds up her long tresses before Krshna and says, shedding copious tears: 'When you talk of peace, remember these tresses that were roughly pulled by Duhshasana. I have spent 13 years containing the raging fire of anger in me; now, hearing the suddenly-virtuous Bheema's tranquil words, my heart is being rendered asunder.'

Krshna comforts her with words of reassurance that she would soon see her husbands destroy their enemies and regain their kingdom. Krshna does his best at Hastinapura to broker an honourable and fair settlement. With great patience and skill, he presents the Pandava case for a fair dispensation after having undergone all the hardship involved in carrying out their severe pledges. He appeals to Dhrtarashtra's sense of duty as the king and family elder to ordain a fair settlement between his greedy sons and his ill-treated nephews, and to save the *Kshatriya* class from annihilation. Finally, he spells out clearly that the Pandavas are prepared to serve him or else to wage war, and that it is for him to make the choice.

The great sages – Parashurama, Kanva, and Narada – who have come down to the Hastinapura court to witness the crucial event, all support Krshna's wise counsel. But Dhrtarashtra, as is his wont, vacillates between the desire to do the right thing and a benumbing incapacity to override Duryodhana's recalcitrance. He finally leaves it to Krshna to try and persuade his son. Krshna, Bheeshma, Drona, Vidura, all try their best, but Duryodhana is unrelenting. To Krshna he says: 'Earlier, being too young, I could not contest the share of kingdom that my father had given. I shall not be so pliant now, and shall not part with even the tiniest bit of land that is marked by the sharp point of a needle.' Even the motherly counsel of the habitually reserved Gandhari, to heed Krshna, abandon greed, and befriend the Pandavas, fails to move him. Instead, he and his coterie chalk out a plan to overpower and bind the wily Krshna and deprive the Pandavas of their main source of strength. But Krshna pre-empts the plan by bedazzling all with the sight of his celestial form, and leaves Dhrtarashtra's court.

ARMS AND THE MAN: THE CONTRARY YUDHISHTHIRA

Duryodhana's rude rejection compels Yudhishthira to join battle. But once on the warpath, he changes beyond recognition.[2.21] Indeed, during those 18 battle-scarred days from the *Bheeshma-parva* (Book 5) to the *Sauptika-parva* (Book 10), a strange twist afflicts Yudhishthira's words and actions. In *Vana-parva*, he had consoled Draupadi by criticising anger and extolling forgiveness, saying: 'It is the quality of forgiveness that holds and sustains the world.' But when hostilities become inevitable, the champion of forgiveness and restraint gets transformed into a warrior-king who thinks in more practical terms.

Gone for a time is the conscientious judge of right and wrong, yielding place to a determined and crafty strategist. He performs some dubiously-motivated deeds that cannot, under any circumstances, be viewed as fair. On the eve of the battle, he makes an inglorious proposal to his maternal uncle Shalya, king of Madra, who had joined the Kauravas, that he should serve as Karna's charioteer and cause him debilitating distraction during his fight with Arjuna. On the ninth day of battle, when the Pandavas are harried by Bheeshma's might, he abandons all vestiges of ethics, conscience and attachment, and personally calling on his affectionate grandfather, elicits from him knowledge about the way to cause his death. And later in *Drona-parva*, under a compulsion-driven Krishna's questionable guidance, he commits that treacherous betrayal of trust, half-whispering those ill-famed words of deception: '*Ashvatthaamaa hatah iti kunjarah,*' a despicable half-lie, as a result of which his previously levitating chariot becomes surface-bound and he would see the illusion of hell on his last journey.

BLESSED ARE THEY WHO MOURN

Such atypical conduct is not normally expected of one hailed as the epitome of righteousness. Indeed, it seems to have been caused by the inner conflict which had afflicted him during the war. At the end of the battle, we see the re-emergence of our familiar pilgrim, the Yudhishthira of the *Vana-parva*. The difference is that now he is overwhelmed with a heavy burden of grief. Yudhishthira, after the battle of Kurukshetra, is without doubt the most penitent figure of the *Mahabharata*. Twice, driven by his almost unbearable sense of guilt, he wants to leave everything and return to the forest – first during the *Shaanti-parva,* and later in the *Aashvamedhika-parva*. On both occasions he is dissuaded by Vyasa and Krshna. The first time his sorrow is alleviated by grandsire Bheeshma's advice on the duties regarding salvation, governance and charity. After Bheeshma's passing, he becomes submerged in a sea of guilt and his mourning and tormented soul finds succour in performing, on the advice of Vyasa, the expiatory rites of the *Ashvamedha Yajna.*

Yudhishthira and Arjuna – the comparison stares at us once again. Arjuna, for all the parricidal and fratricidal destructions directly or indirectly caused by him in the great civil war, remained practically unaffected by guilt,[2.22] because Krshna absolved him by the talismanic assurance: 'I shall release you from all sins; do not lament'. Yudhishthira had no such help. He had to do it all himself, repenting his way to liberation – a self-achieved salvation that was beyond Arjuna. This repentance, this endless thirst for knowledge and purity of conduct, unfolds before us the portrait of a truly blessed man who, with utmost care and self-driven effort, realised the most harmonious fulfilment of the rich promises that were intrinsic to his lofty, but essentially human, soul. This realisation and fulfilment, in turn led to the exalting end of the *Mahaaprasthaanika-parva* and the *Svargaarohanika-parva*, where Yudhishthira lifted himself to the highest peak of human greatness, passed the ultimate test, and earned the right to ascend to heaven in his bodily self.

Yudhishthira's lone ascent to heaven is the final and most noble event in this monumental drama. During the great final journey, one after the other, Draupadi and four brothers fell to their deaths. But the wise and steady Yudhishthira did not look back. He had no desire to descend again into the 'cauldron of great illusion'. The extraordinary traveller forged ahead on his celestial pilgrimage, accompanied by a follower dog. Indra, the heavenly lord, himself came to welcome him aboard the heaven-bound chariot and invited him to leave the lowly dog behind. When Yudhishthira refused, the god-king reasoned: 'You have left your dear brothers and wife to gain access to heaven in your own right; now why are you not leaving this unclean animal?' Yudhishthira replied: 'The dead cannot be brought back to life, nor can one have any attachment to them. I had no power to revive my brothers and wife, and so I left them. I did not forsake them so long as they were alive. In my view, threatening one who seeks shelter, killing a woman, robbing a Brahmana, and killing a friend — the sin that visits from all these offences, visits one who forsakes his follower (*bhakta*).'

These lofty words were the last and noblest of the answers given by Yudhishthira, the scholar extraordinaire. After this, the god Dharma revealed himself, shedding his canine guise: 'My son, in *Dvaita-vana* I once tested you; you sought the life of Nakula rather than Bheema or Arjuna, so that one son of each mother could live. Even in heaven there is none to match you, because you preferred to renounce the heaven-bound chariot for the sake of a devotee dog. Noblest of the Bharata dynasty, you may ascend to heaven in your physical body and be forever in that abode of the blessed.' Such an exalted ending does not leave any scope for doubt. The truth stands out with utmost clarity – that this incomparable epic drama is, in fact, the life story of its super-hero, Yudhishthira.

NOTES & REFERENCES

2.1 In the context of genealogical descriptions, there is a stray reference to another wife and son of Yudhishthira (Aadi; 95), but they do not find any detailed mention in the epic.

2.2 Buddhadev Basu, *Mahabharater Katha* (Bengali), M.C. Sarkar & Sons, Kolkata-73, 1974, pp. 48-55; 71-82; 93-107. Several important aspects of the analysis of Yudhishthira's strengths and weaknesses; his comparison with Arjuna and Rama; the enigma of Dharma, etc. have been sourced from these commentaries.

2.3 On being asked by Yudhishthira the cause for the blood-curdling roar that emanated from the Kaurava army after the unfair killing of Drona, Arjuna reproached him with the following words:

Upaceerno gururmithyaa bhavataa raaijyakaaranaat //
Dharmajnena sataa naama sohdharmah sumahaan krtah /
Ciram sthaasyati caakeerti-strailokye sacaraacare //
Raame vaalibadhaad yadvadevam drone nipaatite /

(Drona; 196. 34.5-35.5)

'You, despite being wise in *dharma*, have deceived your *guru* by lying for the sake of kingdom, and so have committed a grievous violation of *dharma*.' <u>Hence, just as Rama became infamous for his snide killing of Vaalee, you too shall incur lasting infamy for felling guru Drona with a disgraceful falsehood</u> (emphasis author's). However, the underlined verse segment might have been one of the later *Drona-parva* interpolations (linking the two epics), that we shall discuss in the concluding chapter.

2.4 Arjuna's nobility is marred by an episode in his youth when, driven by jealousy of the superior marksmanship of Ekalavya, he inveigled a partial Dronacarya to cause abiding damage to the ambitions of the young tribal (*Nishaada*) archer through the reprehensible act of making the latter cut off his right thumb as his offering to the Acarya, his idolised mentor.

2.5 Arjuna's exile to the forest during the *Aadi-parva* was caused under fortuitous circumstances. On the advice of Sage Narada, in order to avert a possible rivalry between the five brothers for the affection of Draupadi, they agreed that she would stay with each brother for a year at a time, and during that period, the couple's privacy would not be disturbed by the other brothers, failing which, the errant one would suffer 12 years exile. Arjuna was compelled to break the pledge when he disturbed Yudhishthira and Draupadi in order to get his arms (needed to defend the cattle of several distressed Brahmanas), which happened to be where the elder Pandava was then cohabiting with Draupadi. During his first banishment, Arjuna travelled far and wide – from the Ganga-dvaara (Haridwar), where he gratified the amorous advances of *Naga* princess Uloopi, who eventually bore him a heroic son; through many holy sites in the Himalayas; the lands of Anga, Vanga and Kalinga; the Mahendra mountains (Eastern Ghats); along the eastern sea-coast and inland up to the kingdom of Manipur, where he married the princess Citrangadaa and fathered another valiant son; to many holy places on the southern sea-coast; and finally to the western holy coast of Prabhasa before meeting Krshna at Dvaraka, from where, with Krshna's connivance, he eloped with Subhadra, his third bride and future mother of the illustrious Abhimanyu. Arjuna's second *vana-vaasa*, during the *Vana-parva*, was with his other family members after the fateful games of dice.

2.6 Arjuna's two conquests were for Yudhishthira's two great *yajnas* in the *Sabhaa-parva* and *Aashvamedhika-parva*. His three resuscitations were: by the *Naga* princess Uloopi; by Dharma's boon to Yudhishthira; and again by Uloopi, after Arjuna's fatal encounter with his own son Babhruvaahana, in the *Aadi-parva, Vana-parva and Aashvamedhika-parva*, respectively.

2.7 Krshna told Arjuna that the subtle philosophy of supreme *Brahman* that he had described at the beginning of the just war, was a vision seen in a state of yogic absorption and hence could not be retold in full. But he did enlighten Arjuna again on the gist of the *Gita's* message.

2.8 A study of Yudhishthira's evolution and central role as the *Mahabharata's* 'unlikely protagonist', is contained in an essay of that title in the following work: Abhijit Basu, *Prophets, Poets, & Philosopher-Kings: Sketches on India's Literary and Spiritual Heritage*, Celestial Books, Leadstart Publishing Pvt Ltd, Mumbai, 2012, pp. 51-70.

2.9 In the *Nalopaakhyaana* section (Chapters 52-79) of the *Vana-parva*, the sage Brhadashva, on being told by Yudhishthira of the woes he suffered due to his limitations as a dice-player, related the legend of King Nala: how the game of dice caused him to lose everything, including his beloved queen Damayanti, and how he regained all after learning the science of dice. The sage then taught Yudhishthira the same science, so that he never again had to fear any rival in that game.

2.10 Yudhishthira, with his lucidity of intellect, must have been aware of the moral truth that deceit is the essence of gambling. Krshna means the same when, in the *Gita* (Chapter 10) he declares, '*dyootam chalayataam-asmi*' ('of the fraudulent, I am gambling').

2.11 Here is an example of Rama emoting on nature in the exquisite poetry of Valmiki:

Pashya roopaani soumitre vanaanaam pushpashaalinaam /
Srjataam pushpavarshaani varsham toyam-ucaamiva //
Vikshipan vividhaah shaakhaa nagaanaam kusumotkataah /
Maarutashcalitah sthaanaih shatpadair-anugeeyate //
Mattakokila-samnaadair-nartayanniva paadapaan /
Shailakandara-nishkraantah prageeta iva caanilah //
~ Kishkindhyaa; 1.11; 14-15

O Soumitra; behold the beauty of these blossoming woods, showering flowers as clouds shower rain. Many flower-laden branches are swaying in heady wind, trailed by humming bumble-bees. Lo, the trees seem to be dancing in tune with the music of wind gushing out through mountain-caves, accompanied by the melodious cooing of cuckoo.

2.12 Again, one cannot help but compare Yudhishthira's liberal humanism and Rama's rigid orthodoxy, as revealed in the latter beheading Shambuka, the *Shoodra* ascetic, for transgressing the enjoined limitations of his *Varna* by engaging in austerities. However, to be fair to both Valmiki and Rama, that episode of exclusivist persecution is quite plausibly a later casteist addition, appearing as it does in the *Ramayana*'s *Uttara-kaanda*, which is generally believed to be of post-Valmiki origin.

2.13 There is a touch of the bizarre surrealism of a Poe or Conan Doyle in the episode of the lake. The mysterious guard first called itself a bird and then a demi-god. Before uttering its warning to Yudhishthira, it introduced itself saying: '*aham bakah shaibala-matsya-bhaksho*' ('I am heron, lichen and fish are my food'). When an awe-struck Yudhishthira asked if the voice was actually of some god who had felled his four mighty brothers, he heard the reply: 'I am *yaksha*'; then he saw a tall, colossally strong and monstrous-looking spectre, leaning against a tree, addressing him in a stentorian voice. It would seem that the idea behind the 'horror show' was to test Yudhishthira's courage; that was followed by a probe into his character, self-discipline and ethics. The questions thereafter were the final part of this comprehensive evaluation of courage, moral strength and knowledge.

2.14 The device of catechism is primarily employed in the Kena, Prashna, Mundaka, and Shvetaashvatara Upanishads. Similar systems of question-based discussion or debate are also seen in the Katha and Brhadaaranyaka Upanishads — for example, in the dialogues between Yama and Naciketa, and between Yajnavalkya and Maitreyi; or in the debate between Yajnavalkya and other *Brahma-jnanis* on the hallowed sacrificial venue of the royal sage, Janaka.

2.15 To put the story briefly: Vandee, the pundit in King Janaka's court, was a formidable debater, whose precondition for meeting a challenger was that the loser would be drowned. Many scholars, including the young Ashtavakra's father, suffered that fate. But the son was too brilliant, even for the argumentative Vandee. The two engaged in a contest of wits involving the significance of numbers. Starting with the digit one, Vandee said: ' The one and only Agni (fire) is lit in many ways; the one Sun lights up the whole world; the one Indra destroys many foes, and the one Lord of the *pitr*s is Yama.' Ashtavakra promptly replied with his illustrations of the number two: 'Indra and Agni are two brotherly gods; the two *Devarshi*s (divine sages) are Narada and Parvata; the mutually complementing Ashvinee-Kumaras are two in number; a chariot has two wheels, and the Almighty has created wife and husband as the two companions in life.' In this way, they went on with their instant repartees, till it was Vandee's turn to characterise 13. The court scholar, who had never before been so stringently tested, could only form half a couplet:

Trayodashee tithir-uktaa prashastaa trayodasha-dveepavatee mahee ca /
The thirteenth day of a fortnight is considered auspicious; the earth has thirteen islands.

Ashtaavakra promptly completed the other line to win the contest:

Trayodashaahaani sasaara keshee trayodashaadeeny-aticchandaamsi caahuh //

The demon Keshi had fought with Vishnu for thirteen days; the Vedic long metre (*Aticchanda; Ati-jagat…*) contains thirteen syllables.

2.16 A majority of the *yaksha*'s questions are clubbed as quartets, i.e. sets of four questions asked at one time.

2.17 There is also a parallel to be found in the *Brhadaaranyaka Upanishad*: in Yajnavalkya's reply to Gargi, that the firmament (*aakaasha*), is inextricably subsumed in the *Brahman*.

2.18 Yudhishthira's emphasis, on action being integral to true wisdom, is typically illustrative of the timeless significance of his philosophy. The modern Management phrase 'Paralysis through Analysis' sums up the empirical paradox of top managers being unable to act on their conclusions/convictions, even after thorough cogitation. Often the consequences of such knowing inaction are most tragic. Hamlet epitomises the fatal flaw of the tragic hero in his inability to translate thought into action. The history of the modern world also offers several glaring instances of such tragic failure to act despite discernible causality for action – appeasing Hitler, leading to WW II, being a case in point.

2.19 Monier Monier-Williams, *A Sanskrit English Dictionary*, Oxford, Clarendon Press, 1899; Indian Edition: Sri Satguru Publications, Indian Book Centre, Delhi, 1993. p. 846.

2.20 Shamana can signify destruction too, but that significance is more the characteristic of the frenziedly dancing Shiva.

2.21 The analyses of Yudhishthira's war-time change, his post-war repentance, and final journey of salvation, are broadly reproduced from:

Abhijit Basu, *Prophets, Poets, & Philosopher-Kings: Sketches on India's Literary and Spiritual Heritage*, 2012, pp. 66-69.

2.22 Only once, in Book 14 (*Aashvamedhika*; 78), when, in the course of his conquest of Sindhu, he hears the piteous appeal of Jayadratha's widow and Dhrtarashtra's daughter Duhshalaa, does Arjuna utter words of repentance: 'Fie upon the way of *Kshatriyas* that has made me destroy my friends and kinsmen.' But, unlike Yudhishthira, this grief does not burden Arjuna's mind for long.

3

LEGENDS INTERPRETED

YUGANTA: GENERAL FEATURES OF KARVE'S HYPOTHESIS

Among the significant anthropological studies of the *Mahabharata*, the work of Irawati Karve deserves special mention. Karve's well-known book, *Yuganta* (1968), makes interesting reading for a variety of reasons, not the least of which is an approach of practical objectivity, almost bordering on ironical irreverence, in trying to draw rational conclusions based on a clinical analysis of the characters and attitudes of some of the important *dramatis personae* of the great epic. Some of her conclusions, such as the postulation of a secular core with an extraordinarily subtle, but still human Krshna, being later overlaid with moral and devotional accretions, are of a piece with several Western studies.

Some, like her portrayal of the strength and dignity of Draupadi, are admirably sharp and empathetic. Others are controversial, to say the least, as is her iconoclastic depiction of Bheeshma, as one who capitalised on his image of idealism and abnegation to dominate and control events, and heap injustices on several female characters including Amba, Gandhari, and Kunti. Her uninhibited speculation about Yudhishthira being Vidura's son, is also a matter for debate. In particular, two enigmatic subjects, depicted rather intriguingly through Karve's Western-anthropogical prism, offer rich new insight. These are: (i) the fiery destruction of the great Khandava forest; and (ii) the fascinating legend of Krshna-Vaasudeva.

REINTERPRETING THE KHANDAVA HOLOCAUST

Karve's presentation of the analytical implications of the burning of the Khandava forest could impress one with the overall logic of its plausibility.[3.1] A quick relook at the *Mahabharata* story is called for. Khandava,[3.2] in those early days of Aryan ingress, was a great forest on the bank of the Yamuna and its minor tributary, the Ikshumati. *Khandava,* meaning 'made of sugar candy', and *Ikshumati,* translated as 'full of sugarcane' both seem to have associations with sweetness. Puranic annals also mention a certain *Madhu Vana*, meaning 'honeyed forest', located beside the Yamuna. The sweetness may not have been just sugar and honey. Even today, the central Indian forests have large Mahuva trees (the name deriving from the Sanskrit *Madhuka*). The plant is a source of bounty to the local tribals. They make plates from its leaves; extract a heady wine from its fragrant honey-laden flowers, and a variety of sweetmeats from its syrup. But the sweetness, so valued by the aboriginal *Naga* tribes, hardly mattered to the Aryans, who had other designs on the sylvan territory.

The early Aryan migrants hankered for *lebensraum*, a living place. But in those days of yore – from the time of the *Vedas* to the Buddha – north-central India was replete with forests. The *Mahabharata* mentions several great forests: Kamyaka, Dvaita, Khandava and others, separating five small kingdoms in present-day Punjab, Haryana and Delhi; these were: Kuru, North and South Pancala, Trigarta, and Viraata. These were capital settlements, surrounded by a few villages and some grazing pasture for cattle. There were large buffers of forest land separating the kingdoms, whose borders never touched. This topographical separation fitted well with the code of conduct of the ruling *Kshatriyas*, which upheld the hereditary family rights of each dynasty and frowned upon aggressive conquests of other kingdoms. 'Wars were fought, tribute was demanded, but no *Kshatriya* house was deprived of its kingdom. An enemy was spared if he asked for mercy. If he fought and was killed his son was put on the throne. A *Kshatriya* never killed women and children. Nor was he supposed to put to the sword any defenceless person. His most sacred duty was to defend the helpless. The charge that he had not done so was the worst that could be made against him'.[3.3]

But this code, this chivalry, appears to have been reserved only for Aryans; the local forest tribes were conveniently considered beyond its pale; conveniently, because territorial expansion without recourse to aggressive conquest was possible only by burning or razing forests, and exterminating their inhabitants, who could resist or contest the intrusion. Conveniently perhaps, sheer xenophobic contempt for the aborigines reduced them in the eyes of the Aryan invaders to sub-human status, thereby making their decimation a condonable act.

According to the *Mahabharata*, in the forest of Khandava there lived many *Nagas*, with Takshaka, a friend of Indra, as their king. The term *Naga* is generally used for serpents (occasionally also for elephants); but in the *Mahabharata* they seem to be human beings, with a king who ruled over the forest, including its birds and animals. In fact, the narrative mentions a bird-woman living in that forest, bearing children from a Brahmin. It is a reasonable assumption that 'bird' was the name of a clan or group. Similarly, some of the other designated animals might not really have been beasts, but people of other clans.

But clearly, even in the eyes of the Aryans, the *Naga*s were a higher order of being. They represented a ruling class, attempts to gain land from whom would sometimes involve marriage alliances. The Kuru genealogy itself shows two *Naga* princesses as mothers of reigning kings (Arjuna's wife Uloopi was a *Naga* princess). The episode of *Khandava-dahanam*, however, was perhaps another method of gaining land. But before going into that, let us recapitulate the essential story as recorded in the *Mahabharata*.

After marrying Draupadi, the Pandavas gained powerful allies. Duryodhana's nefarious plot to kill them having also failed, Dhrtarashtra was compelled to give the Pandavas, as their share of the kingdom, the forest-bound town of Khandavaprastha, near the border of the Kuru realm. The Pandavas gave it a new name – Indraprastha, meaning 'the city of the king of gods'; but their kingdom was still no match to the splendour of Hastinapura.

Then, shortly after Arjuna's marriage to Subhadra, he took Krshna and his other Yadava wedding guests for an excursion to the nearby woods. There Krshna and Arjuna were engaged in a tête-a-tête when a Brahmin approached them, saying: 'I am very hungry; satisfy my appetite, which has no bounds'. When they offered him food, he revealed himself as Agni, the fire-god, and said: 'Give me the Khandava forest to devour as my repast. Help me burn it; whenever I set about consuming it, Indra sends rain and foils my attempt, so as to save his friend Takshaka'. The two friends agreed to do Agni's bidding and, as a part of the agreement, secured from the divinity a celestial chariot and weapons. Arjuna got a divine horse-chariot with the speed of winds, and his all-conquering bow, the *Gandeeva*, with two inexhaustible quivers; while Krshna received his formidable discus, the *Sudarshana Cakra* and the mace *Koumodaki* – assets that would make them invincible on the battlefield.

Then the all-consuming Agni started devouring the forest, while the two heroes stood guard, butchering all animals that tried to escape the raging fire. Indra came down with his thunderous might but, being thwarted by the formidable guards, and coming to know that Takshaka was safe, desisted from further action. Arjuna's 'special relationship' with Indra would also have been a factor behind the latter's indulgence. The fire raged for a week, with Krshna and Arjuna circling the forest and mercilessly killing all escaping creatures. At last, having gorged on the flesh and fat of almost all the creatures of the forest, Agni went away duly satiated.

The massacre left few survivors, one being Takshaka's son Ashvasena, who lived to thirst for revenge on Arjuna. In contrast, another survivor, the demon Maya, who lived in Takshaka's house, had only gratitude for the Pandava, his life having been spared after he begged for mercy. Maya, an expert architect, repaid his debt by building a magnificent palace of unparalleled splendour at Indraprastha for the Pandavas.

Thus ran the *Mahabharata* account of the building of the grand capital of Indraprastha on the ruins of the Khandava forest, an account that smacks of a factual core overlaid with mythical make-believe. The core of historicity is palpable when one considers that the acts of butchery and devastation that called for such laboured and patently fabulous justification, supposedly involving sanctifying mandates from a Brahmin and the exalted Aryan fire-god, would not have been made up without a vestige of truth.

That brings us back to Irawati Karve's near-iconoclastic interpretation of the Khandava holocaust. Why were all its inhabitants so thoroughly destroyed? How could Arjuna, who took pride in the epithet *Beebhatsu* (one who eschews anything repulsive), indulge in the abominable massacre? A plausible clue lies in the primitive Aryan hunger for land, referred to earlier.

As discussed, the *Naga*s were apparently distinct from other tribes in that they represented a ruling class. The *Mahabharata* mentions the names of various *Naga* chieftains in different regions, stretching from the western Himalayas, through the middle reaches of the Ganga, down to south of the Narmada. The *Naga*s apparently lived along the rivers in the forests, while the pastoral and farming Aryans preferred more open country. The celebrated *Naga* king, Airavata, derived his name from the river Iravati, on the banks of which lay his domain. Normally, the Aryans respected the domain rights of established local houses and left them alone. Instead, some Aryan kings would, rather seek to acquire new lands by burning or cutting parts of a virgin forest not owned by anyone. However, the Khandava episode would seemingly signify a major departure from this practice; there Krshna and Arjuna had a more audacious plan to possess an entire forest, at least a part of which happened to be in the kingdom of the house of Takshaka.

According to the interpretation advanced by Karve, the Pandavas wanted to possess the forest land to augment their modest kingdom by distributing deforested tracts to their own subjects. Arguably, the land was usurped after a massacre, which is presented as a sanctified and valorous deed. The much-vaunted *Kshatriya* ethics were not technically infringed, because the hapless victims were not *Kshatriya*s or their Aryan subjects. Still, as additional fig-leaves to cover the gory act, the epic plays down the human qualities of the *Naga*s and describes the other denizens of the forest as birds and animals. Indeed, the whole episode reads like a week-long hunt. But even the *Kshatriya* rules of hunting were given the go-by, there being no indication that mating animals, pregnant females or suckling young, were spared. *Yuganta* even suggests that Khandava might have been the archetypal precedent of settlers unleashing a pogrom on hapless aborigines, a process of which the Spaniards and Portuguese in South America and the English in North America and Australia are more modern examples. This perhaps is too sensational a view, considering the overall record of assimilation of various ethnic groups into the ancient Hindu fold, with aboriginal tribes being included as *Dasa*s (albeit as a conquered, servile community, as suggested by Basham[3.4]), and with Scythians and even *Yavana*s, being accommodated as *Kshatriya*s.

But the anthropology of Khandava does have a few humanistic angles that are susceptible to radical reinterpretation.

THE LEGEND OF KRSHNA-VAASUDEVA

At this juncture, we should examine another hypothesis Karve presents to explain some of the actions of Krshna, whose super-arching influence pervades the course of events right from the time of Draupadi's *svayamvara* near the end of the *Aadi-parva*, when he first enters the storyline. As with his part in the Khandava episode, Krshna surprises us as the mover, and at times the shaker, of several seemingly controversial turns in the epic drama. Krshna's ruthless yet contrasting roles in the exterminations of Jarasandha and Shishupala offer an interesting study.

While Krshna's Yadava ties of kinship with Kunti, his spontaneous bond of friendship with Arjuna, and his conviction that the Pandavas had, both literally and figuratively, *dharma* on their side (Dharma being also a sobriquet of Yudhishthira), were potent inducements to make common cause with them, there was also the strategic Yadava motive of joining forces with the Pandava-Pancala combine in the struggle against Jarasandha. The mighty king of Magadha was incensed at Krshna for slaying his son-in-law Kamsa, and, after 17 depredations of Mathura, had driven the Yadavas out of their homeland to far-away Dvaraka. For the most part of the *Aadi-parva*, Krshna had his hands full with the long march south-west. Only after regrouping his people at their new location, did he come to witness Draupadi's marriage, when, with his uncanny power of observation, he saw through the disguise of the five Pandavas. He lost no time in greeting Kunti and her sons, and from then on remained their steadfast friend, philosopher and guide. We have already been through the first fruit of the partnership – albeit a somewhat sordid one – in the setting up of the magnificent Indraprastha capital city on the site of the once-sylvan Khandava. Krshna's next step in bolstering the power of the Pandavas was to persuade Yudhishthira to conduct the *Rajasooya* sacrifice, and to convince him that the unquestioned suzerainty the great imperial sacrifice demanded, would not be possible until the implacable Jarasandha was subdued.

Krshna's motive in playing the Pandava card against Jarasandha was threefold. First was his understandable desire for revenge and removal of a person who would have always contested Krshna's own pre-eminence. Second, he had to protect the interest of his Yadava clan, ever threatened by the monarch of Magadha. Third, and importantly for the higher societal good, the destruction of Jarasandha was necessary to preserve and protect the class of *Kshatriya*s, the defenders of the social order. Jarasandha had imprisoned 95 *Kshatriya* kings with the avowed intent of sacrificing them to Lord Shiva, his patron-deity, once he had five more kings to make up 100; this was in cpmplete violation of the *Kshatriya* code, which absolutely forbade such outrageous depredations against other rulers. Krshna did advise him to desist from such heinous and anarchic action and release the imprisoned monarchs. Jarasandha's refusal spelt his own doom. Krshna then felt no qualms about ethical niceties. Jarasandha was too formidable a general to risk a frontal battle with, and was also rendered almost invincible by a boon that protected him from being killed by any weapon. Krshna, therefore, resorted to deceit to overcome the king, manoeuvring things so that Bheema killed him after 27 days of a wrestling duel, by tearing his body into two.

With Jarasandha dead, there remained no viable opposition to solemnising Yudhishthira's all-conquering imperial status by holding the *Rajasooya Yajna*. But in the final hours of the great sacrifice, a sudden hitch arose. One of the assembled *Kshatriya*s was to be felicitated as the best and wisest of all. Yudhishthira, after consulting Bheeshma, chose Krshna. At this, Shishupala, king of Cedi, who bore a personal grudge against his cousin Krshna, rose in protest, insulting Bheeshma and the Pandavas, and denouncing Krshna as a mere cowherd, no king, and hence unworthy of such royal homage. He even incited the assembled kings to stage a walk-out and challenge the Pandavas to battle. Such defiance would have ruined Yudhishthira's sacrifice for royal supremacy, and Krshna nipped it in the bud by beheading Shishupala with his discus. His action, though ruthless, was not premeditated. The situation called for summary measures against Shishupala, who had grossly transgressed the limits of propriety expected of an invited guest and supposed ally. Here lies the difference between the slayings of Jarasandha and Shishupala. In the former, Krshna deliberately plotted the killing of a sworn enemy and an evil oppressor by using the Pandavas as agents with a vested interest in the killing. In the latter case, he was compelled by circumstance to perform the execution himself, as otherwise things would have ended in catastrophe.

These interventions by Krshna were made to serve the common interests of his Yadava clan, his Kshatriya class, and his Pandava friends. But there was probably a deeper personal ambition as well –to become the unchallenged *Vaasudeva*, a position with demigod status. As observed by Karve: 'The Krshna in the *Mahabharata* is definitely not a god, as depicted in later literature. He was, however, an extraordinary man, and his great personal ambition was to be called *Vaasudeva*.' The *Mahabharata* does not elaborate on the significance of the title, other than implying it could be more than just a patronymic (sons of Vasudeva), and apparently be bestowed on only a single person in any age. According to Jain sources and the later *Puranas*, the *Vaasudeva* was a ruler of great valour, splendour, and owned the seven most precious things in the world, as also the most beautiful woman. Three more things are said of him: he lacked nothing, found something good in everything, and never fought standing on the ground. The *Mahabharata*'s Krshna did apparently possess the seven precious things, some of which are mentioned in the epic, and all in the later *Puranas*. The description of his riches and personal splendour also fits the definition. Moreover, he was known as the best charioteer of his time, and a valiant warrior who never fought on the ground.

In fact, on his return to Dvaraka after the *Rajasooya* sacrifice, Krshna found the city devastated by Shaalva, king of Soubha, who unleashed violent attacks on the city, bent on extracting revenge for the death of his brother, Shishupala. Shaalva was a formidable opponent, who could fight from an aerial vehicle, and cast hypnotic spells on his adversaries. After protracted battle, Krshna killed him with his fearsome discus, thus saving his city and people and vindicating his claim to the splendid title of *Vaasudeva*. (Incidentally, he also had to subdue and kill a pretender *Vaasudeva*, the king of Pundra [present-day north Bengal], to consolidate the claim).

Krshna returned, having accomplished everything he wanted for himself, his friends, his clan, and his class. But to his consternation, he found Yudhishthira had gambled away the kingdom he had helped to build with such effort. But with characteristic stoicism, he did not reprimand the eldest Pandava. He only said:

Mayaagate'thavaa veera dyootam na bhavitaa tathaa /
Adyaaham kim karishyaami bhinnaseturivodakam //
~ Vana-parva; 22.43)

Had I been present here, this dice game would never have happened. But now that the dam has been ruptured to let loose the inexorable flood, how can I undo it!

Indeed, his absence during that fateful phase leading to the *dyoota* games in the *Sabhaa-parva*, proved to be a portentous turning point for the future course of events. Yudhishthira's imprudence, Shakuni's trickery, the inaction of Dhrtarashtra and the other elders, and Draupadi's humiliation, could conceivably have been averted had Krshna been present. There lies the true significance of Krshna's role in the great epic, demonstrating the abject poverty its contents would have been reduced to had it been Krshna-less, even in its primordial form.

Krshna, as we shall again see – in the context of the part he played later on in the *Mahabharata*, till its epochal climax of his own passing (causing the perceived onset of *Kali-Yuga*) – seems to be the linchpin of the whole drama, including both its human and philosophical dimensions. He is the *Mahabharata*'s man of destiny, the enigma who, being discovered in ever-newer light by his own and later generations, was also apparently evolving and discovering himself throughout his exceptionally eventful life.

It is no wonder that his deification, causing all those didactic and devotional accretions on the epic, was the work of later generations. He himself perhaps felt the inner urge towards self-actualisation by claiming the modest title of *Vaasudeva*, with occasional displays of the refulgence of a higher divinity. The true greatness of great personalities becomes more evident later, mostly in posthumous light, when the distilled essence of their life-missions, with all their rough and smooth edges, sinks through, with greater objectivity, in the popular perception. This holds true for all of history's Greats – for Christ and the Buddha, for Mohammad, for Ashoka, for Julius and Augustus Caesar, for Lincoln, and for Gandhi.

In one sense, the *Mahabharata's* Krshna strove for a set of lost causes. He could not save his own Yadava clan from their implosive doom; he could not avert the tragic blood-letting at Kurukshetra that wiped out the *Kshatriya* class he had always sought to protect; and he could not prevent the all-round degeneration of values and ethics, both on the battleground and in society at large, that signified the really sad epochal turn. But then, perhaps, there is a deeper significance to it all. Perhaps he, with his moderating presence, was destined to cut what could have been even more grievous losses to a great civilisation; and the philosophy uttered by him (the great syncretistic wisdom distilled from *Samkhya*, *Yoga* and *Vedanta*, that got organised and incorporated at some stage in the *Mahabharata* as the *Bhagavad-Gita*), is surely the one shining beacon of universal truth to sustain mankind on the course of harmonious living and spiritual quest, for generations to come.

A timeless transnational monument to that all-embracing philosophy is the Heliodorus Pillar of 130 BC (also mentioned as 110 BC and 150 BC), with its typically Vaishnavite motif of a surmounting sculpture of *Garuda*. It stands in the ancient city of Vidisha, near modern Besnagar, in central India. Heliodorus, a Greek ambassador of the Indo-Bactrian king Antialcidas, to the court of the Sunga king, Bhagabhadra, was among the earliest of the prominent Greek devotees (*Bhaagavata*, meaning follower of *Bhagavaan*), of Lord Vaasudeva-Vishnu, in whose honour the great stone column was erected. [3.5, 3.6, 3.7] A brief inscription on the pillar strikingly conveys the spiritual message of Krshna to the world at large: *Three immortal precepts (footsteps)... when practised lead to heaven: self-restraint, charity, consciousness.*[3.8, 3.9] [Archaeological Survey of India, Annual Report, 1908-1909]

In this way was the 'legend' of Vaasudeva-Krshna transformed into a deep philosophical faith in the consciousness of people.

NOTES & REFERENCES

3.1 Irawati Karve, *Yuganta* (English), Orient Blackswan Pvt. Ltd., Hyderabad, 2008, Reprint 2011, pp. 97-108.

3.2 The *Khandava* forest, interestingly, was the ancient site that now incorporates one of the busiest areas of the national capital (an area that encompasses the ITO Crossing, the Purana Qila [Old Fort], the Indian Institute of Public Administration, and the appropriately named Indraprastha Stadium). Delhi, like Rome, is replete with historical relics strewn across its thoroughfares. Kurukshetra itself is not far off, being located in the neighbouring state of Haryana, which also includes the district of Gurgaon, meaning the village of Guru Dronacharya. Hastinapura is also close by, in the neighbouring state of Uttar Pradesh.

3.3 Irawati Karve, *Yuganta* (English), Orient Blackswan Pvt. Ltd., Hyderabad, 2008, Reprint 2011, pp. 102-103.

3.4 AL Basham, *The Wonder that was India*, Sidgwick & Jackson, London, 1954; Picador (Macmilan) Edition, 2004, pp. 33, 36. The following extract is relevant to the context: 'As they settled among the darker aboriginals, the Aryans seem to have laid greater stress than before on purity of blood, and class divisions hardened, to exclude those Dasas who had found a place on the fringes of Aryan society, and those Aryans who had inter-married with the Dasas and adopted their ways. Both these groups were low in the social scale.'

3.5 Suvari Jaiswal, *The Origin and Development of Vaisnavism*, Munsiram Manoharlal, New Delhi, 1980, p.116

3.6 Kunja Govinda Goswami, *A Study of Vaisnavism*, Oriental Book Agency, Calcutta, 1956, p.6.

3.7 AL Basham, *The Wonder that was India*, Sidgwick & Jackson, London, 1954; Picador (Macmilan) Edition, 2004, p. 60. AL Basham observes (the conjecture regarding the antiquity of Manu's law-book is, however debatable): 'Thus some of the Greeks, while not completely merging with the local population, soon felt the influence of Indian ways of thought and made many compromises with Indian culture. The author of the law-book of Manu, writing probably a century or two later than Heliodorus, describes the Yavanas as degenerate Kshatriyas, or members of the warrior class, and thus gives them a place in Hindu society.'

3.8 Archaeological Survey of India, Annual Report (1908-1909). Calcutta: Superintendent of Government Printing, 1912, p.129. Here is a reproduction of the ASI Board at the base of the Heliodorous Pillar:

HISTORY OF THE PILLAR
THIS COLUMN IS LOCALLY CALLED KHAMB BABA AND IS
WORSHIPPED ESPECIALLY BY FISHERMEN. IT BEARS TWO
INSCRIPTIONS IN BRAHMI CHARACTERS AND PRAKRIT
LANGUAGE, ONE OF THESE INSCRIPTIONS RECORDS THAT THE
COLUMN WAS SET UP AS A GADUDA PILLAR IN HONOR OF GOD
VAASUDEVA (VISHNU) BY HELIODOROS A GREEK INHABITANT OF
TAXILA WHO HAD COME TO THE COURT OF BHAAGAVADRA KING
OF CENTRAL INDIA AS AN AMBASSADOR FROM ANTIALCIDAS
AN INDOBACTRIAN KING OF THE PUNJAB. HELIODOROS HAD
EVIDENTLY ADOPTED HINDUISM AS HE HAS STYLED HIMSELF A
BHAAGAVATA *i.e.*, A FOLLOWER OF THE VAISHNAVA SECT. THE
APPROXIMATE DATE OF THE COLUMN IS 150 BEFORE CHRIST.
3.9 Journal of the Royal Asiatic Society (London: JRAS, Pub., 1909)
pp.1053-54.

4
HEROINE NONPAREIL

THE DRAUPADI LEGEND

The legend of Draupadi is central to the *Mahabharata* story – so much so that hers is the only name that would come up every time one looks for the principal female character in the drama of the Bhaarata war. Krshna, Yudhishthira, Arjuna – there could be several contenders to claim the distinction of the chief male protagonist, but Draupadi stands apart in wondrous distinction among the illustrious *Mahabharata* ladies, including Satyavati, Gandhari, and Kunti.

There are several valid reasons behind this pre-eminence, each reason corresponding to one or other of the several facets that constitute the persona of the Pandava queen. And there is an intriguing array of variant nuances that makes her a multi-dimensional character of unique significance. As Krshnaa, she rose in the full splendour of her ethereal beauty from the fire of a holy sacrifice; but it was a sacrifice consecrated with the earthly aim of securing King Drupada's revenge against Drona. Her holy 'birth' from the sacrificial altar was heralded by a sinister oracle that she would cause grave danger to the *Kshatriyas* in general and to the Kuru dynasty in particular.

The divine forecast was to be later validated in the shape of an internecine war that had, as one of its causative preludes, her humiliation in the Kaurava court. She bore the marks of that fateful humiliation as symbols of an all-consuming spirit of revenge and gender-nuanced protest against the inequities of a male-dominated socio-cultural order – fretting, fuming, and weeping through her years in the forest, while forcefully chiding her husbands to avenge the insults she suffered. But for all her vengeful wrath, she was also the epitome of conscientiousness – as a dutiful wife to the five Pandava brothers; as a punctilious daughter-in-law carrying out the wishes of Kunti; as a patient and ever-hospitable hostess to many sages and other visitors during her difficult forest-bound years; and as a compassionate family member in consoling Uttaraa after Abhimanyu's death, or in caring for the woe-begotten Gandhari after the tragedy at Kurukshetra.

The authentic Draupadi, as portrayed by Vyasa, was the epitome of grace and dignity in her personal conduct. Flippancy was foreign to her noble nature. The apocryphal story that she burst into laughter at Duryodhana's embarrassing fall into an artfully camouflaged pool at the magical Indraprastha palace, loudly ridiculing the Kuru prince that such blindness was expected of a *blind man's son*, is a canard far removed from the original narrator's description in the *Sabhaa-parva*. That first-hand account only refers to Duryodhana's predicament evoking hilarity among the palace attendants and the Pandava brothers (excepting, of course, Yudhishthira). Draupadi was nowhere in the picture, nor was she, as queen, supposed to be a spectator to that scene.

It would also be incorrect to tar Draupadi with the brush of perceived arrogance. Such a perception is largely based on the one episode of her dismissive rejection of Karna in the *svayamvara* scene with the snobbish public remark: *naaham varayaami sootam* (I shall not accept one belonging to the *soota* class). But aside from what we view today as caste consciousness, was Draupadi's interjection not in keeping with the mores of the time? Was it not a natural enough reaction expected from an exceptionally endowed princess in wishing to choose a social equal as her life partner? Everyone knew of Karna's prowess with arms, but Draupadi did not let matters drift to a *fait accompli*, when Karna could have legitimately claimed her hand after qualifying in that archery test. After all, it was her *svayamvara* and why should we, from the perspective of another age, be judgemental about her expressing her own choice?

Even in her youth, her knowledge and wisdom made her a rarity among women of her time, and a formidable contender in debates – a quality evidenced in her confronting the Kuru elders with a subtle conundrum of right or wrong during her humiliation in the dice hall, as also in her later arguments with husband Yudhishthira during the *Vana-parva*. This very quality of exceptional merit made her a target for attack by her Kuru tormentors, as a woman with false pretensions to wisdom.

She stood out among the women of her time, place and class, in the circumstances of her polyandrous marriage, which provided grist to the mill of her detractors, who exploited her atypical marital status to denigrate her as a woman of easy virtue. It took a miracle to silence the aspersions cast by the forces of male chauvinism, when her tormentor Duhshasana's effort to disrobe her in open court was foiled by the intervention of god Dharma, following her surrendering herself to the protection of an absent Krshna. Given such divine vindication of her virtue, and blessed as she was by an indefinably exquisite bond of friendship with Vaasudeva Krshna, Draupadi has carved a glorious niche for herself in the annals of tradition, being venerated as one of the *pancakanyaa*, alongside Sita, Ahalya, Tara, and Mandodari, remembering whom was believed to wash away sin.[4.1]

INIMITABLE FIRST LADY

Even in that exalted group of five, Draupadi has but one of comparable stature, Sita being her only credible competitor for excellence. Irawati Karve draws a few significant parallels between the two illustrious queens.[4.2] Both had preternatural births; both chose their ideal consorts after they proved their prowess in a *Svayamvara* test; and both accompanied their husbands into exile in the forest. But Draupadi surely had more facets to her remarkable personality than the heroine of the *Ramayana*. Let us review some of those matchless qualities of Draupadi, the miracle-engendered princess of Pancala, marriage with whom provided the Pandavas with the necessary politico-military muscle to face their Kuru rivals.

Rajshekhar Basu provides a fine human sketch of Draupadi.[4.3] Arguably, no other woman in ancient Indian literature can match the qualities that animate her character. Her personal beauty is beyond comparison, and is only enhanced by her dark complexion, perhaps signifying a fire-related characteristic associated with her sacrificial origin. Her ravishing appearance in the *svayamvara* hall cast a powerful spell on all the suitors.

All the five Pandava brothers felt drawn by her enamouring magnetism, and their shared matrimony could well have been an expedient *modus vivendi* to prevent any fissure in fraternal unity, as was the arrangement for her cohabitation with each brother by seasonal turn.[44] Interestingly, the rotational arrangement also helped in fixing the paternal identity of Draupadi's five sons (the Upa-pandavas), which otherwise could have been difficult in such a muddlingly polyandrous situation (without the modern recourse to DNA tests).

Notwithstanding the discipline of such a wife-sharing arrangement by five virile husbands, it certainly would have proved too much for most women.[45] Draupadi, however, discharged her demanding marital role with remarkable success, so much so that Krshna's wife, Satyabhama, keen to establish her own dominance over other co-wives, once asked her (during the *Vana-parva*), if she used some occult rituals or potions to control her five husbands. Draupadi's advice to her could well serve as a model code of conduct for all righteously inclined wives of all ages: 'You ask me about the ways of insincere wives! As one who is loved by Krshna, it is inappropriate for you to think in such terms. A husband, if he comes to know of his wife's intention to exercise occult control, becomes as disturbed as a person who confronts a snake at home. Husbands are never subdued though potions or rituals. Listen to what I do. I never let personal ego, jealousy, desire or anger affect my ministration of my spouses. I never let my marital devotion be distracted by thoughts of other men. I do not bathe, eat or sleep till my husbands do the same. I keep the family utensils, food, and the entire household clean. I do not mix with disreputable women, do not go out much, and do not indulge in frivolous jests or excessive anger. I follow my mother-in-law's advice and my own good sense in dealing with relatives, in serving honoured guests, and in cooking and ceremonial duties. When King Yudhishthira ruled the land, I used to run the household and also to keep track of all income and expenditure of the realm. I have made it a habit to wake up before and to retire after everybody else. Satyabhama, these are my ways of influencing my husbands; the path of impure wives is not mine.'

Does such spousal counsel not remind one of the muse who inspired Alexander Pope's 'Epistle to a Lady': *She who ne'er answers till a husband cools / Or if she rules him, never shows she rules: / ... Reserve with Frankness, Art with Truth ally'd, / Courage with Softness, Modesty with Pride,/ Fix'd Principles, with Fancy ever new/ Shakes all together, and produces---You.'*? Indeed Draupadi, for all her crusades against gender injustice, and for all her related penchant for reproving her guilt-ridden husbands, also personified in herself the eternal values that can inspire an exemplary homemaker.

The husbands, in their turn, admired and adored her. Yudhishthira's words in the *Viraata-parva* sum up that adoration: 'Our wife is dearer than our own lives, as deserving of respect as a mother, as worthy of protection as an elder sister'. Draupadi loved all her husbands, but her affection had shades of difference. Yudhishthira had caused her a lot of trouble; still she held him in the regard due to the head of the family, tinged with the indulgent kindness one accords to an obstinate but well-meaning elder. In times of crisis she would turn to Bheema (at times even manipulating the hefty second Pandava's blind devotion to serve her whims or fancies), who in turn would feel gratified to carry out any mission for her. A kind of motherly instinct pervaded her affection for Madri's twins. But she seems to have been more partial in her love for Arjuna – a human weakness that was commented upon by Yudhishthira as the reason for her fall in their last great journey. [But then, was Yudhishthira's supposition a kind of *'Freudian slip'* caused by his own subjective perception? A moot point indeed.] Her human side is also apparent in her fretful remarks when Arjuna brought home the beautiful Subhadra as bride: 'O *Kaunteya*, you go to Subhadra; a new tie-up weakens old ties'.

There seems to have been an age-defying quality about Draupadi's beauty. Near the fag end of the 12 years in the forest, one look at her caused Jayadratha, the Sindhu king, to lose his head. She was then almost past her youth, yet Jayadratha, considerably younger, was driven by lust to kidnap her, exclaiming in impassioned wonder: 'I need marry none else if this woman becomes mine; after seeing her, all other women seem to be simians in comparison'. There is a striking cross-cultural parallel between her age-defying sex appeal (she was a veritable *Agni-kanya* or 'scorcher' in today's parlance), and her hypnotic effect on even younger men, and the cynic Enobarbus' description of Cleopatra in Shakespeare's *Antony and Cleopatra*: *Age cannot wither her, nor custom stale /her infinite variety. Other women cloy / the appetites they feed. But she makes hungry /where she most satisfies.*

When Draupadi came to the Viraata palace in the guise of *Sairindhree*, Queen Sudeshna told her: 'Crimson is the colour of your palms, your soles, and your lips; bewitching is the melody of your voice; endowed with rich hair and firm breasts, you are as fetching in looks as is a mare of the finest Kashmiri breed. ...You shall be my honoured guest, unless the king himself falls for your charm. All the ladies of this inner chamber are staring at you in rapt wonderment; how can one be sure that men would not be entranced by your comeliness? O fair lady, I fear that seeing your sensual beauty, King Viraata would abandon me and become entirely enamoured of you.' It was precisely for this felt insecurity that Sudeshna agreed to expose Draupadi to the danger of Keecaka's lust. But Draupadi was not one to meekly surrender to brute force; she had the courage and strength to push both Jayadratha and Keecaka and throw them to the ground.

THE LAMENTS OF DRAUPADI

The other facets of her personality are no less remarkable. When it comes to righting wrongs, she is ever impatient, vigorously spirited, and uninhibitedly outspoken – quite capable of stirring passive men to action. The *Mahabharata* bears many a testimony to her rhetorical prowess. Her dramatic laments and reproaches that adorn the *Vana-parva*, *Udyoga-parva*, and *Shaanti-parva*, can be considered priceless gems of world literature. Here are some excerpts:

Naiva me patayahsanti na putraa na ca baandhavaah/ *Na bhraataro na ca pitaa naiva tvam madhusoodana//* *Ye maam viprakrtaam kshudrair-upekshadhvam vishokavat/* *Na ca me shaamyate duhkham karno yat praahasattadaa//* *Caturbhih kaaranaih Krshna tvayaa rakshyaasmi nityashah/* *Sambandhaad gauravaat sakhyaat prabhutvena ca keshava//*	'Husbands, or sons, or friends, or brothers, or father, have I none! Nor have I you, O slayer of Madhu, for you all, beholding me treated so cruelly by inferior foes, sit still unmoved! My grief at Karna's ridicule is incapable of being assuaged! O Keshava, on four grounds I deserve to be ever protected by you: our relationship; your fame and honour; our friendship; and your lordship (over me).[4.6]	Vana (*Arju-naabhigamana-parvaadhyaaya*); 13.112-114 [The 'relationship' that Draupadi refers to is that Krshna is her brother-in-law through Kunti's Yadava connection. Krshna's 'lordship' over her is for reason of his authority to either accord or deny favour to her.]
Ityuktvaa mrdusamhaaram vrjinaagram *sudarshanam/* *Suneelam-asitaapaangee sarvagandhaadhivaasi-tam//* *Sarvalakshmana-sam-pannam mahaabhujaga-varcasam/* *Keshapaksham vara-arohaa grhya vaamena paaninaa//*	'Having said this, the beautiful Krshnaa of deep, dark, teary eyes, and the noble gait of a she-elephant, approached the lotus-eyed Krshna, and holding up with her left hand her own beautiful tresses of curly ends, deep-blue in hue and scented with every perfume, endued with every auspicious mark, and though gathered into a braid, yet soft and glossy like a mighty snake, spoke these words: 'O Lotus, eyed	Udyoga; 82.33-41 [Bheema's uncharacter-istic words of appeasement and reaction of Draupadi and Krshna to the same have already been mentioned in the section captioned 'The failed negotiations' in Chapter 2 ante.]

*Padmaakshee
pundareekaaksham-
upetya gajagaaminee/*

*Ashrupoornekshanaa
krshnaa krshnam
vacanam-avraveet//*

*Ayamte
pundareekaaksha
duhshaasana-
karodhrtah/*

*Smartavyah sarva-
kaaryeshu pareshaam
sandhim-icchataa//*

*Yadi bheemaarjunou
Krshna krpanou
sandhikaamakou/*

*Pitaa me yotsyate
vrddhah saha putrair-
mahaarathaih//*

*Panca caiva
mahaaveeryaah putraa
me madhusudana/*

*Abhimanyum
puraskrtya yotsyante
kurubhih saha//*

*Duhshaasana-
bhujam shyaamam
samcchinnam
paanshugunthitam/*

*Yadyaham-tu na
pashyaami kaa
shaantir-hrdayasya
me//*

one, in the course of all your acts, wishing to find peace with the enemy, you should remember these tresses of mine that were seized by Duhshasana's rude hands! If Bheema and Arjuna, O Krishna, stoop so low as to long for peace, then my aged father with his valiant sons will avenge me in battle. Further, my five heroic sons, with Abhimanyu at their head, will fight the Kauravas. What peace can this heart of mine know unless I behold Duhshasana's dark arm severed and lying in dust? Thirteen long years have I spent, hiding the smouldering fire of wrath in my heart; now that heart of mine is about to be rent asunder by the dart-like words of the mighty-armed Bheema, who now casts his eye on morality!'

Trayodasha hi varshaani
prateekshantyaa gataani
me/ Nidhaaya hrdaye
manyum pradeeptam-iva-
paavakam//

Videeryate me hrdayam
bheema-
vaak-shalyapeeditam/

Yohayam-adya
mahaabaahur-
dharmamevaanupashyati//

Sa tvam bhraatrn-imaan
drshtvaa pratinandasva
bhaarata/

Rshavaaniva sanmattaan
gajendraan-
oorjitaan-iva//

Amarapratimaah
sarve shatrusaahaah
parantapaah/

Eko'hpi hi sukhaa-
yaishaam mama
syaaditi me matih//

Kim punah
purushavyaaghra
patayo me
narar
shabhaah/

Samastaan-eendriaaneeva
shareerasya viceshtane//...

Yeshaam-unmattako
jyeshthah sarve
te'hpyaanusaarinah/

O Bhaarata, felicitate on seeing these brothers of yours who resemble mighty bulls or infuriated elephants. All of them are comparable to the celestials, capable of withstanding and tormenting your foes. To my mind, any one of my husbands can make me happy. O tiger among men, what need I say then, when all five of you, like the five senses inspiring all bodily actions, work together for my sake...

Those whose eldest brother turns mad, can only follow suit. Because of your madness, all the Pandavas are about to become mad. If, O monarch, they were

Shaanti (*Raajadharmaa-nushaasana-parvaadhyaaya*); 14.27-29; 32-33

[Draupadi's words of admonition to Yudhishthira are in the context of the latter's guilt-ridden penitence mentioned earlier under the Section 'Blessed are they that mourn' in Chapter 2.

The same chapter contains detailed reference to her 'debate' with the elder Pandava,

Tavonmaadaan-	in their senses, they	when her bur-
mahaaraaja	would then have	den of woes
sonmaadaah	immured you with	moves her to
sarvapaandavaah//	all non-believers	lament that
	and taken upon	she feels pity
Yadi hi syuranunmattaa	themselves the task	for the weak,
bhraataraste naraadhipa/	of ruling the earth.	because god
		does not look
Badhvaa tvaam naastikaih		after them'.]
saardham prashaaseyur-		
vasundharaam//		

DRAUPADI'S QUESTIONS: FOLLY OR NEW IDIOM?

Draupadi's response to her utterly humiliating experience in being dragged by Duhshasana into the dice hall after Yudhishthira had staked and lost her in his game with Shakuni, was to pose two teary-eyed questions on the legality (and related ethics), of her treatment to Yudhishthira and the assembled elders. The subtlety of the questions, asked in a situation of intense personal trauma, is indicative of her cerebral power and faculty of sharp, logical analysis. Of Yudhishthira, she asked whom he had lost first, himself or her? Of the elders, she enquired what her righteous duty was in the given situation, when Yudhishthira, after gambling away his liberty and becoming himself a slave, had staked his wife in the game of dice. The questions were indeed brilliant. But, given the socio-cultural idiom of the age, they presented a conundrum unamenable to satisfactory solution. No wonder, neither Yudhishthira nor Bheeshma, nor the other elders, had a definitive answer. Even today's commentators seem divided, as seen below.

OPINION X: DRAUPADI'S PERSONAL FOLLY

First, there are analysts like Irawati Karve, who contend that posing the issues was a 'big mistake' on Draupadi's part.[4.7] Her line of argument is that the questions were 'on a difficult and complicated legal point' to which even the Pandava-philic Bheeshma 'was unable to give an answer, perhaps for fear of compromising Draupadi'. What Draupadi contended was that a slave had no property, and hence Yudhishthira could not have staked her as he was a slave. Notwithstanding the logic of her argument, the moot point was that even being reduced to a slave did not take away a man's authority over his wife. 'Moreover, from the most ancient times a slave had the right to accumulate certain property that was entirely his own. The question was thus a tangled one, involving the rights of a master over a slave and a slave over his wife.'

On the above basis, Karve considers Draupadi's questions both 'foolish' and 'terrible', because irrespective of the answer, her position was desperate. Had Bheeshma told her that even though her husband became a slave, she remained in his power and he had the right to stake her, her slavery would have been validated. If, on the other hand, Bheeshma had argued that because of his slavery her husband had no rights over her, then her status would have been even more grievously untenable. The *Mahabharata* vividly portrays her pitiable plight in the dice hall with an evocative turn of phrase – *naathavateem anaathavat*:

Sa taam	And Duhshasana, dragging Krish-	Sabhaa;
paraamrshya	naa of long black tresses unto the	60.24[4.8]
sabhaa sameepam/	presence of the assembly – as if she	
Aaneeya	were helpless, though having pow-	
krshnaam	erful protectors (husbands) – and	
atikrshna	pulling at her, made her tremble	
kesheem//	like the banana plant in a storm.	

Duhshaasano
naathavateem
anaathavat/

Cakarsha
vaayuh kadaleem
ivaartaam//

If indeed Draupadi was to disown relationship with her husband, she would have been in a worse state than a widow. From Rig-Vedic times, there are references to the wretched lot of abandoned wives living in their fathers' house. But there was no precedent of a woman herself denying her husband. For such a woman, getting even a lowly position, let alone an honourable one, in her paternal household, would have been quite impossible.

Karve is critical of Draupadi *'standing there arguing about legal technicalities like a lady pundit when what was happening to her was so hideous that she should only have cried out for decency and pity in the name of the Kshatriya code'*. Interestingly, this line of reasoning is similar to the words of Shakuni to Karna in Pratibha Ray's adaptation of the dice hall scene: *The greatest offence a woman commits is to try to be learned. It is because she became wise and scholarly that her condition is thus! If she had grovelled at our feet and begged, perhaps she might have escaped such a gross insult. Just as knowledge and power enhance a man's attraction, similarly ignorance and helplessness increase the charm of a woman.*[4.9]

OPINION Y: DRAUPADI'S CIVILISATIONAL DISSENT

Irawati Karve's allusion to the practice of treating wives as property or chattel, cannot altogether explain Draupadi being staked in the dice game. One finds no concept of wife being treated as 'property' in the ancient *smrtis*. And of course, there was no gender angle or sense of 'property' ownership in Yudhishthira staking his brothers. Still, Karve's opinion has its validity in the limited context of Draupadi's immediate personal safety. But what Draupadi did must also be seen in a larger societal perspective. She was that rare entity – a woman dissenter against social injustice on women; an upholder of universal human rights against the forces of patrilocal custom. Her protest, viewed from a new angle of radical interpretation, was the progressive assertion of civilisational dissent against the reactionary cultural machismo of the Vedic age. As TRS Sharma points out in an in-depth analysis: *Draupadi's question posed in the assembly of the Elders could only confuse them, and … the prevailing idiom of the time was such that it finds the said question incomprehensible.*[4.10]

VIKARNA ALONE SPEAKS FOR DRAUPADI

But one Kaurava prince in that assembly did indeed raise his voice against the illiberal mindset of the time. Vikarna's ringing note of dissent is a vivid pointer to Vyasa's own intellectual integrity in recording what looks like an authentic and well articulated minority view. This was Vikarna's moment of abiding distinction – a moment that transformed his otherwise minor status in the epic to one of dazzling brilliance, exposing the ethico-legal weakness of the established order of the day that was seemingly upheld by the silence of the assembled elders.

The form and substance of Vikarna's dissent in the dice hall are both indicative of a thinking and sensitive mind, driven to exasperation by the sheer irrationality of the *Kshatriya* code of the time. Modern readers can only marvel at the conscientious acuity with which the epic's ancient narrator has etched that scene for posterity. Vikarna addresses the mute elders, rubbing his hands together and exhaling breaths of intense emotion: 'Whatever you may or may not choose to say, I shall speak out what I consider just and proper. Hunting, drinking, gambling and excessive womanising, these four are our royal indulgences. A person addicted to indulgence is prone to slip from virtue, his deeds are liable to be deemed as misdeeds. Yudhishthira has staked Draupadi in such a state of addictive indulgence. But she is the common wife of all the sons of Pandu, and not of Yudhishthira alone; and he too has offered her as stake after being himself won over. Hence I regard Draupadi as not won'.[4.11]

HELL HATH NO FURY AS A WOMAN SCORNED

But Vikarna's lone voice of conscience was not enough to loosen the iron-hold of the *Kshatriya* code. Rather, Draupadi saved her husbands and in so doing, herself, from servitude (with characteristic dignity, she refused to seek any boon for herself), by invoking a divine power to overawe King Dhrtarashtra. In retrospect, being judgemental about Draupadi's dissent solely from the viewpoint of her personal safety, would mean missing out on the larger socio-cultural message encapsulated in her whole attitude and conduct from that fateful day in the dice hall till the end of the Bhaarata war and the resultant emasculation of ancient India through the wiping out of a whole generation of its defender *Kshatriya*s.

Draupadi was the nonconformist who symbolised and presaged vengeance against the injustice of the prevailing social order. The intensity of her longing for vengeance is almost reminiscent of the all-devouring hunger for revenge that makes Madame Defarge of *A Tale of Two Cities* such a starkly unforgettable character in historical fiction. Of course, Draupadi was far nobler in spirit, and far richer in personal nuances than the Dickensian embodiment of one-dimensional feminine wrath. Still, Draupadi, for all her majestic dignity, does symbolise the spirit of feminist revenge in a manner not seen anywhere except again in the *Mahabharata*. Amba, with her self-immolating and reincarnate hatred of the patriarch Bheeshma, is Draupadi's only parallel in gender-driven vengefulness. Janaki Sreedharan, in a remarkably precise dissection of the anatomy of the epic's 'highly nuanced gender-consciousness', draws our attention to Draupadi's role as an 'overt symbol' of feminine protest on the one hand, and (together with Amba), as central to the vivid dramatisation of the 'narrative of revenge' on the other.[4.12] Draupadi, till the dire end of exacting retribution, 'brazenly preserves the marks of violation on her'. The narrative also dramatises the wrong done to her by repeatedly referring to her physical 'state of ritual pollution' as *rajasvalaa, ekavastraa*, and *muktakeshee* (menstruating, clad in one piece of cloth, and with loosened hair).

Still, one might ask, what after all did Draupadi achieve through her vengeance? In the final analysis, it spelt doom for her near and dear ones – her father, her brothers and most grievously, all her five sons, who met sudden death in Ashvatthama's gory nocturnal revenge. Draupadi, with her all-consuming hatred, was indeed destined to be the tragic heroine in the *Mahabharata*'s human drama, whose pyrrhic triumph came at the cost of the lives of all her young and valiant sons. But is there not a hint here of poetic justice, whereby the avenging angel was reduced to an inconsolable mother?

ABIDING CULT OF DRAUPADI

Draupadi's image, however, is much more than just the stereotypical fury of a woman wronged. Her divine/sacrificial origin, dark (supposedly 'non-aryan') complexion, and harmonious ties with Shri Krshna, could be suggestive of her sharing a larger epochal mission in tandem with the *Blessed Lord* of the *Gita*, as a dark-hued demigoddess in her own right. Over the ages, she has lived in popular psyche as the 'Goddess of Fortune' who, wherever present, removes all scarcity of food. The cult of Mother Draupadi (*Draupati Amman*), is an abiding tradition in certain villages of South India and Sri Lanka, binding people in community worship with unique rituals and mythologies.[4.13]

An ever-fascinating figure in our traditional ballads and rituals, Draupadi, as 'a masterful woman of energy, power and intellect', has now emerged as a powerful exemplar of feminist aspirations in the India of today. She is the inspiration behind the vibrant works of artistes, dramatists and authors like Mallika Sarabhai, Sonal Mansingh, Snaoli Mitra, and Pratibha Ray, all of whom, as observed by Sreedharan, 'have contributed richly to the interpretive lore around Draupadi in recent times.'

NOTES & REFERENCES

4.1 A well-known Sanskrit hymn on the *pancakanyaa* (the five daughters) runs as under:

Ahalyaa draupadee seetaa taaraa mandodaree tathaa /
Pancakanyaah smarennityam mahaapaatakanaashineeh //

Ahalya, Draupadi, Sita, Tara and Mandodari – remembering these five daughters destroys great sins.

Among English references to these fabulous five, the following may be cited: Promatha Nath Mullick, *Mahabharata: A Critical Study 1934*, Kessinger Publishing (Legacy Reprint Series), 31 Oct 2004, pp. 451-452.

4.2 Irawati Karve, *Yuganta* (English), Orient Blackswan Pvt. Ltd., Hyderabad, 2008, Reprint 2011, pp. 73-77.

4.3 Rajshekhar Basu, *Mahabharat Saranuvad* (Bengali), M.C. Sarkar & Sons, 1949 (Bengali Calendar: 1356), Tenth Reprint: 1987, Introductory portion, pp. ix, x.

4.4 The arrangement for rotational cohabitation with Draupadi was decided upon by the Pandava brothers on the advice of the sage Narada, (*Aadi-parva*), so as to preclude any sibling heartburn on that potentially divisive issue. In typical *Mahabharata* fashion, the logic of Narada's counsel was brought home through a frame-tale of Sunda and Upasunda, two otherwise invincible demon brothers, who destroyed themselves by fighting over Tilottama, a woman of incomparable beauty, specially created by the gods to cause dissension between the brothers.

4.5 In SL Bhyrappa's reconstruction in his magnum opus *Parva* (p. 225 of the Sahitya Academy English translation), 2009 (Second Edition), the 'scheme' of rotational sharing of Draupadi was ordained under Kunti's advice to her daughter-in-law. Bhyrappa then presents a sensitive portrayal of Draupadi reminiscing on her unique marital predicament with these words: *The new routine worked more easy on the body. But did this mean any relief from the* *violence on the mind? How would that mother-in-law of mine understand that Krishne is not only a body, but also a mind?*

4.6 The translation of the verse is generally based on Kisari Mohan Ganguli's *The Mahabharata*, Book 3, Section XII, Internet Sacred Text Archive, 1883-1896, p.33, available at: http://www.sacred-texts.com/hin/m03/m03012.htm

4.7 Irawati Karve, *Yuganta* (English), Orient Blackswan Pvt. Ltd., Hyderabad, 2008, Reprint 2011, pp. 88-90.

4.8 *The Mahabharata in Sanskrit*, Book 2, Chapter 60, Verse 24, Internet Sacred Text Archive, 'Parallel Devanagari and Romanization', available on the Internet at: http://www.sacred-texts.com/hin/mbs/mbs02060.htm

4.9 Pratibha Ray, *Yajnaseni*, Tr. Pradip Bhattacharya, 1995, 9th Reprint 2012, p. 238.

4.10 TRS Sharma, Introduction to *Reflections and Variations on the Mahabharata*, Sahitya Academy, New Delhi, 2009, p. 23.

4.11 Vikarna's words here are based on Rajshekhar Basu's Bengali *Saranuvad*, 1949 (Bengali Calendar: 1356), Tenth Reprint: 1987, p. 133, and Kisari Mohan Ganguli's *The Mahabharata*, Book 2, Section LXVII, Internet Sacred Text Archive, 1883-1896, pp. 130-131.

4.12 Janaki Sreedharan, *Imaging Vengeance: Amba and Draupadi*, *Reflections and Variations on the Mahabharata*, Sahitya Academy, New Delhi, 2009, pp. 99-101.

4.13 Alf Hiltebeitel, *The Cult of Draupadi: From Gingee to Kuruksetra*, *1*, Motilal Banarsidass, 1991.

5
EXALTING TRAGEDY

THE IRON HAND OF DESTINY

The way the *Mahabharata* draws to an end is itself a marvel of the great epic. Its last three *Parvas* (Books) are the shortest cantos in this otherwise enormous magnum opus of Vyasa. The *Maushala-parva*, *Mahaaprasthaanikaa-parva*, and *Svargaarohanikaa-parva*, contain just 320, 123, and 323 verses respectively, as against the 11,664 verses of the *Vana-parva*, and the 14,707 verses constituting the largely accreted behemoth of the *Shaanti-parva*.[5.1] The brevity of the last acts is perhaps suggestive of their unadulterated purity. Their tautness stands out in marked contrast to the long-winded meanderings and frame-tales of some of the earlier cantos. Their crisp encapsulation of a plethora of major events and nuances also helps in significantly enhancing the dramatic effect of the epic's conclusion.

One important structural method to enhance that effect is the use of special dramatic devices such as flash-forward and flash-back – both distinctly modern literary techniques that one rarely comes across in ancient story-telling. The technique already has had its striking impact in the *Shrimad Bhagavad-Gita* chapter of the *Bheeshma-parva*, which begins with Sanjaya conveying to Dhrtarashtra the shattering news of the patriarch's death in the starkly unembroidered words: *hato bheeshmah shaantanavo bharataanam pitaamahah* (Bheeshma, son of Shantanu and grandsire to the Bharatas, is dead). It is only after jolting everyone to attention with this tragic end-revelation, that the narrative rolls on, in flash-back mode, with the sightless king asking what his belligerent sons and nephews did at Kurukshetra, and Sanjaya, with the divine sight given him by Vyasa, recounting the battle scene to him.

The *Maushala-parva* too, begins with a similar dramatic jolt. The tragic destruction of the Yadava clan is tersely foreshadowed in Vaishampayana's prefatory words to Janamejaya: 'When the 36th year after the battle was reached, Yudhishthira beheld many ominous portents'. Then, 'Yudhishthira heard of the wholesale annihilation of the Vrshnis caused by the iron bolt'. This staccato message is crisply conveyed to us without indicating who its bearer is. Then again, Vaishampayana resumes his graphic narration of the destruction of the Yadu line and the inundation of Dvaraka.

CURSES AS SIGNALS OF DESTINY

Vaishampayana's detailed narrative is in response to Janamejaya's question about how the Andhakas, Vrshnis and Bhojas, all meet with their collective end in the very sight of *Vaasudeva*. The reason is ascribed to the workings of inexorable destiny; in the come-uppance of two curses, one on Krshna, and the other on his Yadava clan. Indeed, curses play a key role in the *Mahabharata* drama – much more than in the *Ramayana*, though the latter has as a causal prelude, Dasharatha's reminiscence of the curse inflicted by the blind sage, whose son is accidentally killed by the king during a hunt (Ayodhya; 63-64).[5.2] Otherwise, curses do not play much of a role in the 'Little Epic', except of course, in sidelights such as the one about an accursedly invisible Ahalya, who is delivered from her curse by Rama's visit (Aadi; 49). In that way, the *Ramayana* is more an epic of human effort (*purushakaara*), of the righteous actions of Rama, Lakshmana, Hanuman and Bharata, than one of Fate and Time (*Niyati* and *Kaala*). But in the *Mahabharata*, Fate and Time are the primary drivers, despite all the efforts of Krshna, Vyasa, Bheeshma, Vidura, Yudhishthira, Arjuna, Duryodhana and Karna.[5.3]

One can readily count at least six curses that have their telling impacts on the storyline: the one debarring Pandu from sex, that is the precursor to the *kshetraja* birth of the five Pandavas, as also to his own ultimate death; the two curses on Karna that signal his fall in the climactic battle; the pair of curses on Krshna and the Yadavas that foretell the tragedy of the *Maushala-parva*; and Shrngi's curse on Pareekshit, that signals his death from snakebite, which in turn is the cause behind Janamejaya's serpent sacrifice.

There are other curses too – such as the gruesome scourge of 3,000 years of putrid loneliness inflicted on Ashvatthama by Krshna, for his evil deeds in the *Sauptika-parva*; or the forlorn one of women being not able to keep a secret, pronounced by a grief-stricken Yudhishthira upon hearing (in the *Shaanti-parva*), about the secret of Karna's birth, held back by Kunti. Interestingly, one curse turns out to be a blessing in disguise. That is the peevish retribution of asexuality pronounced on Arjuna by a slighted Urvashi, which Indra converts into a one-year sentence of neuterhood to be conveniently used by the Pandava hero as his guise in the *Viraata-parva*. But then, Arjuna is Arjuna, the doubly chosen one, favoured by both Indra and Krshna (and Shiva too, for good measure). More significantly, Arjuna's action of rejecting Urvashi's advances is a righteous one, and therefore does not merit any adverse consequence, unlike the causative acts which bring grief to the others.

Indeed, in a deeper sense, curses in the Indian epics are perceived manifestations of the divine law of cause and effect rather than the cause itself. To put it in a more precise manner, a curse is an articulation of the consequences of someone's errant action, as understood and signalled by the curse-giver. In that sense, Gautama's curse on Ahalya is the sage's articulation of the effect, as perceived by him, of the latter's slippage from marital chastity; Parashurama's curse on Karna is the articulation of Parshurama envisioning the result of Karna's deception of his guru; and the *maushala* (iron bolt) curse on the Yadavas is the articulated consequence of their own arrogant and dissolute ways. Just as in Indian astrology, the 'sinister' nature of *Shani* and *Mangala* lies more in their role as signallers of trouble than as causes, in much the same manner, curses in the Indian epics could be viewed as signals of consequences accumulated by acts of commission or omission, rather than original causalities.

CURSES: A GLOBAL COMPARISON
Interestingly, the role of curses in the world's epics, insofar as they counterweigh human will and volition, offers an intriguing psycho-philosophical theme worthy of deeper study. Comparisons with the Greek epics and tragic drama could be relevant to the context. The death of heroes like Agamemnon and Achilles, the sufferings of Oedipus and Orestes, were results of curses — but there the curses do not just represent a mindset of feared retribution for past misdeeds; rather, in many cases,

they reveal a leitmotif of blatant partiality and favouritism of the gods. Indeed, this theme of the unfairness of divinities seems more pronounced in Greek and Biblical literature than in Indian traditions. The Old Testament Book of Job is perhaps the aptest case in point. That story of awfully cruel punishments inflicted by God on a good man, only for the purpose of testing the limits of his faith and virtue, has little or no parallel in ancient Indian literature, where the causality of poetic justice is normally more at play. The only limited comparison of divine unreasonableness that one can draw from the Mahabharata is perhaps the lot of Karna in being dogged by an unconscionably cruel destiny. But then, Karna's righteousness is that of a generous man and great warrior, and not the pious righteousness of Job.

Reverting to the context of *Maushala-parva*, the fateful curse on Krshna was pronounced during the post-war *Stree-parva* by a woe-begone Gandhari, who blamed him for not having done enough to prevent the tragic war, although he had the resources and ability to do so. The bereaved Kuru queen-mother had invoked the holy power derived from her austere abnegation, to prophecy a fratricidal doom for Krshna's clan, in the same way he had allowed internecine conflict to destroy the Kuru-Pandava clan, adding that the Yadava wives would lament over their dead husbands the same way the Kuru widows had lamented at the killing fields of Kurukshetra, with Krshna seeing all as a mute witness. The anguished Kuru queen then uttered her final words of doom – that Krshna himself would, after 36 more years, die the wretched death of a lowly beast in a forest, in kinless, friendless, and sonless isolation. Krshna tells her with a resigned smile that he already knows her sinister words to be inevitable, because the Yadavas (protected from destruction as they otherwise were), had to be the instruments of their own deaths, aided and abetted by Krshna himself.

THE SHAMVA EPISODE
But by far the weirdest curse in the entire *Mahabharata* is the one pronounced by the sages and forms the backdrop of the *Maushala-parva*. The episode, symptomatic as it was of Yadava hubris, does seem too mind-boggling to have been made up from

nothing, thus suggesting some ancient veracity. A quick review of the episode, as narrated by Vaishampayana, is necessary here to drive home the bizarre nature of what happened at Dvaraka before the advent of the *Kali* epoch.[5.4]

Once, when Vishvamitra, Kanva and Narada came on a visit to Dvaraka, several Vrshni pranksters hit upon a typically irreverent idea of having some fun at their expense. They dressed up Shamva – son of Krshna and Jambavati — as a pregnant woman, and asked the ascetics whether the 'lady' would deliver a boy or a girl. The great yogis saw through the deception and gave vent to their retributive wrath, saying: 'This Shamva, son of Krshna, will bring forth a fierce iron bolt. You Yadavas have become too wicked, too cruel, and much too intoxicated with pride; through that iron bolt you will become the exterminators of your race with the exception of Balarama and Vaasudeva. The blessed plough-wielding hero will enter the ocean, casting off his body, while a hunter named Jara will pierce the high-souled Krshna while he rests, lying on the ground.'

Krshna, who was apprised of the matter by the ascetics, evinced no desire to intervene, telling his Vrshni followers that what the sages pronounced was destiny. The next day, Shamva did deliver a fearsome iron bolt. A distressed King Ugrasena tried some preventive measure by ordering the lump to be ground into fine powder and dumping it into the sea. He, in consultation with Krshna, Balarama, and Babhru, further issued orders to all the Vrshnis and Andhakas, banning manufacture of wines and intoxicating spirits, with the stern warning that whoever violated the orders would be impaled alive with all his kinsmen.

EVIL OMENS AT DVARAKA
However, while the Vrshnis and Andhakas endeavoured to abide by the restrictions, the sinister black and tawny form of *Kaala* (Time/Death) was seen roaming about their houses, immune to all the arrows the Yadava archers shot at him. At the same time, Dvaraka witnessed many evil omens. Rats and mice ate away the hair and nails of sleeping men; asses were born of cows and elephants of mules...and so on. The Vrshnis, with

the exception of Krshna and Balarama, shamelessly committed sinful acts, in utter disregard of the priests and the deities. They insulted and humiliated their preceptors and seniors. There was no sanctity of marriage, with husbands and wives wantonly deceiving each other.

One day, seeing the advent of the new moon on the thirteenth day of the lunar cycle, Krshna told the Yadavas: 'Such portents were seen at the time of the Bhaarata war. It presages our destruction. You all proceed forthwith to bathe in the sacred waters of Prabhasa.' There were other evil portents, even affecting the great lords of Dvaraka. Krshna's formidable discus vanished into the sky in full sight of all; his divine horse-drawn chariot disappeared over the sea, with Daruka remaining a helpless spectator; and celestial nymphs, as if echoing Krshna's command, called aloud to the Yadavas to journey to the Prabhasa coast.

THE END OF THE YADAVAS
It was a journey of collective doom for the Yadavas. They, along with their families, set out on their weird 'pilgrimage', with loads of edibles, meat and drink. Vaishampayana's terse-yet-graphic portrayal of the last acts of the redoubtable Yadava heroes at Prabhasa reads like an orgy of unrestrained self-indulgence rarely seen even in the wildest 'rave' and drinking parties today. Balarama, Yuyudhana-Satyaki, Gada, Babhru and Krtavarma, began drinking right in front of Krshna. Soon the revelry degenerated into a drunken brawl and the immediate result was the rekindling of old antipathies arising from partisanship in the great fratricidal war that had embroiled all of them (except Balarama), 36 years ago.

A thoroughly inebriated Satyaki openly abused Krtavarma with scornful invective: 'Which *Kshatriya* would slay men lying prone in death-like slumber? The Yadavas will never forgive your misdeeds.' Pradyumna (son of Krshna-Rukmini), voiced loud support to the denunciation. An enraged Krtavarma, pointing at Satyaki with his left hand as a gesture of utmost contempt, then said: 'How could you, with all your pretensions as a hero, so cruelly slay the armless Bhurishrava, who had sat down in yogic *praaya* on the battlefield, devoid of all hostile intentions?'

Satyaki retorted by telling Krshna about Krtavarma's role in killing Satraajit (Satyabhama's father), and seizing his celebrated Syamantaka gem. Hearing this, a vengeful Satyabhama stoked Krshna's anger by weeping in his lap. Satyaki then rose up, swearing he would send Krtavarma to follow in the wake of the latter's (and Ashvatthama's), sleeping victims: Dhrshtadyumna, Shikhandi, and the five sons of Draupadi. So saying, he severed Krtavarma's head with a mighty swing of his sword, and proceeded to kill others.

Utter mayhem broke loose. The Bhojas and Andhakas surrounded Satyaki and began hitting him with the pots from which they had been eating. Krshna remained passive, knowing the developing catastrophe as the effect of Time (*kaala*), and remembering Gandhari's dismal prophecy. However his son, Pradyumna, rushed to Satyaki's defence; but both were overpowered and killed. A wrathful Krshna then took up a handful of *eraka* grass, which, in his hand, turned into a terrible iron-bolt of thunderous power. With it Krshna slew all who were before him. The blades of grass turned into iron-bolts, with which the drunken Andhakas, Bhojas, Vrshnis and Kukuras went on a killing spree. Son killed sire, sire killed son, all dying like insects rushing into a fire without any thought of escape. Shamva, Aniruddha, Gada, were all slain in front of Krshna; thereupon, Babhru and Daruka persuaded him to desist from venting his wrath and proceed instead to where Balarama had gone.

THE TIMELESS TRADITION OF 'TIME'

There indeed seems to be a strange inexorability about the way the Yadavas, in full view of their demigod guardian, pushed themselves to sudden self-destruction at Prabhasa. In one sense, true to the *Mahabharata*'s core tradition, the inexorability was ordained by Time (*Kaala*). In another sense, the tradition of yore is overlaid with the palpable reality of inter-personal behaviour dynamics, which seems quite modern in the ever-relevant context of human group interaction. Satyaki's drunken denunciation of Krtavarma; the latter's left-handed gesture of open contempt; Satyabhama's teary instigation of Krshna and Satyaki; the assault on Satyaki and Pradyumna by the Bhoja-Andhaka mob; and, above all else, the all-too-natural wrath transforming, for a while, an almost listlessly resigned Krshna, into a terrible exterminator – all seem to constitute the tragic but credible finale of a timeless reality drama.

ECHOES OF SODOM AND GOMORRAH?

Interestingly, apart from its central theme of Time, the tradition of the *Maushala-parva* seems to have had some wider spatial validity across other ancient civilisations as well. One can perhaps detect some resonance between this epic-Puranic Indian lore of accursed annihilation of the Yadavas and the Semitic-Biblical account of the destruction of Sodom and Gomorrah, contained in the *Book of Genesis* 18-19. The similarities look significant: the sages came on a visit to Krshna, whereas the angels (of God) came to visit Abraham and Lot; the Yadavas had turned arrogant, cruel and dissolute, whereas the Sodomites too had become overweening, selfishly inhospitable and blatantly sinful; at Prabhasa, iron bolts were the instruments of sudden death, whereas in the biblical cities, fire and brimstone caused the abrupt annihilation.

But the difference in the nature of vices sets apart the two accounts. The main vice of the Yadavas was their extreme weakness for the tipple; adultery and sexual promiscuity was a secondary syndrome with them. The Sodomites, on the other hand, were inveterate indulgers in homosexuality[5.5] – at least that is the dominant Christian and Islamic interpretation of their physical 'sin', the Jewish one laying greater stress on their violation of hospitality, blasphemy, robbery and violence. Secondly, in the *Mahabharata*, the Yadavas themselves wield the iron bolts, whereas in the *Bible*, fire and brimstone are sent down by God. One may, therefore, leave the topic of cross-civilisational comparison of the Indian and Semitic tales with the acknowledgement of some commonalities and some differences, in the aberrant natures and lifestyles of the two peoples.

THE EPOCH DIES A DOUBLE 'DEATH'

For all its differences with the Sodom story, there is little that is exalted about the Yadava tragedy, with illustrious heroes like Yuyudhana, Pradyumna and Krtavarma dying unheroic deaths in what resembles a lowly tavern-brawl. But the two silent 'deaths' that follow the Prabhasa mayhem, again prove the *Mahabharata*'s power to amaze readers with the sheer force of its dramatic contrasts that lift a great story to the sublime. Even before the *Maushala-parva*, we come across instances of glorious death – when Bheeshma, after 56 days of self-chosen 'repose' on a bed of arrows, passes away to the ovation of the deities; or when Karna's soul rises high like a fireball to merge with the solar refulgence.

But nothing perhaps can match the eerie grandeur of the yogic imagery of Balarama's death. Krshna's elder sibling chose to stay away from the Bhaarata war, in the manner of a modern 'conscientious objector', only to appear once in a long while, as the voice of conscience – as he did to denounce Bheema for his unethical felling of Duryodhana. To him, the means mattered no less than the end of a 'just war'. Krshna had to exercise all his brotherly influence to persuade him not to break his neutrality. Hailed by the Greeks as the Indian Heracles, and traditionally revered by Indians as an *avataara* in his own right (with some modern exceptions, such as SL Bhyrappa, who makes him into something of a brawny and impulsive character, nursing mixed feelings of grudging respect towards his famed sibling), Baladeva (meaning 'powerful deity'), was Krshna's alter ego. Following the demise of his Yadava clansmen, Krshna (having sent Daruka to Hastinapura to request Arjuna to come and save the women and children), bade his father goodbye with these words of deep melancholy: 'You protect the women till Dhananjaya comes. I am going to Balarama, who awaits me in the forest. I have seen many dying in the Kuru-Pandava war and, now, here. I cannot bear to stay at this Yadava-less Dvaraka; I would rather be a forester and meditate with Balarama.'

And what does Krshna see on his arrival in the forest? He becomes the lone beholder of a supernatural passing – of Balarama sitting in yogic posture, with an enormous thousand-hooded, red-eyed, white serpent emerging from his mouth to enter the ocean nearby, where he is welcomed with great honour by Varuna, Vasuki and other deities of the waters and the netherworld. Indeed, in the *Mahabharata*'s dramatic context,

Balarama's tranquil-yet-awesome end represents the turning point where the epic of myriad moods enters its last phase of *shaanta rasa*.

A lesser poet-playwright would have found it hard to match the surreal grandeur of the imagery of Balarama's last silent journey when portraying Krshna's own death. But here again Vyasa excels with a *tour de force* of dramatic contrast. Krshna, for all his cosmic glory, amazes us with the subtle commonness of his own mortal end. The immeasurably unlimited (*aprameyam*) 'Blessed Lord' shows us, one last time in the *Mahabharata*, his almost inscrutable characteristic of constraining himself now and then within the limitations of perceived human frailty. Krshna, the greatest personage and preserver of the *Dvaapara* order, transits from mortality in a quick and seemingly anticlimactic turn of events. After witnessing the passing away of Balarama, he wanders for a while and then reclines under a tree, restraining his senses in *yoga*, and awaits his own forlorn human end, in line with the dark prophecies of Gandhari and the sages. A hunter named Jara, perhaps mislaid by his yellow robes, takes him for a deer and pierces his heel with a shaft. Krshna absolves the repentant hunter of all wrong, and ascends upwards, 'filling the entire welkin with splendour'. The deities, sages, *siddhas*, *gandharvas*, and Lord Indra himself – all worship him as the illustrious Narayana, as he proceeds to his celestial abode.

KRSHNA, THE *MAHABHARATA*'S DEEPEST ENIGMA

Perhaps the best way, as an objective reader, to reach some understanding of the significance of Krshna's passing, is to review his total role in the *Mahabharata* narrative. Buddhadev Basu, with his razor-sharp analysis, has done just that in his Bengali masterpiece *Mahabharater Katha*.[5,6] Rather than seeking to 'reinvent the wheel', one may therefore try and present, with some additional comments, the eclectic essence of that fine analysis in the present context.

Much of the Krshna-enigma in the *Mahabharata* derives from the seemingly bewildering contradictions inherent in many of his actions in the great epic. In a way, for all the modern talks of interpolation of didactic matters, these Krshna-related 'contradictions' in themselves constitute the core elements of credibility that consistently characterise the basic structure of the traditional Vyasa narrative, which has undergone little or no change in all subsequent accretions. That credibility, in turn, is essentially derived from the credibility of Krshna himself as a towering personality with a human side to his 'demigod-God' characteristics.

One 'inconsistency' that readers may find about Krshna's role, is the seeming gap between what he promised and what he did, in relation to the Kurukshetra war. From the time that war clouds gather on the horizon, we see Krshna working to what appears to be a complex and deliberately considered script. At the start of the *Udyoga-parva* (Book 5; Chapter 4), he professes equal relationship with the Kauravas and Pandavas, but when, shortly thereafter, both Duryodhana and Arjuna approach him for help, his response, involving what is known in popular tradition as Krshna's 'feigned slumber', betrays a latent bias towards the latter (Udyoga; Chapter 6).

Thereafter, once the war begins, even that fig-leaf of impartiality is removed. Krshna, in his words, thoughts and deeds, reveals himself as the foremost facilitator and protector of the Pandavas, especially Arjuna; and the nemesis of the Kauravas. He breaks his own pledge of remaining unarmed and disengaged from active conflict on the third day of the war, when, seeing the Pandava forces in disarray under Bheeshma's onslaught, with Arjuna reluctant to engage the grandsire in serious battle, he resolves on killing the valiant and virtuous Kaurava general himself. Throwing to the winds all pretence of remaining a non-combatant, he jumps down from the chariot and, with the deadly *Sudarshana chakra* raised in his hand, rushes at Bheeshma 'like a lion attacking an elephant in rut'. Arjuna, in trying to restrain him by holding on to his hands, is 'dragged like a tree is dragged by a great storm', and only manages to stop him by forcibly holding his feet and appealing for calm. Again, later in the *Bheeshma-parva*, Krshna makes his bias abundantly clear to Yudhishthira in these words of unequivocal partisanship:
Pashya me vikramam raajan mahendrasyeva samyuge /
Vimunchantam mahaastraani paatayishyaaami tam rathaat //
Yah shatruh paanduputraanaam macchaatruh sa nasamshayah/

Madarthaa bhavadeeyaa ye ye madeeyaas-tavaiva te //
Tava bhraataa mama sakhaa sambandhee shishya eva ca /
Mamsaan-yutkrtya daasyaami phaalgunaarthe maheepate //
~ Bheeshma; 107.31-33

O King, see my Indra-like might in tomorrow's battle. I shall kill and fell Bheeshma, the employer of many great weapons, from his chariot on to the ground.

One who is the Pandavas' enemy is my enemy too — about that there is no doubt. Those who are your friends are my friends; and those who are my friends, know them also as your friends.

O Ruler of the Earth, your brother Arjuna is my friend, brother-in-law, and disciple. I shall even cut my own flesh and dedicate the same for the sake of Phaalguni.

Thus, for all his pledge to stay unarmed, the intent to use weaponry as a last resort is abundantly clear from Krishna's words and actions at Kurukshetra. And his most potent weapons – his cerebral power and his tactical prowess – are actually used to telling effect in almost all the decisive moments of the Bhaarata war. What is even more baffling to any lay reader, is the lack of all normal ethical compunctions in most of these Krshna-driven tactics of war. None else but Krshna could perhaps have hit upon the brilliant, but utterly unscrupulous plan that the way to to kill the invincible Bheeshma had to be elicited from Bheeshma himself.

The disarming and killing of a rampaging Drona through Yudhishthira's half-lie regarding the purported death of Drona's son Ashvatthama – perhaps the most sordid act in the supposedly 'just war' – is again the direct result of Krshna's counsel. It is with a heavy heart that Krshna gives that fateful advice, but the deceitful nature of that patently unethical advice cannot be condoned under any code of morality. Indeed, the single-mindedness with which Krshna drives the 'kill-Drona-at-any-cost' strategy is writ large in his two interventions preceding the reprehensible episode of disarming and killing the Acharya. First, he seeks to persuade Arjuna with the words: 'Only when Drona casts off his weapons can he be slain by humans. Hence, you all should make efforts to kill him by artifice, forsaking inhibitions about slaying your mentor. I think he will cease fighting once he believes that Ashvatthama has been killed;

therefore, let someone go and tell him that Ashvatthama is dead.' (Drona; 190. 11-12)

The upright Arjuna does not find the advice in good taste; but Bheema readily does Krshna's bidding. Drona, however, has his doubts about the veracity of Bheema's message. So Krshna now convinces Yudhishthira, whom Drona regards as the epitome of truthfulness, to do the dirty work:

Yady-ardhva-divasam drono yudhyate manyumaasthitah /
Saatyam braveemi te senaa vinaasham samupaishyati //
Sa bhavaam-straatu no dronaat satyaaj-jyaayo-hnrtam vachah /
Anrtam jeevitasyaarthe vadanna sprshyate-hnrtaih //
~ Drona; 190. 46-47

O King, if the enraged Drona fights for another half a day then, trust my words, your entire army will be destroyed.

Therefore, you save us from Drona; at this grave hour, resorting to untruth is more expedient than adhering to truth. One does not incur sin by telling a lie to save life.

[Here, the pronoun 'us' shows Krshna's personal identification with the Pandava war effort.]

Almost all the formidable heroes on the Kaurava side are slain in battle. But Arjuna stands strong, withstanding myriad assaults, an improbable outcome made possible in large measure by Krshna's shrewd stratagems. Bhagadatta's all-powerful *vaishnavaastra* (Vishnu-weapon) would have certainly proved fatal had it hit Arjuna's breast, as targeted; but Krshna covers Arjuna to take the missile on his own chest, where it turns into a divine garland. A 'distressed' Arjuna cannot help reminding him that such intervention is contrary to his own promise of non-participation in direct battle (Drona; 29.22).

Arjuna's pertinent embarrassment should also remind us, as objectively critical readers, of the ringing last words of the *Gita*:

Yatra yogeshvaro krshno yatra paartho dhanurdharah /
Tatra shreer-vijayo-bhootir dhruvaa neetir-matir mama //
~ Gita; 18.78

Wherever there is Krshna, the Lord of yoga, and Partha (Arjuna), the archer; to my mind, there surely will be fortune, victory, welfare and morality.

The Krshna-Arjuna combine did bring fortune, victory, welfare, and morality to the Pandavas, but all these results came in mixed shades of grey – leading to, as predicted by the dying Duryodhana, 'a disheartened and mournful existence' for them (Shalya; 61.53).

We shall talk about Krshna's practical vision of *dharma*, which motivated his win-at-any-cost approach, a little later. But in the immediate context of his tactics at Kurukshetra, morality and ethics seem to be at a premium. As already seen, his tactics to eliminate Bheeshma and Drona cannot be construed as just and honourable, by any standard of morality. But it is in meeting the threat posed to Arjuna by the valiant Karna, that Krshna amazes us by the core consistency of his adroitly planned battle strategy, which is to evade any direct encounter between the two great heroes until Karna is reduced to a lesser force by expending his main weapon elsewhere. It is mainly due to Krshna's manoeuvres that the Indra-given all-powerful *Shakti* missile, which Karna had carefully preserved for use against Arjuna, is expended in slaying Ghatotkaca.

Krshna's uncharacteristically wild celebration of Ghatotkaca's death drives home the facts of his partisanship and guardianship of the Vedic-Brahminical order. While all the Pandavas are mourning the death of Bheema's demon son, Krshna embraces Arjuna with an ecstatic war cry. Then, after bringing his horses under control, he performs a jig, working up a wild beat by striking his palms together. When a disapproving Arjuna asks the reason for this paradoxical, almost vulgar, elation, Krshna makes a clean breast of how his own masterplan has worked to perfection in Karna being weakened, first by the gifting away of his imperishable armour and talismanic ornaments, and now by his infallible one-strike missile having been used to kill Ghatotkaca. He then makes a significant statement to reveal to Arjuna and to us, his larger scheme of things: 'O Arjuna, it is only for your benefit that I have ensured the destruction, through various means, of Jarasandha, Shishupala, and Ekalavya; as also of demons like Hidimba, Kirmeera, Baka, Alaayudha, Ugrakarmaa, and Ghatotkaca' [Drona; 181].

It is to be noted that of all these characters, only one warrior – Shishupala – was directly slain by Krshna himself. He was not present at the scene when Hidimba, Kirmeera, Baka and Alaayudha, were killed; and when Ekalavya made the death-like sacrifice of his archer's thumb, Krshna had not even entered the *Mahabharata* plot. Obviously, in assuming overall responsibility for all these killings, Krshna is alluding to some divine controlling role on his part, as the unseen mover and shaker of the actions of Bheema, Drona, Arjuna, and others (including Ghatotkaca and Karna themselves, vis-à-vis Alaayudha and Ghatotkaca, respectively). Such a controlling influence seems to be in line with Krshna's other, and significantly deeper, revelations in the *Bhagavad-Gita*:

Tasmaat tvam-uttishtha yasho labhasya /
Jitvaa shatroon bhunksho raajyam samrddham //
Mayai-vaite nihataah poorvam-eva /
Nimittamaatram bhava savyasaachin //
~ Gita; 11.33

Therefore, arise thou and gain glory. Conquering thy foes, enjoy a prosperous kingdom. By Me alone are they slain already. Be thou merely the occasion, O Savyasaachi.

And,
Eeshvarah sarva-bhootaanaam hrddesheh-rjuna tishthati /
Bhraamayan sarva-bhootaani yantraaroordhaani maayayaa //
~ Gita; 18.61

The Lord abides in the hearts of all beings, O Arjuna; causing them to move around by His power as if they were mounted on a machine.

Arjuna, as is his inquisitive wont, asks Krshna how he attributes the aforementioned killings as being to his benefit. Krshna explains that Jarasandha, Shishupala and Ekalavya would otherwise have fought on Duryodhana's behalf; the slaying of the demons was to save the world from the evil depredations of those God-denying entities. As for Ghatotkaca, he clarifies his double-edged strategy. 'Had Karna not done the job, I myself would have killed him, which I had not done out of my attachment to you Pandavas. That demon was a sinful brahmin-baiter, *yajna*-spoiler, and a destroyer of the order of *dharma*. Hence I had him killed through artifice; in the bargain, I have accomplished the task of compelling Karna to spend the sure-shot Indra-given missile, which he had otherwise kept to use against you.'

But in the matter of Karna, Arjuna's most potent adversary, Krshna does not leave things to chance by just weakening him. Knowing that even without his divine missile, Karna is almost invincible in fair and equal battle, he tells Arjuna the only way to kill him. 'When in the course of Karna's battle with you, he is otherwise harassed on account of his chariot-wheel getting accursedly bogged down into the earth – at that very moment you should slay him quickly by following my hints to that effect.'

And that last frontal battle between Karna and Arjuna stands out for the glaring contrast between Karna's punctilious ethics and Krshna's lack of it. Karna, during that fierce final battle, is suddenly gifted with an unexpected opportunity to checkmate Arjuna when, unbidden by him, the revengeful *Naga* Ashvasena (Takshaka's son, who had escaped Arjuna's massacre at Khandava), enters his quiver as a deadly shaft. Quite unwittingly, Karna takes out that shaft, but is advised by Shalya (his charioteer, acting as the Pandavas' agent provocateur), not to use it, as supposedly it would not be capable of decapitating Arjuna. Karna refuses to do Shalya's bidding, citing his *Kshatriya* resolve not to hesitate after aiming an arrow. The awesome missile takes off from Karna's bow with a loud bang, and shoots through the sky, burning an incandescent course, with Arjuna's head as its sure quarry. That would have been the end of Arjuna, but for the quick response by Krshna, who with his feet presses the chariot a spread-palm's length (*kishkumaatram*) into the ground. The four horses kneel, and the infallible serpent-arrow scorches through Arjuna's golden diadem, which falls to the ground.

Thwarted, Ashvasena again seeks to enter Karna's quiver, telling him: 'I could not get Arjuna's head because you shot me unknowingly; now release me again after taking aim, and that shall be the end of our mutual enemy.' But Karna, of righteous valour, refuses, saying:
Na naaga karnodya rane parasya

balam samaasthaaya jayam bubhooshet //
Na sandadhyaam dvih sharam chaiva naaga
yadyarjunaanaam shatameva hanyaam //
~ Karna; 90.47-48

O serpent, I do not desire victory with the might of others, and shall not use that arrow twice even if it could kill a hundred Arjunas; please, therefore, leave my quiver without taking offence.

Karna's end is arguably one of the most glorious deaths depicted in the world's epics. The sheer marvel of Karna's last glory (which almost offsets even his boorish conduct vis-à-vis Draupadi in the dice hall, and his part in the collective slaughter of Abhimanyu), gets heightened when seen in juxtaposition with the unscrupulous – almost infamous – manner in which he is felled by Arjuna under Krshna's overt guidance. Chapter 91 of the *Karna-parva* is epic drama at its best, steeped as it is with the pathos of a true hero's *purushakaara* fighting to the end its losing battle with the cruel forces of destiny. A tired and perspiring Karna looks up from his efforts to lift his chariot wheels that have sunk into the ground, and requests Arjuna for a moment's respite. Left to his own discretion, Arjuna would certainly have heeded the fair call; but Krshna goads him with his stern words: 'Arjuna, intelligent persons do not allow a weakened foe any respite. Make haste to kill Karna when you can.' So Arjuna gets transformed into a murderer (*aatataayee*), and releases his fearsome *Anjalika* missile to behead a tired and distracted Karna. The metaphoric grandeur of the verse describing Karna's decapitation is a jewel of epic literature:

Tatosya deham satatam sukhocitam
svaroopam-atyartham-udaarakarmanah //
Parena krcchena shirah samatyajad
grham mahardheeva susangam-eeshvarah/
~ Karna; 91.53-54)

Then, the exquisitely handsome body of Karna of generous acts, who was worthy of perpetual happiness, let go of that head (of solar refulgence) with the kind of extreme reluctance that is evinced by a wealthy person in leaving his own prosperous home, and by a saintly one in forsaking virtuous company.

KRSHNA'S 'NEW' ORDER OF DHARMA

How can one possibly justify Krshna's seeming lack of compunction in destroying the great Kaurava generals? Bheeshma, Drona, Karna, Duryodhana – all were casualties, not of fair battle, but Krshna's machinations. The answer has to be explored in the macro context of Krshna's overall mission, rather than in the micro analysis of his actions on the battlefield alone. That overall mission is summed up in two nuance-laden statements in the *Gita*. One is that the Lord manifests Himself in every age to establish righteousness:

Dharmasamsthaapanaaya sambhavaami yuge yuge
~ Gita; 4.8

And quite plausibly from this very proclamation of the Lord, there sprouts Arjuna's realisation, after beholding Krshna's cosmic form: *Tvam-avyayahshaashvato-dharmagoptaa*
~ Gita; 11.18
Thou art the undying guardian of the eternal law.

It is this eternal or ultimate law or *dharma* that becomes the dominant principle in a *dharma-yuddha*, requiring the subordination of other principles to attain its end. The *Ramayana* too, tellingly illustrates the point in the variant responses of Ravana's two conscientious brothers, to his war with Rama. Vibheeshana and Kumbhakarna were both confronted with a choice of principles – whether to embrace *bhraatr-dharma* (brotherly duty) and support Ravana, notwithstanding his wrong deeds; or to serve the ultimate *dharma* by joining the righteous side. Kumbhakarna chose to sleep through the unholy war for as long as he could, but finally discharged his brotherly duty by fighting till his own death. Vibheeshana, on the other hand, tried to dissuade Ravana, and only when he was kicked out did he decide to subordinate his brotherly duty to the ultimate *dharma* by crossing over to Rama's camp.

Even in the context of seeking to avoid war, Krshna surely was the foremost emissary of peace in the failed negotiations of the *Udyoga-parva*. There can be no doubt that he did his best to avert the mutually destructive civil war by brokering a settlement that recognised the justified claims of the Pandavas (who, thanks to Yudhishthira's reasonableness, were prepared to forgive and forget all harms caused to them by the Kauravas in return for just five villages). It was only after that fair and right solution was summarily rejected by Duryodhana and his coterie, that Krshna remoulded himself in the role of a master war strategist – to win at any cost in the armageddon forced on the righteous by the intransigence of the unrighteous.

As succinctly put by RN Dandekar, this 'significant trait of Krishnaism' involves a 'new ethical code' that emphasises the desirability and urgency of attaining the right end by any expedient means, even though some of those means may not seem right. It is this new *dharma* propounded by Krshna that Vyasa, as reported by Sauti, seems to be proclaiming near the fag end of the epic:

Urdhvabaahur viraumy esa na ca kashcic-chrnoti me /
Dharmaad arthash-ca kaamash-ca sa kimartham na sevyate //
~ Svargaarohanikaa; 5.49

With uplifted arms I am crying aloud but nobody hears me.
From righteousness is wealth as also pleasure. Why should not righteousness, therefore, be courted?

Paradoxical as it may seem, 'this *dharma* is essentially secular in character; not only does it not reject *artha* (material progress and prosperity), and *kaama* (pleasures of life), but it actually promotes them'.[5.7] There is indeed a certain timeless quality to Krshna's method of upholding this *dharma*, that enjoins the end of winning a 'just war' irrespective of its means. An apt example of this quality of universal relevance is the celebrated 1951 farewell speech of General MacArthur to the US Congress. There, MacArthur recalled his own words on the occasion of the Japanese surrender when (while rueing the inability of the world to establish 'some greater and more equitable system' to promote a fair and humane order of peace between nations), he had championed the cause of a practical war-aim that seems to vibrate with a cross-epochal echo of what was Krshna's method in the context of the *Mahabharata* battle: *But once war is forced upon us, there is no other alternative than to apply every available means to bring it to a swift end. War's very object is victory, not prolonged indecision. In war there is no substitute for victory.*[5.8]

At the same time, one must not forget that Krshna's prescription of a 'win at any cost' approach was in the context of a *dharma-yuddha*, a label which may not apply to the generality of warfare.

A TRAGEDY OF EXALTED TRANQUILLITY

In Peter Brook's internationalist film interpretation of the *Mahabharata*,[5.9] Vyasa calls the epic the 'political history of mankind', because a 'great war' leaves no lasting victory; defeat and destruction are its certain wages. One is reminded of Wellington's doleful utterance on surveying the carnage of Waterloo: *The next worst thing to a battle lost is a battle won.* In the final analysis, however, while subsuming the Kurukshetra war as its core event, the *Mahabharata* is much more than a warrior story, just as it is much more than a didactic, morality tale. The only generic definition that could be applied to this Great Indian Epic, is tragedy – an epic high tragedy, to be more precise.

Reverting to the global trans-cultural context, some of the basic characteristics of the *Mahabharata* tragedy seem to bear a germane concordance with certain characteristics of the tragedy of Aeschylus, as observed by the eminent classicist, Edith Hamilton:[5.10] *When Nietzsche made his famous definition of tragic pleasure, he fixed his eyes, like all the other philosophers in like case, not on the Muse herself but on a single tragedian. His 'reaffirmation of the will to live in the face of death, and the joy of its inexhaustibility when so reaffirmed' is not the tragedy of Sophocles nor the tragedy of Euripides, but it is the very essence of the tragedy of Aeschylus. The strange power tragedy has to present suffering and death in such a way as to exalt and not depress is to be felt in Aeschylus' play as in those of no other tragic poet. He was the first tragedian; tragedy was his creation, and he set upon it the stamp of his own spirit.*

It seems a pity that neither Nietzsche nor Hamilton would have had any familiarity with Vyasa's epic tragedy. But to us, the characteristics of 'reaffirmation of the will to live in the face of death' and of 'the strange power' of tragedy 'to exalt and not depress', sound like the quintessence of the great Indian epic.

Significantly, both the *Ramayana* and the *Mahabharata* are tragedies, whereas a tragic ending was eschewed in almost all later classical Sanskrit drama. The reason lies in the different spreads of dramatic canvas of the epics and classical Indian drama. The *Ramayana* portrays the entire life story of Rama, Sita, Ravana, and its other major dramatis personae. Similarly, the *Mahabharata* presents the whole saga of the lives and times of the Bharata dynasty. Death is the one certain truth in life; and so stories depicting the totality of lives have necessarily to end in bereavements. The other eternal truth about life is its mixed baggage of pleasure and pain; therefore, a great epic must also depict that reality of pain, a reality evocatively described by Keats in his *Ode to a Nightingale*:

Where but to think is to be full of sorrow
And leaden-eyed despairs;
Where Beauty cannot keep her lustrous eyes,
Or new Love pine at them beyond to-morrow.

The *Mahabharata* sensitises us to accept, with a spirit of tranquil detachment, this home truth about the ephemerality of life's pleasures and pains, while pursuing our individual ends of righteousness, wealth, pleasure or salvation. We hear this message, steeped in the stoical sentiment of *shaanta rasa*, in Vidura's words to the bereaved and grief-stricken Dhrtarashtra:

Sarve kshayaantaa nicayaah patanaantaah samucchrayaah /
Samyogaa viprayogaantaa maranaantanca jeevitam //
~ Stree; 2.3

All accumulations end in decay; worldly ascendances end in decline; all unions culminate in separation; and all lives end in death.

Then again, what Vidura says to the blind king after the war is only of a piece with the words of detachment with which Krshna counselled a despondent Arjuna just before it:

Gataasoon-agataasoomsh-ca naanushocanti panditaah //
~ Gita; 2.11

Those who are wise lament neither for the dead nor for the living.[5.11]

But have we not already heard similar wisdom of detachment, as the leitmotif of the *Mahabharata*'s hair-raising cosmic quietism, even before the hurly burly of war, from the lips of the forester Yudhishthira, in his reply to the crane guard:

Asmin mahaa-mohamaye kataahe
Suryaa-gninaa raatridin-endhanena /
Maas-ortu-darvee parighattanena
Bhootaani kaalah pacateeti vaartaa //
~ Vana; 313.118

In this cauldron of great illusion, with the sun as fire, day-night as fuel; using months and seasons as stirrer, Time is cooking all beings – that is the message.

That, indeed, is the marvel of the *Mahabharata* message.

NOTES & REFERENCES

5.1 The numbers of verses correspond to the traditional Aryashastra edition.

5.2 The episode of the curse by the blind sage appears as a flashback in the *Ayodhya-kaanda* (63-64), with Dasharatha relating the incident to Kaushalya, before dying of grief at Rama's banishment.

5.3 Karna alone can perhaps claim the distinction of being the *Mahabharata*'s one great epitome of *purushakaara*. A self-made hero in every sense, his entire life – a saga of heroic effort despite being disowned at birth, being humiliated at every effort of self-actualisation, being deprived of his invincible armour through his own generosity, being exploited by a dissembling Indra, and being afflicted by two great curses (brought about by his own acts of commission and omission) – is one long battle against adversities caused by cruel destiny.

5.4 The subsequent narration of events of the *Maushala-parva* is based largely on the Bengali *Mahabharat-Saranuvad*, by Rajshekhar Basu, M.C. Sarkar & Sons, Kolkata-73, 1949 (Bengali Calendar: 1356), Tenth Reprint: 1987, and the English translation of *The Mahabharata* (Book 16)', by Kisari Mohan Ganguli, Internet Sacred Text Archive, 1883-1896, (to be found at: http://www.sacred-texts.com/hin/m16/index.htm).

5.5 There is also a non-sexual Christian view of the sin of Sodom, which gives a variant interpretation of the word 'know' in this verse of the Genesis: *And they called unto Lot, and said unto him,*

Where [are] the men which came in to thee this night? Bring them out unto us, that we may know them.[Gen 19:5, Holy Bible, King James Version]. Whereas orthodox Christian opinion holds that Lot's brother citizens were making a militant solicitation for homosexual sex, others interpret the demand to 'know' as demanding the right to interrogate the strangers. However, the majority orthodox view of a sexual connotation seems to be borne out by the following appeal of Lot, found only three verses later in the same narrative: *Behold now, I have two daughters which have not known man; let me, I pray you, bring them out unto you, and do ye to them as is good in your eyes: only unto these men do nothing....* [Gen 19:8]. In contrast, there is no reason to doubt that Yadava promiscuity was anything other than of a hetero-sexual nature. Even their dressing up of the apparently good-looking Shamva as a woman seems intended more as a profane prank than as any sex-related Freudian slip.

5.6 Buddhadev Basu, *Mahabharater Katha*, (Bengali), M.C. Sarkar & Sons, Kolkata-73, 1974, Chapter-20 (*Vrddha Kandari*), pp. 220-236.

5.7 RN Dandekar, *Reflections and Variations on the Mahabharata*: *The Human Universal in The Mahabharata*, Sahitya Academy, New Delhi, 2009, p. 45.

5.8 Douglas MacArthur, *Farewell to Congress*, Delivered 19 April 1951. Transcription by Michael E. Eidenmuller; available on the internet at: http://www.americanrhetoric.com/speeches/PDFFiles/Douglas%20MacArthur%20-%20Farewell%20to%20Congress%20Address.pdf

5.9 Peter Brook (born 1925) is an English theatre and film director, who wrote the screenplay and directed his 1989 TV and DVD film, *The Mahabharata*, based on his original 1985 stage play. The film had a large international cast (with Mallika Sarabhai as Draupadi), to show that the Indian epic of destructive confrontation between good and evil is essentially the story of all humanity. The plot is framed as a narrative between the sage Vyasa and the god Ganesha, told to an unnamed Indian lad inquiring about the story of the human race.

5.10 Edith Hamilton, *The Greek Way (1930): Aeschylus, The First Dramatist*, WW Norton & Co, 1930, Norton paperback reissued 1993, pp.179-195. Also available at: http://www.english.emory.edu/DRAMA/Aesch.html

A brief mention of the analogy between the *Mahabharata* and Hamilton's view on Aeschylus' tragedy was made in W. Norman Brown's Foreword to an earlier edition of Irawati Karve's *Yuganta* (English), available at: http://gyanpedia.in/Portals/0/Toys%20from%20Trash/Resources/books/yuganta.pdf

5.11 This aspect of philosophical detachment is a dominantly consistent characteristic of Krshna. He preaches detachment not just as a way of persuading Arjuna on the course of action but even in consoling his own sister Subhadra, after the tragic death of her valiant son and his own dear pupil, Abhimanyu.

PART II

THE HISTORY

CHAPTER OVERVIEW
Detailed Notes & References are appended to the relevant chapters

~~~~~~

PART II: THE HISTORY

6 Search for Historicity

Sauti, in the *Mahabharata*'s prefatory chapter, calls his narration 'history' (*itihaasam*, meaning 'thus it was'). The epic has, as its plausible historical core, the Kuru-Pancala civil war that enervated India of yore by wiping out a generation of heroic *Kshatriyas*. There are also several significant nuances in the book that are too palpably authentic to be just fiction. There are two aspects to the *Mahabharata*'s historicity — one relating to its core event, the battle of Kurukshetra; and the other to its compositional origin and development. On the issue of dating the battle, we encounter a significant divergence between traditional and modern assessment. Popular tradition in India, based on Aryabhata's archaeo-astronomical record of reckoning the onset of *Kali-Yuga*, has long believed the *Mahabharata* war to have had taken place in 3102 BC.

In recent times, other approaches, based on collateral evidence from the *Purana*s, have been attempted. One, based on Puranic references to monarchical reigns, suggests a date of about 1400 BC. However, AL Basham supports a more conservative estimate that places the war in the 10th century BC, i.e. in the Iron Age. But the issue is still far from settled, as revealed by the work of the noted archaeologist, BB Lal, who found evidences of Painted Grey Ware (PGW) at the site of ancient Hastinapura, near Delhi.

One intriguing facet of this seemingly never-ending debate on historicity is the divide between Western and Indian scholars. The former, by and large, tend to push the date forward and place the *Mahabharata* and Krshna in some degree of chronological closeness to the Christian era. The Indian tendency, however, has been a diverse spectrum of views. Leaving out extreme theories, there are three concrete lines of 'evidence': (i) a reference from Megasthenes (which interestingly draws a parallel between Krshna-Balarama and the Greek demigod Hercules); (ii) a Calukya inscription of Pulakesein II (containing an explicit chronological reference to 'the Bharata War'); and (iii) new marine-archaeological explorations at Dvaraka (perhaps the most promising key, based on modern scientific findings). The first two evidences seem to bear out Aryabhata's *Kali-Yuga* tradition of 3102 BC, with the third evidence pointing to a later date of around 15th century BC, as the time of Krshna.

Having examined the various lines of evidence, as also the Iron Age projection cited earlier, we are still left with variances of five centuries and two millennia between 3100 BC and 1500 BC, and Basham's estimate of 1000 BC, as the date of the war. One way out of the imbroglio could be to follow the latest scientific paradigm and look for the 'least implausible' formulation rather than the mirage of the 'most plausible'.

Tracing the epic's origin and development is another ticklish issue, more so because of the quaint Indian syndrome of anonymous interpolations. Given this inherent dynamism, one approach has been to go by the earliest external references to the epic, which include a few fairly direct references found in Panini's grammar of 6th/5th century BC. However, as a logician might say: 'absence of evidence is not evidence of absence'; we cannot, therefore, conclude there was no *Mahabharata* before Panini's time, merely because the evidence is no longer extant.

What we can do is search for the earliest historical forms of the *Mahabharata*'s narration, contained *in situ* in the introductory *Anukramanikaa* sub-chapter of the epic. There, Sauti mentions two different versions, one long, the other short. However, not much of the shorter work, other than the 24,000 verses ascribed to Vaishampayana, are now extant. Moreover, in addition to the two ancient versions, *Mahaabhaarata* and *Bhaarata*, tradition suggests the existence of an older and shorter epic nucleus, *Jaya* (Victory), attributed again to Vyasa.

In light of the above, there are two contrasting views on the long and short versions. Western scholars opine that *Bhaarata* was the original core epic, comprising 24,000 unspecified verses, amenable to recitation in royal courts as a paean on *jaya* (victory). Later, additions may have been made to this core by Brahminical redactors, especially the Bhrgu clan, into whose keeping it came from the narrator *Sootas*. These additions involved increasing insertion of didactic and devotional elements to an original tight narration of the core secular-warrior story.

The above theory is based on the Western text-critical approach, attaching primary importance to manuscript copies, whereas, given ancient India's oral traditions, the *Mahabharata* would have originally been propagated, for thousands of years, as memorised verses. Thus, like many other 'mysteries' of the *Mahabharata*, we do not appear to have a final, open-and-shut scenario of its evolution, there being some points in favour of the traditional Indian belief that Vyasa himself composed the encyclopaedic *Mahabharata* of 100,000 verses and perhaps had a copy scribed by a scholarly amanuensis (later represented as Ganesha), and then his disciples made shorter versions for narration at courts and hermitages.

7 Interpretations Galore

The 19th century, with Western Indologists awakening to India's Sanskritic heritage, became a prolific period for *Mahabharata* research. In India, Bankim Chandra's effort to identify the primitive 'layer' of the pristine *Mahabharata*, by sifting out interpolations, was in refutation of a hypothesis advanced by the German Vedic scholar, Albrecht Weber, that the depiction of Krshna as a personal deity was borrowed from that of Christ. Several other Western studies of the period give interesting, albeit bafflingly varied leads, on the association or otherwise of Krshna in the original, relatively secular, warrior narration and the later didactic/devotional versions of the great Indian epic.

Christian Lassen's was the first systematic study (1837), to suggest there were three major revisions, spreading across both the pre-Buddhist and post-Buddhist periods. Lassen concluded that the poem recited by Sauti was the second (460-400 BC), of the three recensions alluded to in the *Anukramanikaa*. Thereafter, only interpolations with a Krshna emphasis were added. Interestingly, Lassen also noted 'Krshna's connections with both pastoral and warrior groups' (the pastoral being the older).

Sören Sörensen (1883), on the other hand, contended that the *Mahabharata* was originally a secular warrior saga, composed by one author and that the repetitions, digressions, and inconsistencies found now, were due to subsequent grafting of many other sections. The two studies by the Adolf Holtzmanns (1846, and 1881 onwards), ascribed the inconsistencies to what came to be labelled the 'inversion theory'. This suggested that the original version had Duryodhana and the Kauravas (with Buddhism as their guiding faith), as the righteous, and that later editors — proponents of the 'new' divinity, Vishnu — modified the narrative to exonerate Krshna and the Pandavas, while also substituting Shiva for Buddha, as the Kauravas' guiding deity.

EW Hopkins, demonstrating the relative lateness of the didactic portions, called for a more critical approach. In his 1901 book, *The Great Epic of India*, he makes the tentative but reasoned proposition that it was a compilation comprising several layers accreting around a small core that did not have the Pandavas as heroes, or Krshna as god — both being later additions of around 400-200 BC. In the early 20th century, FE Pargiter argued that the war marked the victory of the Krshna-worshipping Pancalas over the cause of Brahmanism, represented by the Kaurava alliance, thereby heralding an infusion of non-Vedic elements into the orthodox tradition.

More credibly based was the thesis of Hermann Oldenberg (1922), linking Pareekshit and Janamejaya with late Vedic literature, and developing the idea that the *Mahabharata* originated as a composition of mixed prose and verse that was later modified into more regular verse. Viewing the epic as literature, Oldenberg analysed its grammatical usages and styles, suggesting the main narrative was based on events that happened around 1200 BC, at the end of the Rig-Vedic period.

Gerrit Jan Held (1935) adopted an ethnographic and anthropological approach, upholding the organic integrity of the epic against the dissection of analysts. Held viewed the Kauravas and Pandavas as analogous to two Hellenic or Iranian 'phratries' (related clans) in a tribe, engaged in perpetual co-operation and rivalry, and saw the whole epic as centred around a potlatch (community feast) ritual. Holding that both dicing and warfare were parts of the potlatch ritual, he proposed that the narrative develops around the fateful *dyoota*, which was the climax to the ceremonial feast, and which Yudhishthira, as the *Dharmaraja* or acclaimed upholder of traditions, was obliged to accept. Held reasoned that the sacred obligation attached to gambling was linked to its social sanctity as the traditional means of ensuring the circulation of tribal wealth.

Interestingly, Held's tribal thesis had some parallels in older Western researches. For example, Hopkins (1901), mentions the apparently incongruous lack of any historical reference whatsoever of a 'Pandu Empire' (which, according to the epic, established its sway after Yudhishthira's two great *yajnas*). He observes that 'before the *Mahabharata*, there were tales of Kurus and Bharats known to antiquity', and further speculates that 'the Pandus appear to have substituted themselves for Bhaaratas and may, in fact, have been a branch of the tribe which, from a second rate position, raised itself to leadership'. Incidentally, while there are references to Janamejaya in later Vedic literature, the same contains no allusion to Pandu or the Pandavas, which, according to Western scholars, indicates post-Vedic vintage of the Pandu legend.

A divergent ethnological view was presented by Walter Ruben in his reconstructive study of the Krshna legend. He observes that the story of Krshna's rivalry with Jarasandha must have had some historical basis since Krshna's mortification there is hardly likely to have been invented. But, in regard to the core *Mahabharata* legend, Ruben argues that Krshna is inessential to its basic plot, and that an absentee hero, who has to come eleven times to the aid of the

Pandavas all the way from Dvaraka, to play a studiedly passive role, strains credulity. But Ruben's Krshna-less *Mahabharata* does not have any textual or manuscript support, and can at best be consigned to a stage preceding the archetype.

8 The Critical Edition

Given the multiplicity of opinions regarding the textual authenticity and significance of the various regional versions of the *Mahabharata*, there arose the need for a common edition of the great epic. The move towards such a 'Critical Edition' was initiated before World War I by the Oxford Orientalist, Moriz Winternitz. After the war, the project was taken up by the Bhandarkar Oriental Research Institute, Pune, in 1919; and finally culminated in the complete 19-volume *Critical Edition*, also known as the Poona Edition, being released in 1966. Hailed as 'one of the most significant events in Indology in the 20th century', the scholastic diligence that went into its making can be understood from the scope of the task, which involved collecting, collating and compiling common portions of the earliest extant manuscripts of the work from Kashmir, Bengal, Uttar Pradesh, Maharashtra, Andhra and Kerala, as also a Nepali and a short Javanese version, and various commentaries.

The objective of the Critical Edition, as stated by VS Sukthankar in his introduction to the first volume, was 'to reconstruct the oldest form of the text... on the basis of the manuscript material available'. The primary criterion for incorporation in the critical text was defined ideally as occurrence in both the Northern and Southern recensions. This meant that the final Edition was closer to the shorter Northern Recension. In cases of variations, the approach followed was to choose the reading found in the largest number of apparently independent versions, with a preference for those coming from Kashmir, which were deemed to have been preserved as relatively more conservative text.

Apart from the fairly extensive spread of manuscripts in various scripts, the other parameter for manuscript selection was their age. However, even then the vintage of manuscripts taken was not very old, the oldest (Nepali), used in *Aadi-parva*, being of 1511AD. Another basic issue is that the 'highest common factor' approach, based on commonalities between manuscripts, is the product of the application of Winternitz's Western methodology to a distinctively Indian problem – that the written manuscripts are far younger in age than the earlier forms of the epic transmitted through the oral tradition, a tradition that was far less prevalent in the West. Hence, some scholars judge the Pune text to be 'an unwarranted simplification of the tradition that has produced an artificial text that never existed for anyone at any time in the past'.

In absolute terms, the net result of the Critical Edition was to reduce the length by about one-fourth — from the traditional size of 100,000 verses to precisely 73,650 verses and 297 prose units. In short, one can say that about a fourth of the verses of the traditional Sanskrit *Mahabharata* could have been accretions on the original.

9 Epics and Epics

The *Mahabharata*'s humongous length makes it an epic in a league of its own when compared to the other great folk epics of the world. But scale apart, when it comes to characterising human attitudes to cross-cultural or trans-civilisational comparison, one often encounters a peculiar dichotomy — between xenophobic exclusivity on one side and internationalist inclusiveness on the other. Quite expectedly, classicists, by virtue of their humanist vision, generally tend towards the latter, more inclusive view of things. This largeness of view could have been the reason behind Megasthenes' perceived discovery of an Indian Hercules, or even behind some of the 19th century European scholars drawing parallels between the child Krshna and the child Christ. A somewhat similar search for parallelism has traditionally driven scholars to examine inter-relationships between the world's great epics. And some of the epic parallels are quite striking, revealing perhaps a deep-seated affinity in ancient thoughts.

Striking indeed are the similarities between the Ionian Odysseus, king of Ithaca and the Sumerian Gilgamesh, king of Uruk (now Iraq). Both went on long and hard voyages, rendered much longer and harder by the curses of divinities. Both travel to the end of the earth and visit the land of the dead. The encounters of Odysseus with Circe and Calypso on their mythical isles, closely resemble the visit by Gilgamesh to the divine woman, Siduri. One can hear similar thematic resonance between the *Epic of Gilgamesh* and the *Iliad*, in the depiction of the after-death experiences of Patroclus and Enkidu, friends of Achilles and Gilgamesh, respectively.

As regards parallelisms between the Indian and Greek epics, Dio Chrysostom (40-120 AD), in illustrating Homeric influence on alien lands, records that 'Homer's poetry is sung even in India, where they have translated it into their own speech and tongue'; and, 'they [Indians] are not unacquainted with the sufferings of Priam, the laments and wailings of Andromachê and Hecuba, and the valour of both Achilles and Hector'. Christian Lassen has suggested that these three striking inter-cultural references relate respectively to Dhrtarashtra's sorrows; the laments of Gandhari and Draupadi; and the valour of Arjuna and Karna. The *Odyssey* and the Indian epics also have things in common. The long providence-driven separation and final reunion between Odysseus and Penelope reminds one of Nala and Damayanti. Similarly, Odysseus stringing a great bow to regain his wife, reads like the story of Rama stringing the bow of Shiva to win Sita's hand in marriage.

The inter-relationship of the two Indian epics is a much debated, but still a somewhat open issue. Notwithstanding the traditional belief that events in the *Ramayana* long preceded those of the *Mahabharata*, the issue is far more complex, as is borne out by more than a century's deep study by eminent Western and Indian scholars. The principal thread of correlation between the epics is in the *Ramopakhyana* section covering 19 chapters of the *Mahabharata's Vana-parva*. This account, of Markandeya relating the story of Rama's travails to Yudhishthira (which, according to scholarly consensus, forms part of the original *Mahabharata* corpus), is a generally faithful summary of the Rama story, sans a few major episodes like Sita's fire-test, as also her exile to the forest and events thereafter.

Interestingly, the events referred to in the Ramopakhyana, can be properly understood only with prior knowledge of the story. For example, the first mention of Vaalee is when Rama promises Sugreeva that he will kill him (with no prior reference to the reason for killing, viz., the rivalry between the *vaanara* siblings). This in turn suggests that the *Ramopakhyana* material could have been sourced from an earlier and more detailed Rama story. There is also the possibility of some reverse flow of material from the *Ramopakhyana* to the *Baala-kaanda* and *Uttara-kaanda* of the *Ramayana*. But the overall modern consensus seems to be that the *Ramopakhyana* is based on an earlier form of the *Ramayana*.

Finally, it is relevant to recall EW Hopkins' summation of the salient points of the inter-relationship between the two epics, which seem as valid today as it did a century or so ago: (i) The story of Rama is older than that of the Pandus; (ii) The Pandu story has absorbed the *Bhaarati Kathaa*; and (iii) The *Bhaarati Kathaa* is older than Valmiki's poem.

Such then is the near-inextricable manner in which strands of the two great epics of India are interwoven — a phenomenon unique to these two. Homer's two epics do not present any such conundrum of chronology. For one thing, both the *Iliad* and the *Odyssey* are ascribable to one poet; for another, the *Odyssey* is quite clearly a sequel to the *Iliad*. In fact, the two Indian epics, though of disparate origins, in different times, stand together to represent the ethos of India as a continuous civilisation.

6
SEARCH FOR HISTORICITY

WHAT THE BARD SAID
Aacakhyuh kavayah kecit sampratyaacakshate pare /
Aakhyaasanti tathivaanye itihaasam-imam bhuvi //
~ Aadi-parva; 1.26)[6.1]
Some scholar-poets have recounted this history in the past; some others are telling it now, and in future too yet more poets shall undertake its narration.

These were the words with which Sauti,[6.2] the celebrated narrator son of Lomaharshana (so named for his 'hair-raising' narration of the ancient *Puranas*), introduced the *Mahabharata* in the prefatory chapter of its *Aadi-parva*.[6.3] Sauti's words were to prove prophetic, as borne out in the millennia which followed. The longevity of the *Mahabharata* (literally 'the great book about the descendants of Bharata'), is amply attested by the fact that, even by conservative reckoning, its core event – the battle of Kurukshetra – took place around 1000 BC.[6.4] By reasonable estimate, the original account was composed not long after the event. We shall undertake a more detailed treatment of the *Mahabharata*'s antiquity, but first, let us examine the fuller implications of what Sauti said in that short prefatory couplet.

RINGS OF TRUTH
Significantly, Sauti of the 'loud voice' (fittingly enough for a story-teller, his actual name was *Ugrashrava*), called his narration 'history' (*itihaasam*, which means, literally, 'thus it was'). It had as its plausible historical core the Kuru-Pancala conflict – a civil war centring round the Kuru-Pandava joint family battle for dynastic succession that enervated India of yore by wiping out a generation of defender *Kshatriyas*. There are also those tell-tale nuances strewn through the great expanse of the book, that strike readers as too palpably authentic to have been invented by flights of imagination. A few examples will illustrate the point. Krpi, Dronacarya's wife, finds just a passing mention in the story, but even in that stray context, she is referred to by her

husband (during his self-introduction to Bheeshma), as a lady with sparse hair:

Naatikesheem mahaaprajnaam-upayeme mahaavrataam /
Agnihotre ca satre ca dame ca satatam rataam //
~ Aadi; 130.49)

(She is) thin-haired, thoroughly wise, observes great asceticism; is ever engaged in fire-worship and in *yajna*s, and is self-restrained.

Why should a peripheral character's lack of hair be mentioned as a distinctive aspect unless it describes a real person? One can detect similar rings of truth elsewhere.[65] Krshna-Dvaipayana Vyasa is himself described as fearsomely ugly, with very dark complexion, uncouth garb, and extremely disagreeable body odour; Bheema the he-man, is bereft of facial hair, and Karna drives the embarrassment home by calling him *toobaraka* on the battlefield; Draupadi's polyandrous marriage is an aberration from the prevalent social norm and had it not been true surely the author would not have made it up; Krshna's inglorious flight from Mathura to escape the wrath of Jarasandha also seems to have a basis of factuality (notwithstanding the subtler significance of Krshna's appellation as *Ranchhod-ji*, implying a strategic retreat to avert bloodshed and conserve strength to fight another day); the Yadavas are depicted as inveterate tipplers; Dvaraka is described as having been submerged in the sea. All these details are plausible strands of truth that sustain the *Mahabharata*'s claim to some proto-historical veracity – thus bearing out Sauti's words to his ascetic listeners at the sage Shaunaka's hermitage in Naimisharanya on that distant dawn, heralding the public release of the holy epic.

DATING THE BHAARATA WAR

Any probe into the historical authenticity of the *Mahabharata* has necessarily to address two distinct, though essentially inter-related, issues. One is the historicity of the epic's core event, the battle of Kurukshetra; and the other is the compositional origin and development of the epic itself. Coming to the issue of actually dating the epic battle, we encounter a significant divergence between tradition and modern assessment. Popular tradition in India, based on the archaeo-astronomical method of reckoning the onset of the *Kali-Yuga*, has long believed the *Mahabharata* war to have had taken place in the late 4th millennium BC. The putative year of the war, based on a reference by Aryabhata (regarding the date of composition of his magnum opus, *Aryabhatiya*), and a collateral estimation according to the *Surya Siddhanta* (ancient Indian calendrical system), was widely reckoned as 3102 BC. Other classical astronomers and historians, such as Varahamihira (author of the *Brhatsamhitaa*), and Kalhana (author of the *Rajataranginee*), however, place the Bhaarata war 653 years after the start of *Kali-Yuga*, corresponding to 2449 BC. Still, as acknowledged by AL Basham and others, 3102 BC, with its epochal significance, has stuck as the date accepted in ancient tradition.[6.6]

In recent times, other approaches based on collateral evidences from the *Puranas* (*Vishnu-Purana* in particular), have been attempted by scholars. One approach, cited first by Bankim Chandra[6.7] and also by AD Pusalker[6.8], is based on Puranic references that there were 1015 years between the birth of Pareekshit (Arjuna's grandson) and the year of accession of Mahapadma Nanda (Chandragupta Maurya's predecessor). The precise *shloka* from the *Vishnu-Purana*[6.9] reads:
Yaavat pareekshito janma yaavan-nandaa-vishecanam /
Etadvarshasahasrantu jneyam pancadashottaram //
~ *Vishnu-Puranam*; 4.24.32
Be it known that from Pareekshit's birth to Nanda's coronation elapsed a period of 1015 years.

By common historical reckoning, Mahapadma Nanda's accession is dated as 382 BC. This leads to a date of about 1400 BC for the *Mahabharata* battle. However, as shown by FE Pargiter,[6.10] this would imply improbably long reigns for the kings listed in the genealogies. Hence, a second approach of reckoning parallel genealogies in the *Puranas* between the times of Adhisimakrshna (Pareekshit's great-grandson), and Mahapadma Nanda, has been attempted. By this method, Pargiter estimated 26 generations by averaging ten different dynastic lists and assuming 18 years for the average duration of a reign, arrived at an estimate of 850 BC for Adhisimakrshna, and thus approximately 950 BC for the Bhaarata battle.[6.11]

Accordingly, on the basis of the approaches mentioned above, the Kurukshetra war would appear to have taken place in the

10th century BC, i.e. in Iron Age India. This view is supported by AL Basham,[6.12] who considers the tradition of placing the war in the 15th century BC as 'several centuries too early in the light of our archaeological knowledge'. He concludes that, 'probably the war took place around the beginning of the 9th century BCE; such a date seems to fit well with the scanty archaeological remains of the period, and there is some evidence in the Braahmana literature itself to show that it cannot have been much earlier.' As contended by M Witzel, the setting of the epic in Iron Age India also gels well with the chronological consensus that the Kuru kingdom was the centre of political power between 1200-800 BC.[6.13] By this line of reckoning, a dynastic conflict during the period could have been the inspiration for the *Jaya*, the core narrative on which the *Mahabharata* corpus is held to have been built, with a climactic battle of the conflict eventually coming to be regarded as an epochal event. This estimate is also supported by Irawati Karve,[6.14] who considers the Kurukshetra battle as 'a real event which took place about 1000 BC'. But, as we will see, the issue is far from settled.

In this context, one must also mention the work of the noted archaeologist (Sanskrit scholar and one-time pupil of Mortimer Wheeler), BB Lal, who found evidences of Painted Grey Ware (PGW) Culture at the site of ancient Hastinapura in Uttar Pradesh, near Delhi, which he initially believed to be representative of the early Aryans in India, assigning the finds to a period around 850 BC. Later, however, Lal revised his view, as he came across similar ceramic artefacts from excavations in the Middle Ganga Valley, still upholding a broad time-band for the *Mahabharata* PGW (between Northern Black Polished Ware whose beginning went back to the 6th-7th century BC, and a lower stratum, with a break in between, of Ochre Colour Ware of the early 2nd millennium BC), but delinking it from the Aryan invasion hypothesis.[6.15]

MEDLEY OF OLD RECORDS, NEW 'EVIDENCES' AND CONCLUSIONS

One intriguing facet of the seemingly never-ending debate on the antiquity of the *Mahabharata* war is the divide between Western scholars and their Indian counterparts. Among the former, as we shall see with some of the European theories covered in the following chapter, one finds a tendency to push the date forward and place the *Mahabharata* and Krshna in some degree of chronological closeness to the Christian era. The Indian tendency, on the other hand, is a diverse spectrum of views, in which, alongside some upholders of the Western projections, and some diehard sceptics dismissing almost all traditions as mythology, there are also shades of the other extreme, with a penchant of a few to stretch the date a long way back. However, by and large, Aryabhata's astronomical calculation of 3102 BC as the year of the war holds a strong sway on the Indian mind.

While some of these opinions have been sought to be bolstered with collateral historical, astronomical, and astrological arguments, newer evidences, especially relating to the marine-archaeological relics found at Dvaraka (Dwaraka), seem to throw additional light on the antiquity of Krshna and the *Mahabharata* war. Here, leaving out the more extreme antiquarian theories (one of which puts the war at 5561 BC[6.16]), let us briefly examine three 'evidences', the first two of which seem to bear out the *Kali-Yuga* tradition of 3102 BC, ascribed to Aryabhata, with the third marine-archaeological evidence pointing to a later date of around 15th century BC, as the time of Krshna. These evidences, in seriatim, are: (i) a reference from Megasthenes; (ii) a Calukya inscription of Pulakesein II; and (iii) the new Dwaraka marine-archaeological discoveries.

MEGASTHENES' REFERENCE TO THE INDIAN 'HERCULES'
Arrian, the Roman historian (Flavius Arrianus; ca. AD 86-160), cites the following reference from *Indica* of Megasthenes (ca. 350-290 BC),[6.17] the illustrious Greek ethnographer and ambassador of Seleucus I to the court of Chandragupta Maurya: *From Dionysus to Sandracottus the Indians reckoned 153 kings, and 6,042 years. ...They say that Dionysus was earlier than Heracles by fifteen generations, and that no other ever invaded India for war, not even Cyrus, the son of Cambyses, though he marched against the Scythians, and in other matters was the most meddlesome of the kings of Asia. However they admit that Alexander came and overcame in battle all the nations whom he visited, and that he would have conquered them all if his army had been willing. But none of the Indians ever marched out of their own country for war, being actuated by a respect for justice.*

Now, there is no dispute that 'Sandracottus' was the Greek equivalent of Chandragupta Maurya. As regards the references to 'Dionysus' and 'Heracles' in the Indian context, there seems to be a certain belief, supported by a few collateral similarities in exploits and names, that they represented the assimilation of the Indian legends of 'Indra' and 'Krshna' respectively, into Greek legendary traditions. Here, since our interest is centred on Krshna, let us quickly review his 'Heracles' association. The American Indologist Edwin Francis Bryant, in his recent (2007) work on Krshna,[6.18] has observed:

According to Arrian, Diodorus, and Strabo, Megasthenes described an Indian tribe called Sourasenoi, who especially worshipped Herakles in their land, and this land had two cities, Methora and Kleisobora, and a navigable river, the Jobares. As was common in the ancient period, the Greeks sometimes described foreign gods in terms of their own divinities, and there is a little doubt that the Sourasenoi refers to the Shurasenas, a branch of the Yadu dynasty to which Krishna belonged; Herakles to Krishna, or Hari-Krishna: Mehtora to Mathura, where Krishna was born; Kleisobora to Krishnapura, meaning "the city of Krishna"; and the Jobares to the Yamuna, the famous river in the Krishna story. Quintus Curtius also mentions that when Alexander the Great confronted Porus, Porus's soldiers were carrying an image of Herakles in their vanguard.

The association is nothing new. For example, Colonel James Tod, in his well-known *Annals and Antiquities of Rajasthan* (1873), cited an etymologically ingenious parallelism between Heracles and the sibling pair of Balarama (Baladeva) and Krshna:[6.19] *How invaluable such remnants of ancient race of Harikula! How refreshing to the mind yet to discover, amidst the ruins on the Yamuna, Hercules (Baldeva, god of strength) retaining his club and lion's hide, standing on his pedestal at Baldeo, and yet worshipped by Suraseni! This was the name given to a large tract of country round Mathura, or rather round Surpura, the ancient capital founded by Surasena, the grandfather of the Indian brother-deities, Krishna and Baldeva, Apollo and Hercules. The title would apply to either; though Baldeva has the attributes of 'god of strength'. Both are es (lords) of the race (kula) of Hari (Hari-kul-es), of which the Greeks might have made the compound Hercules.*

Hercules, the Greek superman and demigod, drawing his supposedly original signification of name from the patently

Indian *Hari-kul-esh*! Can there be a more intriguing projection of ancient globalism? But whatever may have been the truth behind the cross-cultural association, the plausible point in our present context is that the Indian 'Heracles' referred to by Megasthenes is quite likely to have been Krshna (or even Balarama, who, in any case, belonged to the same generation). Hence, from the fragment of the afore-cited extract from *Indica: From Dionysus to Sandracottus the Indians reckoned 153 kings, and 6,042 years. ...They say that Dionysus was earlier than Heracles by fifteen generations* – it would follow that between Krshna and Chandragupta Maurya, there intervened 153 minus 15, i.e. 138 generations.

The other figure of 6,042 years in the same extract is somewhat problematic. First, it is not clear whether it means the chronological gap between reigns (coronations), or between years of birth. Second, it would seem to suggest too long reigns. In fact, taking 6042 years as the period of 153 reigns, the average per generation works out to 39.50 years, which in turn would yield a time scale of 5,451 years (138 x 39.50) between Krshna and Chandragupta Maurya; adding the latter's coronation date of 320 BC, one gets 5771 BC as the date of Krshna. Although this date has been supported by some Indian scholars,[6.20] such a projection of antiquity does not seem free from doubt. Instead, we may here go by the majority view of 20 years per generation (à la Pergiter's assumption of 18 years per reign), leading to 2,760 years (138 x 20), and so, 2,760 + 320 = 3080 BC as Krshna's date, which would fit snugly with Aryabhata's calculations, though admittedly, it would still be a very speculative fit.

'HARD' EVIDENCE OF THE CALUKYA INSCRIPTIONS

One important indigenous source for researchers in ancient Indian history since Ashoka's time, has been the rock inscriptions strewn here and there across the sub-continent. Regarding the historicity of the *Mahabharata* war, scholars often refer to a 634 AD inscription (found in a Jain temple at Aihole, Karnataka), in praise of Pulakesein II, the illustrious Calukya king in whom the great Harsha is said to have met more than his match. The inscriptions are in Sanskrit, written in the old Kannada script. Here are literal translations of four relevant verses, appearing in *Epigraphia Indica*, officially published by the Archaeological Survey of India:[6.21]

Verse 23 – Harsha, whose lotus-feet were arrayed with the rays of the jewels of the diadems of hosts of feudatories prosperous with unmeasured might, through Him had his mirth (harsha) melted away by fear, having become loathsome with his rows of lordly elephants fallen in battle.

Verse 33 – (Now) when thirty (and) three thousand and five years besides, joined with seven hundred years, have passed since the Bharata war;

Verse 34 – And when fifty (and) six and five hundred years of the Saka kings also have gone by in the Kali age;

Verse 35 – This stone mansion of Jinendra, a mansion of every kind of greatness, has been caused to be built by the wise Ravikirti, who has obtained the highest favour of that Satyashraya whose rule is bounded by the three oceans.

In a seemingly straightforward way, the arithmetic of Verses 33 and 34 tells us that the temple came up 30 + 3000 + 5 + 700 = 3,735 years after the Bhaarata war; and after 50 + 6 + 500 = 556 years of the *shaka* calendar. Taking the standard date of 78 AD as the beginning of *shaka* era, the inscription can be assigned to 556 + 78 = 634 AD, which is consistent with the historically accepted reign of Pulakesein II (610-642 AD). As regards the phraseology, *have gone by in the Kali age*, the same could have been intended to put an additional solemn touch to the recorded chronology.

The date of the inscription having thus been reasonably established as 634 AD, the precise indication of '3,735 years after the Bhaarata war', would yield a date of 3735 – (minus) 634 = 3101 BC as the date of the war – again vindicating the venerable Aryabhata's ancient calculations. Of course, the inscribed chronology itself was likely to have been based on the Aryabhata date as its starting landmark, which should establish the abiding sway of the pioneer astronomer in ancient India.

There are several valid reasons why the Aihole Inscriptions should be taken seriously in the context of dating the Bhaarata war. For one, it is, of course, both literally and figuratively, old and 'hard' evidence, which is a rarity in ancient history. Second, the figures recorded are too precise, up to the units' place of decimal numbering, to be dismissed as inaccurate, especially taking into account that they represented 'official' chronology authenticated by the imprint of an important monarch. And finally, there is no cause to suspect deliberate fudging of the calculations since they had no bearing on the eulogy of achievements otherwise recorded in the inscription.

MARINE ARCHAEOLOGICAL FINDS AT DVARAKA

Perhaps the most promising key to unravelling the *Mahabharata*'s historicity, lies buried in the undersea ruins at Dvaraka. The place has always held a magical sway over the minds of generations of Indians, cemented by faith and reinforced by a deeply entrenched civilisational memory. After all, traditions hold this to be the place where Krshna, after his strategic retreat from far-away Mathura, built an impregnable stronghold for his Yadava clan; the place from which he made those dozen trips to counsel the Pandavas at the turning points in the great drama of the *Mahabharata*; the place where he lived for 36 years after the Bhaarata war; and again, the place where a climactic tragedy of that epochal drama occurred, with the self-destruction of the Yadavas, the providential passivity and ultimate passing away of Krshna, and with the submergence of the fabulous city shortly thereafter.

The starkly concise *Maushala-parva* gives a graphic picture of the event. Here is an adaptation conveying the pathos of Arjuna's rescue mission in a Dvaraka devoid of its presiding Lord:[6.22] *The sea rushed into the city. It coursed through the streets of the beautiful city. The sea covered up everything in the city. Even as they were all looking, Arjuna saw the beautiful buildings becoming submerged one by one. Arjuna took a last look at the mansion of Krishna. It was soon covered by the sea. In a matter of a few moments it was all over. The sea had now become as placid as a lake. There was no trace of the beautiful city which had been the favourite haunt of all the Pandavas. Dwaraka was just a name; just a memory.*

The *Shreemad-Bhaagavatam* also records Shuka telling Pareekshit about the fateful submergence in the poignant *shloka*:[6.23]
Dvarakam harinaa tyaktaam
samudro 'plaavayat kshanaat /
Varjayitvaa mahaaraaja
shreemad-bhagavad- aalayam //
~ SB; 11.31.23

As soon as Dvaraka was abandoned by the Lord Hari, the ocean flooded it on all sides, O King, sparing only the Supreme Lord's palace.

Visitors to Dvaraka are likely to sense the spell the place, with its majestic Dvarakaadheesh temple, surrounded by miles of barren land on one side and an enigmatically placid sea with its mild waves chopping around the island temple site of Bet Dvaraka on the other, exerts on receptive minds. The place can indeed bring to mind Coleridge's 'miracle of rare device'.

On-shore and off-shore archaeological explorations have been going on at Dvaraka for nearly 50 years, the first excavations by a Deccan College Pune team having been conducted in 1963. But the real breakthrough was achieved by a marine archaeological project conducted by a team of experts under the leadership of renowned archaeologist-oceanographer, Dr. SR Rao. The ambitious project, mounted jointly by the National Institute of Oceanography and the Archaeological Survey of India, employed 'the technique of geophysical survey, combined with the use of echo-sounders, mud-penetrators, sub-bottom profilers and under-water metal detectors'. This team carried out twelve marine archaeological expeditions between the years 1983 and 1992, and articles/artefacts recovered were sent to the Physical Research Laboratory for dating. By using thermo-luminescence, carbon dating and other modern scientific techniques, these were found to belong to the period spanning 15th - 18th century BC. The following are some of the important findings recorded by Rao.[6.24]

(i) The land for building the city of Dwaraka had been reclaimed from the sea between 16th to 15th century BC and a fortified city was built on boulder packing with outer gateway to the sea and inner gateway to Gomati River.
(ii) The thermo-luminescence dating of lustrous Redware Pottery items found during explorations revealed that these were 3,520 years old, i.e. around 16th-15th century BC.
(iii) The most famous rectangular seal with engraved motifs of bull, unicorn and goat found in trench UW6 in the sea bed was dated as belonging to 16th century BC. The seal corroborates the references made in the ancient manuscripts that every citizen of Dwaraka was required to carry a mudra (seal) as a mark of identification.

(iv) Stone anchors with double holes and triangular prismatic stone anchors recovered from under the sea were similar to the ones found in Lothal excavations belonging to 23rd century BC.

Thus, according to the celebrated marine archaeologist, the underwater explorations prove that the reconstructed city of Dwaraka was a prosperous port town and that it was in existence for about 60-70 years in the 15th century BC before being submerged in the year 1443 BC. In this context, the following extracts from a detailed article in *The Hindu* of Feb 7, 1988, is of interest:[6.25]

The sixth marine archaeological expedition of the National Institute of Oceanography, Goa, led by Dr. S.R. Rao, Emeritus scientist, has claimed the discovery of hitherto unknown features of the legendary Dwaraka of Sri Krishna, submerged by the Arabian Sea 3,500 years ago.

During the current season (November 1987 to February1988 the expedition said it came across the inner and outer gateways of the proto-historic port city, flanked by circular bastions built of massive blocks of sandstone. From the inner gateway a flight of steps led to the Gomati river, the submerged channel of which has been traced over a length of 1.5 km in the seabed. According to Dr. Rao, the occurrence of smaller three-holed stone anchors of triangular shape weighing 100 to 140 kg suggests that small boats used to sail up the Gomati while the larger ones were moored farther away from the outer entrance gate.

.....

If the number, size and variety of stone anchors are any indication of the size of the port, it can be said that Dwaraka was the largest port of the second millennium B.C. on the Indian coast. As many as 50 stone anchors are visible. But several hundred must have been buried in the sediment.

.....

Nine courses of stone masonry of the massive fort wall are still intact at many places. It must have been much higher in ancient times to prevent further erosion by the sea.

The construction technique is interesting. Large trapezoidal blocks built course by course formed the outer shell holding together the rubble filling in the core. This gravity well was specially designed to serve as anti-erosion structure in the sea, and is certainly a bolder experiment than that of their predecessors, the Harappans.

.....

The occurrence of late Harappan artefacts such as chart blacken and perforated vessels suggests the <u>existence of a settlement earlier than the Dwarka of Sri Krishna</u>, to which reference is made in the epic. Thus <u>we have in Bet Dwarka the Mahabharata (before 1,500 B.C.), the Mahabharata (1500-1400 B.C.) and post Mahabharata (third century B.C. onwards) settlements</u>. The former two were submerged by the sea. [Emphasis by author]

A POSSIBLE WAY TO RESOLVE THE DATING CONUNDRUM

Having examined the three evidences (Megasthenes, the Pulakesein inscription, and the new Dvaraka archaeological discoveries), as also the Iron Age projection, we are still left with gaping differences of five centuries and two millennia, between the recurrent Indian projection of 3100 BC, the recent Dvaraka finds suggesting 1500 BC, and Basham's Western estimate of 1000 BC, in dating the Bhaarata war. Each line of evidence has some reasonable basis. One way out of the conundrum could be to attach greater credence to the median projection of 1500 BC, by virtue of its being supported by physical tests like thermo-luminescence and radiocarbon dating. But then, such scientific tests are susceptible to a margin of error which, in absolute terms, may be significant in the case of very ancient proto-historic samples, where dates are reckoned on the millennial scale.

A better course, perhaps, could be to more rigorously examine the intrinsic as well as relative merits of the various evidences. While doing so, one could adopt the new 21st century paradigm of physics and look for the 'least implausible' formulation rather than the mirage of a 'most plausible' theory. With this as a considered view, we have, willy-nilly, to leave the challenge of resolving the dating question to future researchers.

THE DYNAMIC NATURE OF THE EPIC'S EVOLUTION

We have by now delved enough into the still mystery-laden historicity of Shri Krshna and the Bhaarata war. But tracing the history of the epic's origin and development is another issue that has provided fertile ground for much scholastic research. What adds a ticklish dimension to the exercise is that the *Mahabharata* is much more than history. According to Tagore, 'it is not just history authored by one individual; rather, it is the spontaneous and holistic self-history composed by an entire nation'. Again,

Sauti was proved right about future poets recounting the same 'history' over and over again. In the process of such retellings, and in a quaint Indian syndrome that was the very antithesis of modern plagiarism, many later poets found soulful gratification in interpolating their anonymous contributions into the revered narrative. Some of these accretions are great philosophy; some are good literature; some merely unhistorical and preternatural concoctions, while others are mythical folklore.

One rationale that can be adduced to put these 'creative' latitudes in perspective is that, unlike the *Vedas,* which had to be preserved verbatim, the epic was a popular work whose reciters would conceivably make contemporaneous changes in language, style and even in the substance and slant of presentation. Given this inherent dynamism, one basic approach to dating the original work has been to go by the earliest external references we have to the epic, which include a few fairly direct references found in Panini's stupendously perfected grammar of 6th or 5th century BC vintage (*Ashtaadhyaayee, sutra* 4:2:56; 4:3:98; 8:3:95).[6.26, 6.27] Another relevant reference is found in the Vedic *Aashvalaayana Grhya Sutra* of 4th century BC vintage, which we shall discuss in a later section.

Now, if we take it that the work called *Mahabharata,* in some form, was known in Panini's time, the question arises as to which form was prevalent in the late-Vedic age (600-500 BC), that is generally taken to be the period when the pioneering grammarian lived and ushered in the age of classical Sanskrit that followed. That, unfortunately, we cannot say for sure. Moreover, as a logician of the Aristotelian school would say, *absence of evidence is not evidence of absence;* [6.28] we cannot thus say that there was no *Mahabharata* before Panini's time, merely because the evidence is no longer extant. What we can do is reach some preliminary conclusions based on the indicative evidence of the earliest historical forms of the *Mahabharata's* narration, contained *in situ* in the introductory *Anukramanikaa* sub-chapter of the epic's *Aadi-parva* itself.

THE SAUTI EVIDENCE
To start with, Sauti, in Verse 51 of the *Anukramanikaa,* spells out the rationale for composing two different versions, one long, another short:

Visteeryaitan-mahaaj-jnanam rshih samkshipya caabraveet /
Ishtam hi vidushaam loke samaas-avyaasa-dhaaranam //
~ Aadi; 1.51
The sage (Vyasa) has narrated this great knowledge in both
expanded and abridged forms;
Because scholars of this world prefer practising (their subject of
study) in both short and long manner.

This is followed by indication of three standard starting points,
corresponding to three stages of abridgement (or expansion) of
the narrative, also referred to as an 'encyclopaedia', which true
scholars can explain (comment upon), others can only commit
to memory:
Manvaadi bhaaratam kecid-aasteekaadi tathaa pare /
Tatho-pari-caad-anye vipraah samyag-adheeyate //
Vividham samhitaa-jnanam deepayanti maneeshinah /
Vyaakhyaatum kushalaah kecid granthaan dhaarayitum pare //
~ Aadi; 1.52-53
Some Brahmanas study the Bhaarata thoroughly from its
invocation with Manu [the opening hymn, i.e. *naaraayanam
namaskrtya* etc.]. Some others study it from the episode of
Aasteeka; still others begin the narrative from the section on
Uparicara.
Sagacious scholars depict this encyclopaedia of wisdom in
different lights. Some can explain it well; others can only commit
its words to memory.

As regards ancient redactions of the pristine work, the
Anukramanikaa itself indicates that there is a core portion of
24,000 verses; and the complete *Mahabharata*, as traditionally
known to people, of 100,000 verses, and also a summary in 150
verses, the *Anukramanikaadhyaaya*. The following are the relevant
lines recited in this context by Sauti:
Idam shatasahasram tu lokaanaam punya-karmanaam /
Upaakhyaanaih saha jneyam-aadyam bhaaratam-uttamam //
Caturvimshati-saahasreem cakre Bhaarata-samhitaam /
Upaakhyaanair-vinaa taavad bhaaratam procyate budhaih //
Tatohpy-ardha-shatam bhooyah samkshepam krtavaan-rshih /
Anukramanikaadhyaaam vrttaantam sarvaparvanaam //
~ Aadi; 1.102-104
It should be known that including the episodes, this ancient

Mahabharata contains 100,000 sacred verses. Excluding all episodes (stories) the encyclopaedia of Bhaarata contains 24,000 thousand verses. Wise men call this digest the Bhaarata proper. Thereafter, again the sage (Vyasa) composed a condensed introductory chapter of 150 verses. It contains a summarised account of all the Parvas.

THE VAISHAMPAYANA EVIDENCE

But Sauti, according to his own indication, heard the narrative from Vaishampayana in Janamejaya's *Sarpa-satra*. So it is relevant to check what Vaishampayana himself has to say on the subject. In Chapter 63 of the *Aadi-parva*, after the episode of Vyasa's birth (already referred in Chapter 1), Vaishampayana mentions five students of Vyasa while naming the presenters of separate encyclopaedias of the Bhaarata:

Vedaan-adhyaapayaamaasa Mahaabhaarata-pamcamaam /
Sumantum jaiminim pailam shukam caiva samaatmajam //
Prabhur-varishtho varado vaishampaayanam eva ca /
Samhitaastaih prthaktvena bhaaratasya prakaashitaah //
~ Aadi; 63. 89-90

Vyasa taught the *Vedas* and the *Mahabharata* as the fifth *Veda* to Sumantu, Jaimini, Paila, his own son Shuka, and to his blessed disciple Vaishampayana. They, in turn, composed separate encyclopaedias of the Bhaarata.

So we get the names of five ancient sages, of whom Shuka appears to have been the memoriser of his father's original version, and the four others may have been the original co-organisers of the *Vedas* and the *Mahabharata*. A collateral clue in this regard is to be found in the *Aashvalaayana Grhya Sutra* (3.4.4):[6.29, 6.30]

sumantu-jaimini-vaishampaayana-paila-sutra-bhaashya-bhaarata-
Mahaabhaarata dharmaacaaryaah.

This suggests that Sumantu was the framer of the aphorisms; Jaimini, the commentator; and Vaishampayana and Paila, the presenters of the *Bhaarata* and the *Mahabharata* respectively. But we are still left with the problem that not much of the works other than the one ascribed to Vaishampayana, are now extant. Some textual reference or indication of those missing versions could have been of great help in re-verifying the excised portions of the Critical Edition, which we shall discuss in a later chapter. More problematic is the non-availability of a clearer indication as to which were the 24,000 verses that comprised Vaishampayana's *Bhaarata*.

THE 'OBSCURE' VERSES

In addition to the two ancient versions, *Mahaabhaarata* and *Bhaarata*, tradition suggests the existence of an older and shorter epic nucleus, named *Jaya* (Victory), attributed again to Vyasa and containing 8,800 verses. In fact, the epic itself carries a few references to this name, the most prominent one being the grandly alliterating invocatory hymn appearing at the beginning of all the *Parvas*:

Naaraayanam namaskrtya naram caiva narottamam /
Deveem sarasvateem caiva tato jayam-udeerayet //

Only after paying obeisance to Narayana, Nara (Brahmaa), Narottama (Prajapati), Devi (Durga) and Sarasvati, one should recite *Jaya* and the *Puranas*.

The reason for associating the name *Jaya* with a core of 8,800 verses is the following couplet in the same *Anukramanikaa* section, indicating that the said number of verses were definitely known only to Vyasa himself and to Shuka, the latter being Vyasa's own son, who was the first to learn the Mahabharata from his father, even before it was taught to the sage's disciple Vaishampayana:

Ashtou shlokasahasraani ashtou shlokashataani ca /
Aham vedmi shuko vetti sanjayo vetti vaa na vaa //
~ Aadi; 1.81

This book has 8,800 verses, (the meaning of) which I know, Shuka knows, and Sanjaya may or may not know.

But a reference to its actual context will show that this verse does not relate to the first redaction of the epic as is misconstrued by some, perhaps due to association with the first listener-recipient Shuka's name. Its actual context is the number of *koota*, or intricate verses (8,800), which Vyasa deliberately injected in his composition to slow down the scribe, Lord Ganesha, who had consented to do the job on the condition there would be no break in Vyasa's dictation unless Ganesha himself needed to pause to understand the meaning. However, this particular verse, for all its ingeniously dramatic, though seemingly mythical, context of its incorporation, now stands excised in the modern critical form of the epic, apparently due to lack of authentic textual support.

CONTRASTING VIEWS ON THE LONG AND SHORT VERSIONS
In light of the above, Western scholarly view (now accepted by many Indian scholars following the publication of the *Critical Edition*), is that both *Jaya* and *Bhaarata* may actually refer to the same originally concise form of the epic. This *Bhaarata* (of 24,000 unspecified verses), may have been the real core of the epic, which would have been amenable to recitation in royal courts as a paean on *Jaya* (victory), as also to being sung by wandering minstrels. Later additions may have been made to this core by Brahminical redactors, especially those of the Bhrgu family clan, into whose keeping it was placed by the narrator *Sootas* (as suggested by VS Sukthankar, about whose work we shall discuss later); these redactions, or rather amplifications, were apparently carried out with some regard for thematic and contextual consistency, but with increasingly greater insertions of didactic and devotional elements, which did not exist in the original tight narration of the secular-warrior story of a profoundly tragic, but compellingly fascinating dynastic war of succession.

This line of reasoning appears to have some validity, but one must also bear in mind that it is based more on the occidental approach, attaching primary importance to manuscript copies, whereas, given ancient India's oral traditions, the *Mahabharata* would have been propagated for thousands of years as memorised versions. We shall discuss this problem with manuscripts in a later chapter (on the *Critical Edition*). But the short point one can make here is that, like many other 'mysteries' of the *Mahabharata*, we do not appear to have a final, open-and-shut scenario of its evolution. There are indeed arguable points in favour of the traditional Indian belief that Vyasa had himself composed the larger encyclopaedic *Mahabharata* of 100,000 verses, including the 'frame-tale' episodes and much of the didactic-devotional matter. For one thing, such a large work with devotional content could reasonably be expected from an exceptional scholar famed for his remarkably voluminous corpus of religious works (including classification of the *Vedas*, composition of 18 *Puranas*, etc). Secondly, and perhaps more importantly, as we have already seen (Aadi; 1.51 and 63.89-90), Vyasa is directly credited by both Sauti and Vaishampayana as the original creator of the long form of the epic which has 100,000 verses.

It is doubtful if any of the ancient 'interpolators', given their own devotional traditions, would have dared to doctor the pristine verses of the epic merely to concoct a surreptitious association with the original Guru of Indian spiritual scholarship. Rather, a more credible hypothesis would be to 'suspend disbelief' and not to dismiss the inlaid clues that suggest the Guru created the long form, perhaps got one copy scribed by a scholarly amanuensis (later represented as Ganesha), and then tasked his disciples to make shorter versions amenable to readier narration in courts and hermitages. A hypothesis indeed, but with some basis to serve as a researcher's counterpoint to the text-critical point already mentioned.

Another basic point in our working hypothesis on the origin of the *Mahabharata* story is not to discount Vyasa as a 'mythical' figure, as has been done by some Western analysts and even by Indian scholars such as VS Sukthankar (who basically belongs to the Western text-critical school of his mentor, Moriz Winternitz). Unlike the lack of collateral evidences that makes the identity of Homer a matter of considerable doubt, Vyasa had left such a trail of personal legend (including his unique interventions in the core events of the great epic itself), and such a voluminous corpus of great works in myriad ancient cross-references, that to doubt his very existence would be carrying scepticism beyond reasonable limits.

Incidentally, one more aspect of the said text-critical point needs to be mentioned before we wind up this longish chapter. As observed by Irawati Karve and others, the present composition of the work into 18 *Parvas*, seems to be an artificial structural frame brought in later due to a certain perceived mystical sanctity attached to the number eighteen. It is relevant to note that the battle of Kurukshetra itself lasted 18 days, and involved 18 armies. Of course, the subtle scriptural significance of the numerological association would be more apparent when one considers that, apart from the 18 chapters in the epic's philosophical crown jewel, the *Bhagavad-Gita*, there are also 18 *Puranas* and 18 main *Upanishads*. By the same logic, and in line with the traditional 'counter-point' already mentioned, it could also be argued that the holy numerology of 18 is consistent with the long form having been composed by Vyasa, who composed the 18 *Puranas*.

If, however, as suggested by some, the rigidity of 18 is removed, the book itself could perhaps be recast into a more secular and primitive form by removing some of its seemingly later additions, such as the long and patently instructional *Shaanti-parva*. But, given the limitation of available evidences, such radical speculations on dismembering a massive epic built on centuries of tradition, would not be desirable or practicable. Instead, we would be better advised to acquaint ourselves with the phenomenal quantity of global work that has already been done on the study of the historical evolution of the *Mahabharata*.

NOTES & REFERENCES

6.1 *Maharshi Vedavyaasa-racitam Mahaabhaaratam*, Aryashastra Publications, 1968 (Bengali Calendar: 1375), Kolkata.

6.2 Sauti means 'son of *Soota*'. The *Sootas*, as a class, were narrator-bards (of *Puranas*), or charioteers. Sauti was the sobriquet of Ugrashrava, meaning 'loud-voiced', as ideal an attribute in a narrator as was 'hair-raiser', in case of Sauti's father, Lomaharshana.

6.3 Sauti heard the account from Vyasa's disciple Vaishampayana, at the famous *Sarpa-Satra* (serpent sacrifice), of King Janamejaya.

6.4 The date (1000 BC), is mentioned in the Introduction (p. 4), of Irawati Karve's interesting anthropological treatise, *Yuganta*, Orient Blackswan Pvt. Ltd., Hyderabad, 2008, Reprint 2011. More detailed chronological references are given in Notes 6.6 and 6.7 below.

6.5 Several such details have been mentioned in the brilliantly analysed introductory portion of the abridged Bengali translation (*Mahabharat-Saranuvad*), by Rajshekhar Basu, M.C. Sarkar & Sons, Kolkata-73, 1949 (Bengali Calendar: 1356), Tenth Reprint: 1987.

6.6 AL Basham, *The Wonder that was India,* Sidgwick & Jackson, London, 1954; Picador (Macmilan) Edition, 2004, p. 40. Basham mentions the 'most popular' tradition of placing the *Mahabharata* war in 3102 BC, as also a later tradition of the 15th century BC, but finally attaches greater credence to its placement 'around the beginning of the 9th century BC'.

6.7 Bankim Chandra Chattopadhyay, *Krishna-Charitra* (in Bengali), Chapter 5, in *Bankim Rachanavali (Part Two)*, Model Publishing House, Kolkata-73, 1997, pp. 506-510. Here, Bankim Chandra has cited several *shloka*s from Part 4, Chapter 24 of the *Vishnupurana*. However, the ones (*shloka*s 33, 34 and 39), relating to the astronomical positions of the stars *Maghaa* and *Purvaashaadaa* vis-à-vis the *Saptarshi* (Great Bear) constellation at the times of Yudhishthira /

Pareekshit and Nanda/ Chandragupta Maurya, give inconclusive results; hence, Bankim Chandra went by the *shloka* 32 cited in the text.

6.8 AD Pusalker, *History and Culture of the Indian People*, Bharatiya Vidya Bhavan, 1966, Vol I, Chapter XIV, p. 273.

6.9 *Vishnu-Puranam*, Aryashastra Publications, Kolkata. In translating the *shloka*, *sahasra* has been taken to mean a 'thousand' and not just 'many', as otherwise *pancodashottaram*, meaning 'fifteen more' cannot make sense.

6.10 FE Pargiter, *Ancient Indian Historical Tradition*, London 1922 [Reprint Motilal Banarsidass, 1997], p. 180. He shows estimates of the average as 47, 50, 31 and 35 years for various versions of the lists.

6.11 Pargiter, *ibid.* pp. 180-182.

6.12 Basham, *The Wonder that was India*, Sidgwick & Jackson, London, 1954; Picador (Macmilan) Edition, 2004, p. 40.

6.13 M Witzel, *Early Sanskritization: Origin and Development of the Kuru State*, EJVS (Electronic Journal of Vedic Studies), Vol.1 No.4 (1995).
Monograph available at: http://laurasianacademy.com/ejvs/ejvs0104/ejvs0104article.pdf

6.14 Irawati Karve, *Yuganta* (English), Orient Blackswan Pvt. Ltd., Hyderabad, 2008, Reprint 2011, p. 4.

6.15 BB Lal, *Inaugural Address delivered at the 19th International Conference on South Asian Archaeology, held at University of Bologna, July 2-6, 2007: 'Let not the 19th century paradigms continue to haunt us!'* This is available on the internet at: http://www.archaeologyonline.net/artifacts/19th-century-paradigms.html The following witty reference to Lal's own mentor, the illustrious Mortimer Wheeler, may be of incidental interest: *Then came the master stroke. In 1946, my revered guru Mortimer Wheeler (later knighted) discovered a fortification wall at Harappa and on learning that the Aryan god Indra had been referred to as puramdara (destroyer of forts) he readily pronounced his judgment (Wheeler 1947: 82): 'On circumstantial evidence Indra [representing the Aryans] stands accused [of destroying the Harappan Civilization].' In further support of his thesis, he cited certain human skeletons at Mohenjo-Daro, saying that these were the people massacred by the Aryan invaders. Thus was reached the peak of the 'Aryan Invasion' theory.* Setting aside the 'Aryan Invasion' or 'Indigenous Aryan' controversy, Lal's address brings out other germane areas of archaeological knowledge that may be worth knowing.

6.16 PV Vartak, *The Scientific Dating of the Mahabharat War*, Veda Vidnyana Mandala, Pune, 1989, 2004. A monograph of the same title is available at:

http://www.hindunet.org/hindu_history/ancient/mahabharat/ mahab_vartak.html The paper contains detailed references to Greek records, inscriptions, archaeological finds, and ancient astronomical and astrological sources; however, the accompanying analyses, though copious in content, perhaps tend to present a maximal antiquarian projection.

6.17 Arrian, *The Indica, in Anabasis of Alexander, together with the Indica*, E. J. Chinnock, tr., Bohn, London, 1893, Ch. 1-16; at: http:// www.shsu.edu/~his_ncp/Indica.html The quoted portion appears near the end of section 9. The following two extracts from sections 5 and 8, respectively, contain the actual Megasthenes suggestions on an indigenous Indian Heracles resembling Krshna, which are relevant in the context of the two succeeding references (1.17 and 1.18) as well:

Section 5 *And besides, in the land of the Sibians, an Indian race, because they saw the inhabitants clothed in skins, they said that the Sibians were those who had been left behind from the expedition of Heracles. The Sibians also carry cudgels, and the figure of a club was branded upon their oxen; this too they explained to be a commemoration of the club of Heracles. If anyone gives credit to these tales, this must not have been another Heracles, the Theban, nor the Tyrian, nor the Egyptian; but some great king of a land situated in the interior not far from India.*

Section 8 *This Heracles is especially worshipped by the Sourasenians, an Indian nation, in whose land are two great cities, Methora and Cleisobora, and through it flows the navigable river Jobares. Megasthenes says, as the Indians themselves assert, that this Heracles wore a similar dress to that of the Theban Heracles.* [It has also been suggested that *Cleisobora,* or Krishnapura, as mentioned in the succeeding reference by Edwin Bryant, could be another name for Vrja, or Vrndavana).

6.18 Edwin Francis Bryant, *Krishna: a sourcebook*, Oxford University Press, New York, 2007, pp. 5.

6.19 James Tod, *Annals and Antiquities of Rajasthan*, Higginbotham, Madras, 1873, Reprint: Asian Educational Services, New Delhi, 2001, pp. 35-40.

6.20 Vartak, *ibid.*

6.21 Durga Prasad Dikshit, *Political History of the Chālukyas of Badami*, Abhinav Publications, New Delhi, 1980, p.8.

6.22 SR Rao, *The Lost City of Dvaraka*, Aditya Prakashan, New Delhi,1999.

6.23 Bhaktivedanta VedaBase: *Shreemad Bhaagavatam, Canto-11, Chapter-31*; available on the internet at: http://vedabase.com/en

6.24 These details of the marine archaeological finds have been taken from the following blog posting, which, in turn cites SR

Rao's book (see Note 6.22 above): Saroj Bala, blog posting: *Amazing facts about Ancient India;* http://sarojbala.blogspot.in/2007/09/shri-krishnas-dwarka-submerged-in-1443.html

6.25 The Ancient: *Dwaraka: Sri Krishna's City, Excerpt from The Ooparts Collection;* available at:
http://www.thelivingmoon.com/43ancients/02files/India_Ancient_City_Dwakara.html

6.26 Panini, *Ashtaadhyaayee or Sutrapaatha;* available at: http://sanskritdocuments.org/all_pdf/aShTAdhyAyI.pdf

Sutra 4.3.98: *vaasudevaarjunaabhyaam vun* ('After the words *Vaasudeva* and *Arjuna, vun* is to be added to denote the sixth case').

Sutra 8.3.95: *gaviyudhibhyaam sthirah* ('After the words *gavi* and *yudhi,* the '*Sa*' of '*sthira*' becomes '*sha*'; e.g. *Yudhishthira*'). These and a few other examples from Panini have been cited by Bankim Chandra Chattopadhyay, in his *Krishna-Charitra,* Chapter 7, of *Bankim Rachanavali* (Part Two), Model Publishing House, Kolkata, 1997.

6.27 Panini, *Ashtaadhyaayee,* Books 6-8, translated by Chandra Vasu, Benares, 1897 (Sanskrit/English); *Sutra* 6.2.38, p. 1154, contains a reference to the word *Mahaabhaaratah* as an example of *Karmadhaaraya* accent. Internet link:
http://archive.org/stream/ashtadhyayitrans06paniuoft#page/1154/mode/2up The period of Panini, shown as 6th or 5th century BC, is in conformity with Encyclopaedia Britannica (2004).

6.28 This type of Aristotelian syllogism (deductive reasoning), was propounded by John Locke as the 'Argument from Ignorance' (*argumentam ad ignorantium*) in his *An Essay Concerning Human Understanding* (1689). In recent times others, notably Carl Sagan, the eminent modern cosmologist, popularised it.

6.29 *Aashvalaayana Grhya Sutra,* 3.4.4; available at:
http://www.hinduwebsite.com/sacredscripts/hinduism/grihya/asva.asp#fr_532

6.30 *The Grihya-Sutras: Rules of Vedic Domestic Ceremonies,* Aashvalaayana Grhya-Sootra, 3.4.4; translator: Hermann Oldenberg, 1886; available at: http://merki.lv/vedas/Grihya%20Sutras%20(eng).pdf

7
INTERPRETATIONS GALORE

PERSPECTIVES OF THE 19TH CENTURY

With Europe and the world waking up to India's Sanskritic heritage, the 19th century became a prolific period for research into the *Mahabharata*. In India, Bankim Chandra, in his search for hard evidence on the historicity and antiquity of Krshna, attempted an analysis aimed at identifying the primitive 'layer' of the pristine *Mahabharata*, by sifting out the interpolations or *prakshipta* portions.[7.1]

Bankim Chandra's effort was in the nature of a spirited refutation of a late 19th century hypothesis advanced by the German Vedic scholar, Albrecht Weber, who sought to establish a parallelism between Krshna, the pastoral child-god, and Christ. Referring to the similarity in the story of nativity of the two child divinities (both providentially rescued from infanticidal designs of tyrants), Weber suggested that Krshna was a later addition to the Puranic narrative, and went on to argue that the depiction of Krshna as a personal deity was borrowed from that of Christ. While one might agree with Bankim Chandra that this part of Weber's thesis is highly debatable, his later effort (1891), to trace the origin of the story back to Vedic literature, appears more tenable, given the important parts played by Yudhishthira's *Rajasooya* and *Ashvamedha* sacrifices and Janamejaya's *Sarpa Yajna*, in the development and dissemination of the epic narrative.

We need to also mention here the other important hypotheses relating to the *Mahabharata* that were adduced by scholars of the 19th century and thereafter. Several of these studies give us more plausibly interesting leads than Weber's, on the association (or otherwise), of Krshna in the original, relatively secular, warrior-narration and the later didactic/devotional versions. A quick summary of some of these studies, based largely on a fairly detailed treatment contained in John Brockington's 1998 work, *The Sanskrit Epics*,[7.2] as also a briefer analysis in a more recent article, *The Mahabharata: The Global Epic* by Saroja Bhate,[7.3] would enable readers to put into perspective the somewhat baffling variety of yesterday's European-rationalist views on the historicity of the composition of the *Mahabharata*.

The trend of *Mahabharata* studies by historical and comparative methods was set by the German Indologist Franz Bopp, who translated into Latin the *Nala* and *Savitri* episodes in 1819 and 1829 respectively. For example, he observed that: *The Mahabharata legend of the flood and the fish is more archaic than its counterparts in other Puranas.*[7.4] However, Christian Lassen's was the first systematic study (1837) of both the *Ramayana* and the *Mahabharata*. Lassen was, in fact, the first scholar to suggest there were three major recensions (revisions based on plausible sources), of the poem, spreading across both the pre and post-Buddhist periods. On the whole, Lassen's analytical approach is in line with '*the traditional Indian approach recorded in the epic itself*. And interestingly, *according to him, the names Pandu and Krshna which signify white and black colours respectively are symbolic of tribes.*[7.5]

Basically, Lassen concluded that the poem recited by Sauti to Shaunaka was the second of the three recensions alluded to in the *Anukramanikaa* (the second recension being also cited in *Aashvalaayana Grhya Sutra*, which mentions a *Bhaarata* alongside a *Mahaabhaarata*), and that, '*since Aashvalaayana can be dated to 350 BC and was a pupil of Shaunaka, this second recension can be dated to 460 or 400 BC. Thereafter only interpolations with a Krshna emphasis were added, whereas the epic in its original form is pre-Buddhist.* Interestingly, Lassen noted *Krshna's connections with both pastoral and warrior groups*, averring that *these represented two layers of one tradition (with the pastoral one being the older), and suggested that the name Vaasudeva was not actually a patronymic*, but that its simple form, *Vasudeva*, meant *Gott der Vasu* (The God Vasu).[7.6] As we have already seen in Chapter 3, this suggestion is not just a stray speculation, but has some weighty collateral evidences in its support.

Sören Sörensen (1883), on the other hand, contended that the *Mahabharata* was originally a secular warrior-saga, composed by one author and that the repetitions, digressions, and inconsistencies found now, were due to subsequent grafting. On this logic, Sörensen drastically pruned the mammoth epic to only 8,000 stanzas. Brockington observes that although the somewhat arbitrary reduction has not found scholarly acceptance, *the main idea of an ancient warrior-saga as the original basis of the epic is still widely accepted.*

The two studies by the Adolf Holtzmanns (conducted by the uncle in 1846, and the nephew from 1881 onwards), ascribed the inconsistencies to what came to be labelled (by Hopkins), as the 'inversion theory', suggesting the original version had Duryodhana and the Kauravas (with Karna as the hero, and, according to the younger Holtzmann, with Buddhism as their guiding faith), as the righteous side, and that it was later redactors (editors), proponents of the 'new' divinity Vishnu, who modified the narrative to exonerate Krshna and the Pandavas from guilt, while substituting Shiva for Buddha as the Kauravas' guiding deity.

But in the absence of any reliable evidence, the Holtzmann theory fell through. Instead, in 1895, the Jesuit Joseph Dahlmann, rejecting altogether the suggestion of later accretions (external additions), asserted the fundamental unity of the text as a combination of narrative and didactic (morally instructive) content wrought by one author to present a popular saga of a conflict of good and evil. But Dahlmann's view of monolithic unity of the epic did not withstand peer scrutiny, mainly because of plausible indications that several elements of the story came from different periods. EW Hopkins, persuasively demonstrating the relative lateness of the didactic elements, called for a more critical approach. In his 1901 book, *The Great Epic of India*,[7.7] which marks the culmination of 19th century research on the subject, he makes the 'tentative' proposition, based on differences in language, prosody and style between different segments of the epic, that it was a compilation comprising several layers accreting around a small core that did not have the Pandavas as heroes, or Krshna as god – both being later additions of around 400-200 BC.

It would be pertinent to quote here what Hopkins has to say in summing up his scheme – *We may tentatively assume as approximate dates for the whole work in its different stages: Bhaarata (Kuru) lays, perhaps combined into one, but with no evidence of an epic before 400 BC. A Mahabharata tale with Pandu heroes, lays and legends combined by the Puranic diaskeuasts, Krshna as a demigod (no evidence of didactic form or of Krshna's divine supremacy), 400-200 BC. Remaking of the epic with Krshna as all-god, intrusion of masses of didactic matter, addition of Puranic material old and new; multiplication of exploits, 200 B.C. to 100-200 A.D.*

In putting the earliest date of the work as 'not before 400 BC', Hopkins apparently ignored the Panini evidences we have referred to. In any case, Hopkins's plausible approach of dissecting the *Mahabharata* into an older narrative and its later didactic components, as also its mechanism of growth, set the trend for subsequent research. But for all that, Hopkins himself acknowledged that the material was so tightly interwoven that to try to divide it into earlier and later parts would be difficult in the extreme.

20th CENTURY VIEWS TILL THE *CRITICAL EDITION*

Among the few studies of the early 20th century, mention may be made of the work of FE Pargiter, who, applying his theory of Puranic genealogies (conflict between *Brahmanas* and *Kshatriyas*), in the context of the *Mahabharata*, argued that the war marked the victory of the Krshna-worshipping Pancalas over Brahmanism, represented by the Kaurava alliance, thereby heralding an infusion of non-Vedic elements into the orthodox tradition. His view met with mixed reception, with Grierson in favour, and AB Keith in opposition.

Notwithstanding the lack of scholarly consensus on Pargiter's thesis, it was based on some logic and method. These elements were conspicuously absent in several other theories of the time, which seem to have been the products of imagination run wild. One such construction, cited by Brockington, was an allegorical wonder proposed by J. Kennedy in 1907-08. According to this hypothesis, there were several Krshnas. One was the demon-slaying hero of solar myths, linked to the dark sun, rains and storm, whose seat of Dvaraka was located 'where the sun dips into the boundless western ocean'; the other was 'the original Krshna of the Indus Valley, non-Aryan hero and semi-Aryan god, Aryan only in name'. For good Christian measure, Kennedy also added the theory that the legend of the child Krshna originated from apocryphal gospels imported to the Mathura area by the Scythian Gurjars; in a later (1917) article, he assigned the child Krshna to the Gupta era. Needless to say, such freewheeling fiction did not cut much ice with serious classicists.

More credibly based was the thesis of Hermann Oldenberg, appearing in a posthumous publication (1922), linking Pareekshit and Janamejaya with late Vedic literature, and developing the idea that the *Mahabharata* originated as a composition of mixed prose and verse that was later modified into regular verse form. Viewing the epic as literature, Oldenberg analysed its grammatical usages, the differences in metres employed by later redactors, as also the style of the work. He suggested that the main narrative is based on events which happened around 1200 BC, at the end of the Rig-Vedic period.

THEORIES OF ETHNOLOGY, SYMBOLISM AND CONTEMPORANEITY

Gerrit Jan Held (1935) discounted the utility of the debates between synthetically and critically oriented scholars as subjective theorising. Instead, he adopted an ethnographic and anthropological approach, raising his voice for the organic integrity of the epic against the dissection of analysts. Held viewed the Kauravas and Pandavas as analogous to two Hellenic or Iranian 'phratries' (related clans) in a tribe, engaged in a perpetual mode of cooperation and rivalry, and saw the whole epic as centred around a potlatch (community feast) ritual. Holding that both dicing and warfare were parts of the potlatch ritual, he proposed that the narrative develops around the fateful *dyoota*, or gambling tournament, which was the climax to the ceremonial feast, and the call to which Yudhishthira, as the *Dharmaraja*, or acclaimed upholder of traditions, was obliged to accept. Held reasoned that the sacred obligation attached to gambling was linked to its social sanctity as the traditional means to ensure circulation of tribal wealth.

Held drew a parallel between his theory of conflict and cooperation of the Kauravas and Pandavas, and the way the *Devas* and *Asuras* were in conflict but cooperated, in the ritual churning of the ocean. Interestingly, several scholars have, in various ways, drawn a parallel between the *Mahabharata* battle with the primordial conflict of the *Deva*s and *Asura*s – some viewing the conflict as that between the Aryans and the aborigines. Held also suggested that in this symbolic engagement, Vishnu (Krshna) sides with the Pandavas and Shiva with the Kauravas. Importantly, Held sought to project an elaborate theme of initiatory relationships in the epic – between Nara-Arjuna and Narayana-Krshna, between Arjuna and Shiva, and between Markandeya and the child-Krshna – averring that teaching being integral to the initiation process, the didactic and narrative elements were not artificial conjuncts but belonged *ab initio* together (we can add here the extensive student-teacher interactions of Yudhishthira with the sages Brhadashva, Lomasha and Markandeya). Held's central idea was that the epic reflects the reality of contemporaneous society (which he considered to be of the Vedic Braahmana period), and that the organic unity of the epic represents the unity of that society. The persuasive logic of the idea is hard to dismiss.

RECURRENT THEME OF THE PANDU TRIBE
Looking back, Gerrit Held's 1935 thesis, emphasising the centrality of tribal feasts and associated serious dice games, in the main plot of the *Mahabharata*, had interesting parallels in older Western researches suggesting the actual tribal identity of the Pandavas. During the 1890s, Alfred Ludwig, a student of Weber, argued that the original epic was about the triumph of the Bhaarata clan in Kurukshetra, and that *the Pandavas were not historical and were in fact members of different tribes, only later linked under the patronymic of Pandava*.[7,8] Concluding that the purpose of the narrative is not historical, Ludwig went off a tangential spin, ascribing the whole plot to a far-fetched seasonal allegory, in which sons of the pale sun Pandu fight those of the blind sun; also speculating, even less convincingly, that Krshna represents the spring sun, rendered dark by sacrificial smoke.

The theory that the Pandavas were not the original heroes but only figured in a secondary development of the epic, was also put forth by others, such as Holtzmann (1846) and Hopkins (1901). Hopkins mentions the apparently incongruous lack of any historical reference whatsoever of a 'Pandu Empire' (which, according to the epic, firmly established its sway after Yudhishthira's two great *yajna*s), pointing out that the concept of empire itself was unknown in India before Ashoka of the Buddhist period. Hopkins asserts that *even Manu has no idea of an empire; his king is a petty Raj.* Observing that *before the Mahabharata there were tales of Kurus and Bharats known to antiquity,* Hopkins speculates that *the tales which told of Kurus and Bhaaratas became the depository of the Pandus, who appear to have substituted themselves for Bhaaratas and may, in fact, have been a branch of the tribe, which, from a second rate position, raised itself to leadership.*[7.9] In this context, it needs to be noted that while there are references to Janamejaya in later Vedic literature, the same contain no allusion to Pandu or the Pandavas which, according to these Western scholars, indicates post-Vedic vintage of the Pandu legend.

RUBEN'S 'KRSHNA-LESS' *MAHABHARATA*

A divergent ethnological view was presented by Walter Ruben in his study on Krshna, which concludes our own survey of Western *Mahabharata* studies before we move on to the *Critical Edition.* In his effort to reconstruct the earliest and original form of the Krshna legend, Ruben assumed that the core of the traditions relating to Krshna and the Pandavas was historical but mythicised, on the model of the *Deva-Asura* battle. In particular, he observed that the story of Krshna's rivalry with Jarasandha, the king of Magadha, must have had some historical basis since Krshna's mortification in it is hardly likely to have been invented. Ruben further suggested that on this historical base, there grew three layers of tradition from three independent cycles of legend: first, the Mathura chapter, in which various folk traditions accrete around the conflict with Kamsa and Jarasandha; second, the Dvaraka material based on Krshna's flight from Mathura (perhaps originally about a different mass leader); and finally, an amalgamation of these two parts with the Hastinapura material, again embellished with folk tradition with its pre-moral ethics, which explain some of Krshna's questionable stratagems.

One implication of this theory is that the *Mahabharata* may have been originally bereft of Krshna. In fact, Ruben argues that Krshna is inessential to its basic plot, and that an absentee hero, who has to come eleven times to the aid of the Pandavas all the way from Dvaraka, just to play a studiedly passive role, strains credulity. Ruben obviously is not swayed by the

Mahabharata's unique oriental-mystic nuance of a super-arching personality (contemporaneously revered and later deified), who guides events on a pre-destined course. Ruben's Krshna-less *Mahabharata* does not, however, have any textual or manuscript support, and can at best be consigned to a stage preceding the archetype. The quest for that manuscript archetype needs now to be discussed.

NOTES & REFERENCES

7.1 Bankim Chandra Chattopadhyay, *Krishna-Charitra* (Bengali), Chapters 9-11, in *Bankim Rachanavali* (Part Two), Model Publishing House, Kolkata-73, 1997.

7.2 John Brockington. *The Sanskrit Epics*, Leiden, Boston, 1998, pp. 43-55.

The book contains, *inter alia*, a concise analysis of the various 19th century studies, including those by Christian Lassen, H.H. Wilson, Adolf Holtzmann (elder and younger), Albrecht Weber, Sören Sörensen, Joseph Dahlmann, EW Hopkins and others.

7.3 Saroja Bhate, *The Mahabharata: The Global Epic, Text and Variations of the Mahabharata*, *Sameeksheekaa* Series No. 2, Ed. Kalyan Kumar Chakravarty, National Mission for Manuscripts (Co-publisher: Munshiram Manoharlal Publishers) New Delhi, 2009, pp. 37-48.

7.4 Bhate, *ibid.*, p.38.

7.5 Bhate, *ibid.*, p.41.

7.6 John Brockington. *The Sanskrit Epics*, Leiden, Boston, 1998, p. 43.

7.7 Edward Washburn Hopkins, *The Great Epic of India: Character and Origin of the Mahabharata*, 1901. Reprint by Motilal Banarsidass, Delhi (1993). The quoted portion: pp. 397-398.

7.8 Brockington, *ibid.*, p.46.

7.9 Hopkins, *ibid.*, pp. 396-397.

8
THE *CRITICAL EDITION*

NEED FOR A TEXT-CRITICAL APPROACH

What with all the divergence of opinion regarding textual authenticity and significance, there was a felt need for an agreed common edition to be developed on the basis of the texts available in the form of the main northern and southern recensions (reconstructed intermediate editions) and other regional versions of the great epic. The first call in this direction was voiced by Moriz Winternitz, the Austrian orientalist from Oxford, who had the distinction of assisting Max Muller in preparing the second edition of the *Rig Veda* in 1890-92. Winternitz, who raised the matter in the XIth, XIIth, and XIIIth, International Congress of Orientalists at Paris (1897), Rome (1899), and Hamburg (1902), records that initially the idea of a critical edition of the *Mahabharata* met with considerable scepticism. Most scholars felt it would be impossible to recover a critical text of the great, yet inextricably synthetic, epic. Despite doubts and hesitations, some funds were allocated by academies at Berlin, Vienna and Göttingen, and in 1908, a specimen fascicle (part published separately), based on 29 manuscripts held in European libraries, was presented by Heinrich Lüders, who succeeded Winternitz as the Librarian of the Indian Institute, Oxford. The preliminary results were encouraging, and a sum of £6,000 was raised, before the whole project was brought to a standstill by the outbreak of World War I. Subsequently, the collations of Lüders, called *Mahabharata 1908*, were forwarded to the Bhandarkar Oriental Research Institute, Poona/Pune.

MAKING OF THE 'PUNE' EDITION

It was at the Bhandarkar Institute that the signal breakthrough in modern *Mahabharata* research was achieved. The Institute, founded in 1917, resolved to take up the challenging task of compiling a critical edition. The project, which began in 1919, continued for nearly half a century, culminating in the *Critical Edition*, also known as the *Poona* (Pune) *Edition*, being released in 1966. The scholastic diligence that went into its making can be well understood from the scope of the task, which involved collecting, collating and compiling common portions of the earliest extant manuscripts of the work from Kashmir, Bengal, Uttar Pradesh, Maharashtra, Andhra and Kerala, as also a Nepali, and a short Javanese version, and various commentaries.

It would be appropriate to delve a little into the making of the *Critical Edition*, which has been hailed as 'one of the most significant events in Indology in the 20th century, as well as a matter of legitimate pride for Indian scholars'.[8.1] The first promising outcome of the project had been the experimental publication, in 1923, of the *Viraata-parva*, edited by NB Utgikar, who, at many places, produced a better text than the vulgate. Then, in August 1925, VS Sukthankar became the director of the project. Sukthankar was a former student-associate of Winternitz, and adopted his mentor's methods of textual criticism to brilliant effect. The end results were the *Critical Edition* proper, published in 19 volumes (13,000 pages) from 1927 to 1966, followed by the *Harivamsha* in another two volumes, and six index volumes. All but one of the volumes was edited by Indian scholars (the *Sabhaa-parva* was edited by Franklin Edgerton).

Scholarship and resourcefulness went hand-in-hand in the accomplishment of the noble mission. SK Belvalkar, who edited part of the *Shaanti-parva* 'concerning the origin and functions of the State', records: *I thought it would be opportune and quite in the fitness of things to request Shri Jawaharlal Nehru to secure from the Government of India a special grant towards the printing expenses of the Parvan. The grant was promised and paid in three instalments, and the editorial work on the Raajadharma section of the Shaantiparvan was straightway commenced on the 15 August 1947. The first format of the final edition was actually printed on 15 August 1948, the first anniversary of India's independence.*[8.2] This little anecdote bears testimony to the positive spirit of enterprise with which the makers of the *Critical Edition* harnessed the impulse of national regeneration that animated India at the dawn of her freedom.

SPREAD OF MANUSCRIPT MATERIAL
In his *Prolegomena* (critical introduction) to the first volume, Vishnu Sukthankar remarks: 'It is useless to think of reconstructing a fluid text in a literally original shape, on the basis of an archetype and a *stemma codicum*. What then is possible?

Our objective can only be to reconstruct *the oldest form of the text which it is possible to reach* on the basis of the manuscript material available'[8.3] [emphasis in original]. That manuscript evidence is somewhat late, given its post-oral (written) composition and given the harsh Indian climate, which makes the preservation of old manuscripts problematic; still, this minimalist record itself is impressively extensive. In fact, as many as 1,259 manuscripts, written in 12 different scripts, were examined, and 734 actually used (with reference to the legendary 17th century Marathi scholar Neelkantha's Varanasi-based text, commonly known as the Northern Recension, as the vulgate).[8.4]

The primary criterion for incorporation in the critical text was defined ideally as occurrence in both recensions. This meant that the final edition was closer to the Northern Recension, since the Southern one was appreciably lengthier. In cases of variations, the approach followed was to choose the reading found in the largest number of apparently independent versions, with a preference for those coming from Kashmir (both in the *Shaaradaa* script, or transcript in Devanagari, written on birch-bark), which were deemed to have preserved a relatively more conservative text. In a broad sense, Sukthankar and his team believed that all standard manuscripts of the *Mahabharata* are basically derived from a single written source, and that the *Critical Edition* was the closest approximation to this archetype that could be achieved, of course with many uncertainties of detail caused by the complexities of textual transmission. Even if this claim is not accepted at face value, the fact remains that the *Critical Edition* is free from many of the accretions apparent in other versions.

PROBLEM WITH MANUSCRIPTS
Apart from the fairly extensive spread of manuscripts in various scripts (although some scripts, like Kannada and Oriya, could not be covered), the other parameter for manuscript selection was their age. Sukthankar observed that, *old manuscripts, even though fragmentary and partly illegible, were selected in preference to modern-looking manuscripts, though complete, neatly written and well-preserved.*[8.5] However, as pointed out by Brockington,[8.6] *this admirable principle was not always entirely adhered to.* Thus, the oldest dated manuscript, a Nepali one, used in *Aadi-parva*, was of AD 1511, whereas the only Maithili manuscript used for that

volume was of AD 1528. This illustrates the handicap of lateness of the manuscript evidence mentioned earlier.

The following extract from a paper by MA Mehendale, brings out a few 'limitations' recorded by two of the editors of the *Critical Edition*:[8.7] *The first limitation is that the critical edition "is not anything like the autograph copy of the work of its mythical author, Maharshi Vyasa. It is also not an exact replica of the poem recited by Vaishampayana before Janamejaya. It is further wholly uncertain how close it approaches the text of the poem said to be recited by the soota (or Sauti) before Shaunaka and the other dwellers of the Naimisha forest" (V.S. Sukthankar, Prolegomena, p. c iii). The critical edition presents only that text which is as old as the extant manuscript enables us to reach. The text cannot be accurately dated nor assigned to any locality or any one author. It gives us a text which really once existed and from which all manuscripts are directly descended (F. Edgarton, Sabhaaparvan p. xxxvi).*

UNIQUE ESSENCE OF ORAL TRADITION COMPROMISED?

There is another basic issue that needs to be mentioned in this context. Although the *Critical Edition* has been a remarkable achievement in what could be described as the 'highest common factor' approach based on different manuscripts, yet that approach in itself was the product of Sukthankar's application of his mentor Winternitz's Western methodology to a distinctively Indian problem. The distinctiveness came from the fact that the written manuscripts were far younger than the earlier forms of the epic, which, for centuries together, had been transmitted through the oral traditions which were much less prevalent in the West. Even with manuscripts, many were perhaps destroyed by invading hordes at old north Indian seats of learning like Nalanda in modern-day Bihar. This could have been one reason for the Southern Recension being lengthier than its northern counterpart, the north having always borne the brunt of invasion by marauders and their depredation against centres of 'infidel' culture. In these peculiarly 'Indian' circumstances, exclusion of the 'additional' Southern portions from the main *Critical* text has been questioned by some.

The following extract from a nuanced review of the *Pune Edition*, appearing in a Department of Classics, Brown University publication is relevant:[8.8] *Several scholars have argued that the*

Mahabharata textual tradition is too complex, too rooted in living, oral traditions, to be amenable to edition on the basis of principles developed in the more simply literary traditions of Western texts. These scholars judge the Pune text to be an unwarranted simplification of the tradition that has produced an artificial text that never existed for anyone at any time in the past. At the same time the Pune edition (though only in its complete version, that is, with its full apparatus) makes available not only the editorially determined critical text, but all the variants to that text and all the passages that were judged to be additions to the putative original text. This text is the basis of most contemporary Western scholarship on the Mahabharata, but at the same time few such scholars, if any, take the critical edition simply at face value.

NET RESULT

In absolute terms, the net result of the compilation of the *Critical Edition* was to reduce the length by about one-fourth – from its traditional 100,000 verses to precisely 73,650 verses and 297 prose units in 1,995 *adhyaayas* (the average length of an *adhyaaya* being 37 verses). In other words, as a very broad thumbrule based on text-critical result, we can say that about one-fourth of the verses of the traditional Sanskrit version of the *Mahabharata* could have been accretions on the original.

NOTES & REFERENCES

8.1 Brockington, *The Sanskrit Epics*, Leiden, Boston, 1998, p.57.
8.2 *The Critical Edition of the Mahabharata,* Bhandarkar Oriental Research Institute, 1933-66: *vol. XVI, The Shaantiparvan,* Ed. SK. Belvalkar, Introduction, CC-CCI.
8.3 VS Sukthankar, *Prolegomena* to *the Mahabharata*, Bhandarkar Oriental Research Institute, 1933, p. lxxxvi. Emphasis is in the original. *Stemma Codicum*, in the methodology of Textual Criticism, means the family tree of manuscripts, descending from one archetype or original.
8.4 Bhandarkar Oriental Research Institute, Poona, 1917-67, Golden Jubilee Souvenir, May 17, 1968, p.4.
8.5 *The Critical Edition of the Mahabharata,* Bhandarkar Oriental Research Institute, 1933-66: vol. I, Ed.VS Sukthankar, vi.
8.6 Brockington, *The Sanskrit Epics*, Leiden, Boston, 1998, p.60.
8.7 MA Mehendale, 'The Critical Edition of the Mahabharata', *Text and Variations of the Mahabharata, Sameekshikaa Series No. 2,* National

Mission for Manuscripts, Ed. Kalyan Kumar Chakravarty, 2009, p.14.
Sukthankar's reference to Vyasa as 'mythical author' is debatable,
as already mentioned in Chapter 1. Also debatable is the categorical
assertion of Edgerton that 'all manuscripts are directly descended
from the *Critical Edition* text.

8.8 JL Fitzgerald, Das Professor of Sanskrit, Department of
Classics, Brown University. The following link is relevant. *Reading
Suggestions: The Critical Edition of the Sanskrit Text: The Mahabharata
for the First Time Critically Edited*; available at:
http://www.brown.edu/Departments/Sanskrit_in_Classics_at_
Brown/Mahabharata/MBh2Biblio.html#Poona

9
EPICS AND EPICS

FOLK EPICS OF 'ONE WORLD'

Where does the *Mahabharata* fit among the great folk epics of the world? Monier-Williams gives us this revealing comparison of scale: *Virgil's Ænid consists of 9,000 lines, Homer's Iliad of 12,000 lines, and the Odyssey of 15,000, whereas the Sanskrit epic poem* Mahabharata *contains at least 200,000 lines, without reckoning the supplement called* Harivamsha.[9.1] But scale apart, when it comes to characterising human attitudes in regard to cross-cultural or trans-civilisational comparisons, one often encounters a peculiar dichotomy between xenophobic exclusivity on one hand and internationalist inclusiveness on the other. Quite expectedly, classical historians and scholars, by virtue of their largeness of humanist vision, generally tend towards the latter, more inclusive view of things. This vision (helped perhaps by a centripetal cultural pull), could have been the reason behind Megasthenes' perceived discovery of an Indian Hercules, or some 19th century European scholars drawing parallels between the child-Krshna and the child-Christ. A somewhat similar search for parallelism has traditionally driven scholars to examine inter-relationships between the world's great epics. Indeed, some of the epic parallels are too striking to disregard, arguably revealing a deep-seated affinity of thought among ancient civilisations.

COMPARATIVE MYTHOLOGY OF SUMERIAN AND GREEK EPICS

What else but cross-cultural affinity or influence can explain the similarities between the Ionian Odysseus, king of Ithaca, and the Sumerian Gilgamesh, king of Uruk (modern Iraq)? Both went on long and hard voyages, rendered much longer and harder by the curses of divinities. The parallels do not end there. Both Odysseus and Gilgamesh travel to the end of the earth, and on their journeys visit the land of the dead. The encounters of Odysseus with Circe and Calypso on their mythical isles, also closely resemble the visit by Gilgamesh to the divine woman Siduri, who keeps an inn in a marvellous garden of the sun-god near the shores of the ocean. Like the two Greek witch-goddesses, an enamoured Siduri tries to dissuade Gilgamesh from pursuing his journey further, by dangling the pleasures of life; but the firm resolution of the hero compels her to help him cross the waters of death. One can hear some echo of the *Epic of Gilgamesh* in the *Iliad* as well, where Patroclus, who dies as a substitute for his dearest friend Achilles, and then gives Achilles a description of the miserable condition of man after his death, bears striking similarities to Enkidu, Gilgamesh's[9.2, 9.3] friend.

PARALLELS BETWEEN THE INDIAN AND GREEK EPICS

The celebrated Greek writer Dio Chrysostom (40-120 AD), in his *53rd Discourse: On Homer*, made the following point to illustrate Homeric influence on alien lands:[9.4] *For example, it is said that Homer's poetry is sung even in India, where they have translated it into their own speech and tongue. The result is that, while the people of India have no chance to behold many of the stars in our part of the world – for example, it is said that the Bears are not visible in their country – still they are not unacquainted with the sufferings of Priam, the laments and wailings of Andromachê and Hecuba, and the valour of both Achilles and Hector: so remarkable has been the spell of one man's poetry!*

Of course, the reasonable conclusion here is not the naïve construct that somehow the *Iliad* got translated into Sanskrit or its offshoots! Rather, scholars have generally taken this as evidence for the existence of a *Mahabharata* at this date, whose episodes Dio or his sources identify with the story of the *Iliad*. The Indologist Christian Lassen, in his *Indische Alterthumskunde*, suggested that the reference to 'the laments of Priam', is linked to Dhrtarashtra's sorrows; the 'wailings of Andromachê and Hecuba' to those of Gandhari and Draupadi; and the 'valour of Achilles and Hector', to that of Arjuna and Duryodhana / Karna. The suggestion was supported by Max Duncker,[9.5] and further endorsed in such standard references as Albrecht Weber's *History of Indian Literature*.

Certain thematic similarities between the *Odyssey* and both the *Ramayana* and the *Mahabharata*, have also been noted by scholars. The long providence-driven separation and final reunion between Odysseus and Penelope finds a parallel in the story of Nala and Damayanti.[9.6] Similarly, the theme of Odysseus stringing a great bow and beating all competitors to regain his wife, rings like the one of Rama stringing the bow of Shiva to win Sita's hand in marriage.

INTER-RELATIONSHIPS OF THE TWO INDIAN EPICS

The name of Rama is the cue for us to take up the much debated but still open issue of correlation between the two great Indian epics featuring Rama and Krshna. The traditional belief is that events in the *Ramayana* long preceded those in the *Mahabharata* – the former happening in the *Tretaa Yuga*, and the latter in the twilight phase, when *Dvaapara* was yielding place to *Kali Yuga*. But the issue is far more complex than that, as is borne out by more than a century's deep studies by such eminent Western and Indian scholars as Weber, Hopkins, Jacobi, Sukthankar, Vaidya, van Buitenen, and more recently, Brockington. In fact, so interwoven is the relationship between the two basic narratives, and between the two epics proper, that the whole matter bears the look of a chicken-or-egg conundrum.

The principal direct thread of correlation between what Hopkins calls the 'Great' and the 'Little' epics[9.7] (meaning of course, the *Mahabharata* and the *Ramayana* respectively), is to be found in the *Ramopakhyana* section of the *Mahabharata*'s *Vana-parva*, covering 19 chapters (viz. Chapters 273-292 of the traditional Aryashastra edition, generally referred by this author). In this section, in answer to a despondent forest-bound Yudhishthira's question as to whether there had ever been a king more woebegone than himself, the visiting sage Markandeya recounts to him the story of Rama's travails (and travels). This account is a generally faithful and competent summary of the Rama story, with special emphasis on the *Ramayana*'s *Yuddha-kaanda* events, sans a few major episodes like Sita's fire-test, as also her exile and other episodes of the *Ramayana*'s *Uttara-kaanda*.

A second thread of connection is woven earlier in the *Vana-parva*, in the chapter (*Hanumad-bheemasenayor-aalaapah*) relating to the conversation between Bheema and Hanuman. Bheema is out in one of his many errands to humour Draupadi – this time to get her the divine lotus of a thousand petals. But his search takes him too close to the way to heaven, which exposes him to fatal risk. Out of brotherly concern, the immortal Hanuman blocks his advance by lying down on his way. Bheema asks the unfamiliar but impressive figure to move aside, saying he could easily have crossed over him like Hanuman crossed the sea, but desisted as such action would be contrary to the scriptures. Hanuman feigns ignorance and asks to be enlightened about the one who leaped across the sea. Bheema proudly proclaims:

Bhraataa mama gunaashlaaghyo buddhi-sattvabalaanvitah /
Raamaayane'tivikhyaatah shreeman vaanarapungavah //
~ *Vana; 147.11*

My brother Hanuman is praised for his qualities, his intelligence and noble strength. He is the best of *vaanara*s and is greatly famed for his role in the *Ramayana*.

Hanuman, in the next chapter, briefly describes to Bheema the missions he had accomplished for the great Rama, and the blessing of longevity he had secured from his master. Three more chapters cover Hanuman's discourse with Bheema on matters not directly related to the *Ramayana*.

The above meeting of Bheema with Hanuman is a relatively rare instance in the earlier segment of the *Mahabharata*, where the 'little epic' finds mention by name. It is, however, possible that this too, like the later instances of such naming in the *Shaanti-parva* and the *Anushaasana-parva*, as also in the *Harivamsha*, can be attributed to possible accretion.

A third notable connectivity is found in a chapter[9.8] of the *Drona-parva*, where Yudhishthira, again sorrow-stricken after the tragic death of Abhimanyu, is consoled by Vyasa with the story of Rama (among other great yet mortal kings), as told by Narada to king Srnjaya, who was similarly grief-stricken on losing his son. This story, however, is just an adjunct to a Puranic fable about the inevitability of death and other related frame-tales; the Narada sub-tale itself is a short and sketchy outline of the Rama narrative, devoting only 10 verses to concrete Rama events, and the remaining 15 verses to eulogies about Rama, the ideal man and model king, who 'had ruled for 11,000 years'. Brockington[9.9] cites 'the inflated state' of the *Drona-parva* in the context of this inclusion, as also several other stray allusions to the Rama story contained therein. He observes that these 'casual allusions', found in the *Vana-parva* as well, 'often appear in the form of similes', which 'implies considerable familiarity of the story on the part of the audience as well as the poet or performer'. However, the possibility of later accretion may also explain that familiarity, irrespective of the relative age of the original epics. Many of these similes have, in fact, been excised from the *Critical Edition*.

Yet another small but significant link between the two narratives lies snuggled in one line of the *Gita*'s tenth chapter where, as one of the many divine manifestations of one (monist) God, Krshna tells Arjuna: *Ramah shastrabhrtaam aham* (Among wielders of weapons, I am Rama). But while the line bears its own subtle implications, it may not be enough to build a substantial concordance.

RAMOPAKHYANA: ORIGINAL CONNECTOR OF THE TWO EPICS?

We are thus left with the *Ramopakhyana* as our main inlaid clue to the inter-relationship of the two epics. One interesting aspect is that at certain places, the events referred to in the *Ramopakhyana* are properly understood only with prior knowledge of the story. For example, the first mention of Vaalee is when Rama promises Sugreeva to kill him (with no prior reference to the reason for killing, *viz.* the rivalry between the *vaanara* siblings):

Pratijajne ca kaakutsthah samare vaaleeno badham /
Sugreevashcaapi vaidehyaah punaraanayanam nrpa //
~ Vana; 280.14

Markandeya tells Yudhishthira: O King, Kakutstha (Rama) gave Sugreeva his pledge to kill Vaalee; Sugreeva too promised to bring back Sita.

The above line of argument suggests that the *Ramopakhyana* material is likely to have been sourced from an earlier and more detailed form of the Rama story. Interestingly, Brockington cites a possibility of some reverse flow of material as well, referring to the detailed genealogy and divine origin of Rama (along with the genealogy and origin of invincibility of Ravana), contained in the *Ramopakhyana*, and suggesting this could have been later expanded and accreted as the *Baala-kaanda* of the *Ramayana*. He also suggests a similar reverse sourcing for much of the apparently later *Uttara-kaanda* as well.[9,10]

But the overall consensus seems to be that the *Ramopakhyana* is based on an earlier form of the *Ramayana*. In this context, Brockington cites a 1941 article by Sukthankar, which demonstrated, on textual grounds, the *Ramopakhyana*'s basic origin from the *Ramayana*. There, with reference to his larger work on the *Critical Edition (Vana-parva)*, Sukthankar provided 86 verbal parallels between the two, and suggested that the source of the *Ramopakhyana* was a memorised version of the *Ramayana*. Brockington notes that this view, though modified by later scholars, has not been seriously challenged. Thus, RV Vaidya has suggested that the *Ramopakhyana* as a 'genuine part' of the *Mahabharata*, was much older than Valmiki's poem.[9.11] JAB van Buitenen has broadly validated this view by asserting that the *Ramopakhyana* is not a summary of the *Ramayana*, but rather it is 'a brief, tersely stated compendium that the storyteller would know by heart and on the basis of which he would elaborate and improvise the full narrative'.[9.12]

TAILPIECE: INSEPARABLE TRADITIONS
In the end, it would be germane for us to remember EW Hopkins' brilliant summing up of the salient points of the inter-relationship of the two epics, which looks as valid today as it did a century ago.[9.13] In the first place, Hopkins makes the significant point that the decidedly older parts of the *Mahabharata* recognises the Rama story, but associates the same with 'an ascetic', and not with a poet named Valmiki (or Bhargava, as Valmiki was named in the later *Parvas* of the *Mahabharata*). This could mean that Valmiki actually created his poetic masterpiece (set in *anushtubh* and portraying, *inter alia*, the urban splendour of Ayodhya, which clearly pertains to a period much later than that of the largely pastoral *Mahabharata*), by adapting an older narrative.

Secondly, Hopkins observes: *In regard to the final growth of each (epic), it may be said at once that neither epic was developed quite independently of the other. The later Ramayana implies the Mahabharata, as the later Mahabharata recognizes the Ramayana of Valmiki. It is not, then, a question of absolute separation, but only of the length we may go in separating.*

Thirdly: *Ramayana recognizes Janamejaya as an ancient hero, and knows Kurus and Pancalas and the town of Haastinapur (ii, 68, 13).*

Indeed, a quick cross-check into the *Ayodhyaa-kaanda* (description of the route traversed by Vashishta's messengers to Bharata in Kekaya), bears out Hopkins chapter and verse:

Te haastinapure gangaam teertvaa pratyanmukhaa yayuh /
Paancaaladesham-aasaadya madhyena kuru-jaangalam //
~ Ramayana; Ayodhya; 68.13

In this way they (the five messengers) went first to Haastinapura, where they crossed the Ganga; after further crossing the Pancala land they proceeded westward along the road that runs through the Kuru kingdom and its neighbouring forest.

Finally, Hopkins reaches the following significant conclusions:
The story of the Pandus, the gist of the present epic, is presumably later than the story of Rama; the former everywhere recognizing the latter as an ancient tale.[9.14] *We must therefore on these data make the following distinctions:*

1. *The story of Rama is older than the story of the Pandus.*
2. *The Pandu story has absorbed the Bhaarati Kathaa.*
3. *The Bhaarati Kathaa is older than Valmiki's poem.'*

Such then is the near-inextricable manner in which strands of the two great epics of India are interwoven. This indeed is a phenomenon unique to the Indian epic pair. The only other such pair, *viz.* the two epics of Homer, does not present any such conundrum of chronology. For one thing, both the *Iliad* and the *Odyssey* are ascribable to one poet; for another, the *Odyssey* is quite clearly a sequel to the *Iliad*. But the two Indian epics, though of disparate origins in different times, stand together to represent the ethos of India as a continuous civilisation. Tagore put the matter with telling effect in one succinct sentence: *In the simple anushtubh metre of these pan-Indian epics, one can hear the heartbeats of millennial India.*

NOTES & REFERENCES

9.1 Monier Monier-Williams, A Sanskrit English Dictionary, Oxford, Clarendon Press (1899); Indian Edition: Sri Satguru Publications, Indian Book Centre, Delhi, 1993 (Reprinted: 1998, 2001, 2005), Introductory Chapter. Here 200,000 lines correspond to 100,000 verses (couplets) in the traditional *Mahabharata*.

9.2 *Early patterns of development (from epic), The Greek epic, Eastern* *influences,* Encyclopaedia Britannica, Deluxe Edition, 2004 CD-ROM.

9.3 Martin West, *The East Face of Helicon: West Asiatic Elements in Greek Poetry and Myth*, Oxford, 1997, pp. 402-417.

9.4 Dio Chrysostom, *The Fifty-third Discourse: On Homer*, 53.6-7, trans. H. Lamar Crosby, Loeb Classical Library, 1946, Vol. 4, p. 363; available at: http://penelope.uchicago.edu/Thayer/E/Roman/Texts/Dio_Chrysostom/Discourses/53*.html#6

9.5 Max Duncker, *The History of Antiquity*, trans. Evelyn Abbott, R Bentley & Son, London, 1880, Vol. 4, p. 81. Also available as Reprint from the University of California Libraries, Jan 1, 1877.

9.6 Wendy Doniger, *Splitting the difference: gender and myth in ancient Greece and India*, University of Chicago Press, 1999, ISBN 978-0-226-15641-5.pp.157ff.

9.7 EW Hopkins, *The Great Epic of India: Character and Origin of the Mahabharata*, 1901. Reprint by Motilal Banrsidass, Delhi (1993), p. 58.

9.8 *Maharshi Vedavyaasa-racitam Mahaabhaaratam*, Aryashastra Publications, 1968 (Bengali Calendar: 1375), Kolkata, *Drona-parva*, Chapter 58.

9.9 Brockington, *The Sanskrit Epics*, Leiden, Boston, 1998, p. 473.

9.10 Brockington, *ibid.*, p. 476.

9.11 RV Vaidya, *A Study of Mahabharat; A Research*, Poona, A.V.G. Prakashan, 1967.

9.12 Johannes Adrianus Bernardus Buitenen, *The Mahabharata*, three volumes (translation / publication incomplete due to his death), University of Chicago Press, 1978.

9.11 EW Hopkins, *The Great Epic of India: Character and Origin of the Mahabharata*, 1901. Reprint: Motilal Banarsidass, Delhi (1993), pp. 58-63.

9.14 Here, Hopkins cites several verses from the Mahabharata bearing allusions to the Rama story. The following are three such couplets, reconciled chapter and verse with the Aryashastra *Mahaabhaaratam*:

Vaali-sugreevayor-bhraatror-yathaa streekaankshinoh puraa /
Sheershayoh patitaa vrkshaa vividhur-naikadhaa tayoh // (Vana; 11.48)
'Just as the brothers Vaalee and Sugreeva had fought to secure a woman, likewise there ensued a battle with trees as weapons between Bheema and Kirmeera; as a result many trees in the forest were felled.'

Tathaa poulastya-tanayo raavano naama raakshasah /
Raamena nihato raajan saanubandhah sahaanugah // (Shalya; 31.11)
(Krshna urges Yudhishthira to resort to appropriate measures to

destroy a hiding Duryodhana) 'O King, the *rakshasa* Ravana, son of Pulastya, was killed, along with his relatives, friends and followers, by Rama.'

Tato gaccheta raajendra shrngavera-puram mahat /
Yatra teerno mahaaraaja raamo daasharathih pura // (Vana; 85.65)

(Narada cites to Yudhishthira what Pulastya had told Bheeshma) 'O Best of Monarchs, then you should proceed to the beautiful Shrngavera-pura; where in ancient times Rama had crossed the Ganga.'

NAMES & PLACES
IN THE *MAHABHARATA*

Alaayudha	A demon (*rakshasa*) fighting on the Kaurava side. The name means 'one whose weapon is the sting from a scorpion's tail'.
Amba (Ambaa)	Eldest princess of Kashi. Reborn as Shikhandi to take revenge on Bheeshma.
Ambalika (Ambaalikaa)	Third daughter of the King of Kashi. Wife of Vicitraveerya and mother of Pandu.
Ambika (Ambikaa)	Second daughter of the King of Kashi. Wife of Vicitraveerya and mother of Dhrtarashtra.
Anga	Kingdom of Karna in the area around modern Bhagalpur; alternatively the area of Bengal.
Arjuna	Pandu's third son. Born of Kunti through *kshetraja* (assigned) union with Indra.
Aryavarta (Aaryaavarta)	Land of the early Aryans in Northern and Central India located between the Himalaya and the Vindhya mountains.
Ashtaavakra	Scholar-sage. His body was deformed (bent, *vakra*) in eight (*ashta*) places, and hence the name. Son of Kahoda, whom he, as a young prodigy, rescued by defeating King Janaka's court scholar in debate.
Ashvasena	Son of the *Naga* king, Takshaka. Having escaped the Khandava holocaust, he sought to kill Arjuna by entering Karna's quiver as a deadly shaft. But the upright Karna refused his help.

Ashvatthama (Ashvatthaama)	Son of Drona and Krpi.
	Duryodhana's last general in a residual Kaurava army of three. His longing to avenge his father's unethical killing made him launch an inglorious nocturnal attack on the Pandava camp. In his effort to counter Pandava retribution, he released his infallible celestial missile which got diverted to Uttaraa's womb. Krshna restored the child Pareekshit to life and cursed Asvatthama to three thousand years of a diseased and lonely existence.
Babhru	A Yadava (Vrshni) hero.
Babhruvaahana	Son of Arjuna-Citrangadaa.
Balarama	Krshna's elder step-brother. Son of Vasudeva and Rohini.
Bhagadatta	Son of Narakasura. King of Pragjyo-tishapura (present Assam). Fought on the side of his son-in-law Duryodhana, astride his formidable elephant named Suprateeka. Was killed by Arjuna after Krshna saved the Pandava from his *Vaishnavaastra*.
Bheema	Pandu's second son. Born of Kunti through *kshetraja* union with the god Pavana.
Bheeshma (Devavrata)	Son of Shantanu and Ganga. Grand patriarch, revered for his legendary sacrifice and valour.
Bhurishravaa	Son of the Balhika king, Somadatta. A Kuru warrior controversially killed by Satyaki.
Brhadashva	Ancient sage. In the *Vana-parva* he told Yudhishthira the story of King Nala (*Nalopaakhyaana*), and taught him the secret of dice play.
Cedi (Chedi)	Kingdom of Shishupala near present-day Jabalpur, located between the rivers Narmada and Godavari.

Citrangada (Citraangada)	Son of Shantanu-Satyavati. Elder brother of Vicitraveerya.
Citrangadaa	Daughter of Citravahana, king of Manipur. Arjuna's wife and Babhruvaahana's mother.
Daruka	Krshna's charioteer.
Dhaumya	Family priest of the Pandavas. Younger brother of sage Devala.
Dhrshtadyumna	Son of Drupada. Draupadi's brother.
Dhrtarashtra	Blind Kuru king. Eldest *kshetraja* son of Vicitraveerya, born of Ambika's union with Vyasa.
Draupadi	Daughter of king Drupada. Common wife of five Pandavas. Also called Krshnaa, Pancali, and Yajnaseni.
Drona	Son of sage Bharadvaja. Arms instructor of Kauravas and Pandavas. Krpa's brother-in-law.
Drupada	King of Pancala. Father of Dhrshtadyumna, Shikhandi and Draupadi.
Duhshalaa	Only daughter of Dhrtarashtra-Gandhari. Wife of Sindhu King Jayadratha.
Duhshasana	Second son of Dhrtarashtra-Gandhari.
Duryodhana	Eldest son of Dhrtarashtra-Gandhari. *Mahabharata*'s anti-hero.
Dvaraka (Dvaarakaa)	Capital of Yadava domain set up by Krshna on the westernmost point of modern Gujarat; said to have been submerged by the sea.
Dvaitavana	Forest located beside the ancient river, Sarasvati, in Punjab.
Ekalavya	Son of an aboriginal *Nishaada* (hunter) king, whose prowess as an archer, which rivalled Arjuna's, was thwarted by Drona asking for his right thumb as an offering.
Gada	Yadava hero. Younger brother of Krshna.

Gandhara (Gaandhara)	Ancient kingdom around the Indus and Kabul rivers. Alternatively, the area southwest of modern-day Peshawar, comprising modern Kandahar. Panini is said to have belonged to Gandhara.
Gandhari	Daughter of King Subala of Gandhara. Dhrtarashtra's queen. Mother of Duryodhana and other Kaurava brothers.
Ghatotkaca	Demon son of Bheema-Hidimbaa. Killed by Karna.
Hastinapura	Ancient Kuru capital founded by King Hastin to the northeast of modern Delhi (near Meerut); on the banks of an old channel of the Ganga.
Hidimba	*Rakshasa* killed by Bheema.
Hidimbaa	Bheema's demon wife. Sister of Hidimba and mother of Ghatotkaca.
Indraprastha	City near Delhi, built on the site of the old Khandavaprastha.
Janamejaya	Kuru king. Son of Pareekshit; grandson of Abhimanyu.
Jarasandha	Mighty king of Magadha. Kamsa's father-in-law and Krshna's arch enemy.
Jayadratha	King of Sindhu (Sind). Husband of Duhshalaa.
Kalinga	Ancient kingdom on the Coromandel coast (modern Odisha and Andhra) extending from Mahanadi River to Godavari River.
Kanka	Pseudonym adopted by Yudhishthira in disguise.
Karna	One of foremost Kaurava generals. Born of a maiden Kunti through union with god Surya; nurtured by a charioteer named Adhiratha and his wife Radha. Also called Radheya and Vasushena. A grateful Duryodhana made him king of Anga.

Keecaka	Brother-in-law and army chief of King Viraata.
Khandava	Ancient forest in the vicinity of Delhi. Burnt down by Krshna and Arjuna to build the new Pandava capital called Indraprastha.
Kimpurushavarsha (Kimnaravarsha)	Central Asian territory north of the Himalayas.
Kirmeera	*Rakshasa* killed by Bheema.
Krpa	Son of sage Sharadvaana. Early instructor of the Kuru-Pandava princes. Brother of Drona's wife Krpi.
Krpi (Krpee)	Krpa's sister. Drona's wife.
Krshna	Son of Vasudeva and Devaki. Stepbrother of Balarama and Subhadra. Maternal cousin and protector of the Pandavas. Leader of the Yadavas. Revered as Vaasudeva (demigod) and worshipped as the 'Blessed Lord' of the *Bhagavad-Gita*.
Krtavarma(a)	Yadava chieftain of the Bhoja line. Fought with the Kauravas.
Kunti	Also called Prthaa. Vasudeva's sister, who was the adopted daughter of King Kuntibhoja. Pandu's queen consort. Mother of Yudhishthira, Bheema and Arjuna.
Lomasha	Ancient sage. Accompanied the Pandavas during their pilgrimage in the *Vana-parva*, when he told Yudhishthira many legends. The name actually means 'hairy'.
Madra-desha	Shalya's ancient kingdom, located between the rivers Chandrabhaga (Chenab) and Irawati (Ravi) in Punjab. The Madra people were known for their uninhibited ways, as evidenced by Karna's taunts at his charioteer Shalya.

Madri (Maadri)	Sister of Madra King Shalya. Pandu's second wife, who ascended her husband's funeral pyre. Mother of Nakul and Sahadeva.
Magadha	Ancient land near modern Patna and Gaya. Kingdom of Jarasandha.
Manipura	Ancient town on India's eastern sea coast. Distinct from the modern Manipur.
Mandavya (Maandavya)	An ancient sage whose vow of abstaining from speech prevented him from informing royal guards about a theft, which led to his being impaled along with the thieves. When the king came to know of his identity, he was released with profound apologies. But the sage had to carry the broken end of the spike in his body. He was thenceforth called *Anee-Maandavya* (*anee* = end of a spike). One day he asked the god Dharma the reason why he had been given such a punishment. The deity replied that it was retribution for a childhood offence of inserting a stem of grass in the tail of a grasshopper. Mandavya then said: 'You have given a disproportionately severe punishment for a child's prank. You shall suffer its consequence by being born as a *Shoodra*; and henceforth no act committed by a child till the age of twelve shall be counted as a sin.' It was due to this curse that the god Dharma was born of a *Shoodra* mother as the righteous Vidura.
Matsya-desha	Land of King Viraata; situated west of Dholpur in Rajasthan. Alternatively, modern Jaipur.
Maya	Demon (*Asura*) architect; also versed in magic. Builder of the fabulous Indraprastha palace of the Pandavas.

Markandeya (Maarkandeya)	Ancient sage. Narrator of the *Markandeya-Purana*. Fabled to have been blessed by Shiva with everlasting youth.
Nahusha	Ancient king (father of Yayaati). His virtuous acts elevated him to Indra's seat as the lord of heaven. But he then developed the weakness of arrogance. He ordered sages to carry his palanquin, which they did. The great sage Agastya was the lead carrier, and the impatient Nahusha urged him to move faster by touching the sage's head with his foot. Agastya then cried out in anger: 'Fall, thou serpent'. Nahusha fell in a headlong plunge from heaven and became a serpent. But Agastya, at the supplication of the wretched king, moderated the punishment by declaring that he would one day be released from the curse through the instrumentality of the profoundly virtuous King Yudhishthira. And that is what happened in Yudhishthira's encounter with the python in the Mahabharata's *Vana-parva*.
Narada (Naarada)	Ancient sage. Supposed to be a messenger between gods and men.
Naimishaaranya	Site of an ancient holy grove at Sitapur in Uttar Pradesh where Sauti related the Mahabharata; present-day Nimsar. The name derives from the legend that an *Asura* army was destroyed there in a twinkling (*nimesha*).
Nakula-Sahadeva	Pandu's fourth and fifth sons, twins. Born of the assigned union of Madri with the Ashvinee-Kumaras.
Pareekshit	Son of Abhimanyu-Uttaraa, who was resuscitated by Krshna as the lone heir of the Kuru dynasty; grandson of Arjuna. Father of Janamejaya.
Pandu (Paandu)	Second *kshetraja* son of Vicitraveerya, born of Ambalika's union with Vyasa.

Pancala (Paancaala)	Land between Ganga and Yamuna, spreading from Ganga-dvaar (Haridwar) to the Chambal river.
Parashara (Paraashara)	Great sage and scholar. Grandson of Vashishta, son of Shakti and father of Veda-Vyasa.
Parvata	Ancient sage. Associated with Narada as a messenger of the gods. The name also means 'mountain'.
Prabhasa	Pilgrimage site on the Kathiawad sea co-ast, where the Yadavas met their sad end.
Pradyumna	Yadava hero. Son of Krshna-Rukmini.
Praagjyotisha-desha	Kamrup or Assam.
Pundra-desha	North Bengal.
Sanjaya	Dhrtarashtra's attendant and charioteer *soota*. Receiver of divine sight from Vyasa and narrator of the *Gita*.
Satyaki (Saatyaki)	Yadava hero of the Vrshni sub-clan. Krshna's trusted follower; Arjuna's friend and student. Also called Yuyudhana.
Satyabhama	Daughter of Satraajit. One of Krshna's eight wives. Provoker of Yadava quarrels.
Satyavati	Daughter of a fisherman chief. Mother of Vyasa. Later became King Shantanu's queen and mother of Citrangada and Vicitraveerya.
Sauti	Sobriquet of Ugrashrava, the narrator *soota*; son of Lomaharshana. He recited the Mahabharata to assembled sages in the hermitage of Shaunaka in Naimishaaranya.
Shakuni	Gandhari's brother; Duryodhana's maternal uncle and foremost adviser.
Shaalva-desha	Probably in modern Rajasthan. Its sev-eral kings were also called Shaalva. The Mahabharata's Shaalva was fabled to fight from an aerial (magic) city called Saubha. Killed by Krshna.

Shalya	Madra king of the Balhika dynasty. Brother of Madri. Penultimate Kaurava general.
Shamva (Shaamva)	Son of Krshna-Jaambavati.
Shantanu	Kuru king. Son of Prateepa. Father of Bheeshma, Citrangada and Vicitraveerya.
Shaunaka	A great sage. He did a 12-year-long *yajna* at his hermitage in the Naimis-haranya, where Sauti came and made his first narration of the *Mahabharata* to the assembled sages.
Shikhandi	King Drupada's son; Amba, princess of Kashi in a previous birth.
Shishupala	King of Cedi and one-time protege of Jarasandha. Also Krshna's cousin and jealous detractor. Killed by Krshna.
Shrngi (Shrngee)	Virtuous but acerbic son of sage Sha-meeka. Once during a hunt, King Pareekshit, while chasing a deer which he had wounded with his arrow, came to Shammeka's cottage and asked him about the deer. The sage was then in a vow of abstinence from speech, and so did not reply. The annoyed king then picked up a dead snake lying nearby with the end of his bow and slung it on the silent saint's neck. Shameeka forgave the king, because he was tired and did not know of the vow. But when his son Shrngi returned to the cottage and came to know from a forester of his ascetic father's humiliation, he pronounced the curse: 'The sinner who put that dead snake on my innocent father will himself die within seven nights from the venomous bite of the serpent Takshaka.'
Sudeshna (Sudeshnaa)	Princess of Kekaya. Queen of King Viraata. Mother of Uttara and Uttaraa.

Subhadra (Subhadraa)	Krshna's step-sister. Arjuna's wife. Abhimanyu's mother.
Takshaka	*Naga* king, who sought vengeance on the Pandavas for the destruction of his family habitat at Khandava. His killing of Pareekshit in turn led to the famous serpent sacrifice of Parrekshit's son Janamejaya, where the Mahabharata was first narrated by Vaishampayana.
Ugrasena	Father of Kamsa. Was reinstated as the Yadava king by Krshna after Kamsa's death.
Uloopi	Daughter of *Naga* king Kauravya. Arjuna's wife.
Upaplavya	A town in Matsya territory where the Pandavas camped while preparing for the battle of Kurukshetra.
Urvashi	Heavenly nymph (*apsara*) in Indra's court. She made an advance which Arjuna politely turned down, because he held her as a mother figure by virtue of having been once the consort of his ancestor Pururavaa (an episode immortalised by Kalidasa in his play, *Vikramorvashi*). Urvashi felt humiliated and cursed Arjuna to become a eunuch. Indra, however, reduced the curse and made it effective for only a year.
Uttara	Son of King Viraata.
Uttaraa	Daughter of King Viraata. Abhimanyu's wife. Pareekshit's mother.
Uttarakuru-varsha	Land to the northwest of Tibet. Fabled as the country of eternal beatitude. Its description in *Bheeshma-parva* (Chapter-7) evokes the picture of a veritable Shangri-la.
Vaka-rakshasa	A demon killed by Bheema.

Vandee (Bandee)	Scholar in the court of Mithila's King Janaka. He was a great debater, but was conceited and cruel. His condition for debate was that the challenger, if defeated, would be imprisoned under water. He met more than his match in the young sage Ashtaavakra, who beat him in debate and rescued his father from watery prison.
Vanga-desha	Eastern part of modern-day Bengal.
Varanavata (Vaaranaavata)	A town located near Prayaag (present-day Allahabad), where Duryodhana made his abortive attempt to burn the Pandavas in a house of lac.
Vaishampayana (Vaishampaayana)	Foremost disciple of Vyasa. First narrator of the *Mahabharata* in Janamejaya's serpent sacrifice.
Vasuki (Vaasuki)	Divine lord of serpents. Son of sage Kashyap and Kadru. Also called Ananta-naga.
Vicitraveerya	Son of Shantanu-Satyavati. Stepbrother of Bheeshma.
Vidura	Wise adviser of the Kurus. Born of Ambika's maid and Vyasa.
Vikarna	Brother of Duryodhana. Lone Kaurava dissenter to Draupadi's humiliation at the dice hall.
Viraata	King of the Matsya country. Father of Uttaraa.
Vyasa (Vyaasa)	Krshna-Dvaipayana. Son of sage Parashara and fisherwoman Satyavati. Genetic father of Dhrtarashtra, Pandu and Vidura. Original chronicler of the Mahabharata. Illustrious splitter and disseminator of the *Vedas*.

Yudhishthira   Eldest son of Pandu. Born of Kunti's
assigned union with the god Dharma.
Central figure in the epic's twists and
turns.

Yuyudhana   Another name of Satyaki.

GLOSSARY

Aaditya	Sun. Also, the common name of twelve sons of Aditi and Kaashyapa (Vivasvaan, Aryamaa, Pushaa, etc.)
Aakaasha	Sky. Firmament.
Aashvalaayana Grhya sutra / Grhya-sootra	Collection of domestic ritual texts ascribed to sage Ashvalaayana, a disciple of Shaunaka. They deal with rituals for conception, birth, Brahminical initiation, marriage, death etc.
Aaryabhatiya (Aryabhatiya)	Sanskrit astronomical treatise composed by Aryabhata, the 5th century Indian mathematician. It gave the world the system of decimal place value notation. The work was translated into Arabic around 820 AD, and later led to the adoption of the Hindu-Arabic numerals in Europe in the 12th century.
Aatataayee	Murderer. A person who is about to kill someone.
Abhicaara-mantra	Occult incantation of spell to control someone.
Agni	Fire. The fire-god.
Agnihotree	A Brahmin who preserves sacred fire for daily vedic rites at home.
Aksha-hrdaya	Subtle science of dice play.
Akshauhinee (Akshauhini)	A division of army in ancient India, comprising 109,350 foot soldiers, 65,610 cavalrymen, 21,870 elephant-mounted fighters, and 21870 charioteers.
Andhaka	A descendant of Yadu and ancestor of Krshna and other members of the Yadava tribe of that name.

Anjalika missile	The weapon used by Arjuna to kill Karna. Its use is mentioned four other times in the Mahabharata: in the *Bheeshma-parva,* when the Pandavas shoot *anjalikas* against the Magadha elephant forces, and Bheeshma likewise employs it against the Pandavas; then in the *Drona-parva,* when Ghatotkaca uses it twice, first against Ashvatthaamaa, and again against Karna. In the *Bheeshma-parva,* these missiles are described as 'arrows with crescent-shaped heads'. [Ref: Edwin F Bryant, *Krishna: A Sourcebook,* Oxford University Press, New York, 2007, p.70].
Anushtubh (Anush-tup)	A Sanskrit metre, consisting of four *pada*s or quarter-verses used in invocation and poetic works. Supposedly invented by poet Valmiki.
Aprameyan	Unlimited. Immeasurable. An epithet of Vishnu / Krshna.
Artha	Wealth. Meaning.
Ashvinee-Kumaras	Twin deity. Divine physicians.
Ashtaadhyaayee	Book containing eight chapters. Title of Panini's Grammar.
Ashvamedha Yajna	Vedic horse sacrifice.
Asura	Demon. Mighty entities hostile to gods.
Avataara (Avatara)	Divine incarnation. God descending on earth in human form.
Baka-yaksha	A demigod guard disguised as a crane (stork).
Beebhatsu	One who eschews any repulsive act. Name of Arjuna.
Bhakta	Devotee. Follower.
Bharata	Celebrated monarch of India (*Bhaarata*). Son of Dushyanta and Shakuntala. The first of 12 *Cakravartins* (universal emperors). Ancestor of the Kauravas and Pandavas, who were also called *Bhaaratas.*
Bhaarati Kathaa	Another name of the *Mahabharata.*

Bhayaavaha	Terrible. Dreadful.
Bheeshana	Severe.
Bhoja	A Yadava sub-clan, ruled by king of that name.
Bhraatr-dharma	Brotherly duty.
Brahmaastra	Ultimate infallible weapon. Divine missile which could never be warded off. [refer Supplementary Notes]
Braahmana (Brahmana)	A Brahmin. A part of the Vedas laying down religious rites.
Brahmashira	An even deadlier version of the *Brahmaastra*. [refer Supplementary Notes]
Brahma (Brahman)	The Absolute Entity. God.
Brahma (Brahmaa)	The 'creator' god.
Brhat-samhitaa	Literally meaning the 'great encyclopaedia', it is one of the most important works of Varahamihira, the 6th century Indian scholar (reputedly one of the 'nine jewels' in the legendary ruler Vikramaditya's court). Its 106 chapters cover a wide range of subjects, including astrology, planetary movements, eclipses, rainfall, clouds, architecture, growth of crops, manufacture of perfume, matrimony, domestic relations, gems, pearls, and rituals.
Buddhimaan	Endowed with understanding. Intelligent. Wise.
Devarshi	One who is both a god and a saint. Celestial sage. Honorific of Narada.
Draupati-Amman	Mother Draupadi (vernacular).
Daanadharma	Duty of liberality/ charity.
Daasa (Dasa)	Non-Aryan. Servant/slave.
Deva	Deity (god).
Dharma	Duty. Righteousness. The ultimate Law. Another name of *Yama*, the Lord of death and self-restraint.
Dharmaraaja (Dharmaraja)	Exemplar/upholder of duty. Honorific of Yudhishthira.

Dharma-yuddha	Just war. Holy war to establish righteousness. War to uphold the ultimate Law. War of good against evil. War fought in the right manner. [refer Supplementary Notes]
Dveepa	Island.
Dyoota	Game of dice. Gambling.
Eeshvara	God.
Ekavastraa	Clad in one piece of cloth.
Gaandeeva (Gande-eeva)	Arjuna's bow, which he received from Agni, the fire-god (who, in turn, had borrowed it from the god Varuna), to serve his earthly mission.
Gandharva	A class of demigods proficient in music and war.
Garuda	Name of a prince of birds on whom Vishnu rides.
Grhastha / Grhee/ Grhi	Householder.
Guna	Quality. Attribute. Characteristic.
Hrshi	Sage. Ascetic.
Ikshumati	A tributary of Yamuna River. Its name means 'full of sugarcane'.
Ikshvaaku (Ikshvaku)	Name of first king of the solar dynasty in Ayodhya (son of Vaivasvata Manu). A descendant of that line.
Indra	King of gods. Putative appellation of early Aryan hero.
Itihaasa (Itihasa)	History ('Thus it was').
Janaka	Name of several illustrious kings of Mithila.
Jaya	Victory. Name of short form of the Mahabharata, which was sung in courts as paean to victory.
Jnana	Knowledge.
Jnana yogi /yogee	One engaged in austere search for knowledge to attain salvation.
Jnani (Jnanee)	Achiever of knowledge. Wise.
Kaala	Time. Death.

Kaama	Desire. Sexual urge. Lust.
Kali Yuga	The fourth or last stage of creation. Age susceptible to sins.
Karma yogi / yogee	One engaged in austere pursuit of action for purification of the soul.
Kirata (Kiraata)	One of an uncivilised mountain tribe of ancient India who lived by hunting.
Kishku-maatram	Only 24 thumbs' breadth. (*Kishku* is a kind of hand/palm measure)
Kleeva	Impotent. Emasculated. A eunuch. A neutered entity.
Koota	Intricate. Obscure. Subtle.
Koumodaki	Divine mace received by Krshna from the fire-god Agni.
Kshatriya	Defender of the society against injury (kshata). A member of the military or reigning order, which later constituted the second caste.
Kshattaa	Son of a maidservant (*daasa* woman) and a person of higher class. Charioteer (*Soota*). Form of addressing Vidura.
Kshetraja	Child born of one's wife by another man (usually appointed by the husband).
Kukura	Name of a Yadava prince. The sub-clan named after him.
Kula dharma / Kulaa-caara	Traditional customs and practices of a family. Familial duty.
Mahadeva	Shiva's name, meaning the Great Deity.
Maharshi	Great sage.
Manomala	Impurities of the mind. Impure thoughts and desires.
Markandeya-Purana	One of the 18 major *Purana*s (Hindu religious texts), ascribed to a discourse by the sage Markandeya, which contains the celebrated *Durga Saptasati* or 700 verses on the goddess Durga.
Matsya	Fish. Name of Virata kingdom.

Mokshadharma	The law or rule of eternal emancipation. Way to attain salvation. The name of a section of the 12th book (*Shaanti-parva*) of the *Mahabharata*.
Muktakeshee	A woman with loosened (unbraided) hair.
Muni	A sage practising ascetical meditation (usually in solitude). A hermit.
Naathavateem anaathavat	'A woman who is helpless (like an orphan), though having powerful protector or husband'. An evocative description of Draupadi's plight in the dice hall scene of the *Sabhaa-parva*.
Naga	Serpent. Elephant. In Indian mythology, *naga*s are supposed to have a human face with serpent-like lower extremities, whose kings are Vasuki, Shesha, and Takshaka. Buddhists, however, represent them as ordinary men. Perhaps they were actually aboriginal tribals of the ancient Indian forests.
Nalopakhyana	The fascinating ancient legend of King Nala, his loss of kingdom and separation from Queen Damayantee through an accursed addiction to dice, and their eventual reunion. Name of an important section of the Mahabharata's third book (*Vana-parva*).
Nimesha	The time taken to drop and open an eyelid. A twinkling of time.
Nishaada (Nishada)	Hunter. One of an uncivilised tribe of ancient India chiefly living on hunting.
Niyati	Predestination (destiny). Fate. An inevitable occurrence.
Niyoga	An act of engaging, appointing, or assigning. A social practice in ancient India, of appointing the brother or any near kinsman to produce issue to a deceased husband by marrying /impregnating his widow. In more general terms, appointing another male to produce a *kshetraja* child by union with a bride of the clan.

Pancakanyaa	Five illustrious women ('daughters') of ancient India – viz., Ahalya, Draupadi, Sita, Tara and Mandodari – remembering who is believed to wash away great sins.
Pandita	Scholar. Person of learning. Wise person.
Pitrs / Pitris / Pitaras	Heavenly sages from whom the human race has evolved. Manes of the forefathers of mankind or of an individual. Deceased ancestors or forefathers.
Pootikaa (Poothikaa)	A species of culinary plant. A variety of spinach.
Praaya	Sitting down (without food) and calmly waiting the approach of death.
Pravrajyaa	Wandering asceticism. Migration away from home.
Purushakaara	Humanly effort. Use of one's own abilities without depending on destiny or divine help.
Raajadharma	Duties of an ideal king or ruler. Name of a section in the *Mahabharata's* 12th book (*Shaanti-parva*).
Rajasooya (Raajasooya) Yajna	Important vedic sacrifice performed by great monarchs to establish supremacy or suzerainty over other kings.
Rajasvalaa	A menstruating woman.
Raakshasa (Rakshasa)	A supposedly malignant demon or fiend, who is an enemy of the gods. One of a non-Aryan anthropophagus (cannibal) race of ancient India.
Ranchhod-ji	A vernacular sobriquet of Krshna, alluding to his leading the great escape of the Yadavas from Mathura in the face of the mighty attacks by Jarasandha's army. It actually was a brilliant strategic retreat to far-away Dvaraka to avert bloodshed and conserve strength, so as to fight another day.

Rudra (Shiva)	The destroying and reproducing deity, who constitutes the third god of the Hindu *Trimoorti* or triad, the other two being Brahma 'the creator' and Vishnu 'the preserver'. In the Veda, the only name of 'the destroyer' deity was Rudra, 'the terrible god', but in later times it became usual to give that deity the name Shiva, 'the auspicious', and to assign him the role of reproduction as well as dissolution.
Saamkhya (Samkhya)	One of the principal divisions of vedic philosophy, which is ascribed to the sage Kapila. It is an enumerationist philosophy (reckoning 25 *tattvas* or true entities) that regards the universe as comprised of two realities, *Purusha* (consciousness) and *Prakrti* (phenomenal realm), the former being bonded to the latter through desire. The end of this bondage is *moksha* or liberation, which is held to be the ultimate goal.
Saattvika	Relating to purity and goodness. One driven by the quality of *sattva-guna*, the purest of the three modes of mind (*sattva, rajas, and tamas*).
Samyama (Sanyama)	Self-restraint. Control over organs (senses).
Sannyaasi	Ascetic. Mendicant. Renouncer of worldly attachments.
Sarvabhoota	All created beings.
Shaanta rasa	The sentiment of quietism or tranquillity, or mood of detachment (rhetoric).
Shaka	An era (calendar), beginning AD 78, introduced by King Shalivahana. The Scythian race.
Shakti	Power. Name of a celestial missile of great destructive strength.
Sharanaagata	A seeker of shelter or refuge.
Shloka	A couplet or verse.
Shoodra	The fourth of the four *varnas* (classes).

Shrotriya	A *Brahmana* versed in the Vedas.
Siddha	A semi-divine entity who has achieved that holy status through austere religious practice.
Soma	The sacred vedic sacrificial wine (*soma-rasa*) produced from a special herb (*soma-lataa*). Also, the name of the lunar deity.
Soota	A charioteer, master of the horse, and attendant on a king. Also, a royal herald or bard whose job was to narrate (from practised memory), the heroic ballads of the king and his ancestors while he drove his chariot to battle, or on state occasions. He was usually of mixed birth, with parents hailing from different classes.
Sudarshana cakra	The formidable circular weapon (disc) wielded by Vishnu and Krshna to destroy sinners.
Suraa	Common spirits or liquor. A kind of ancient beer.
Surya (Soorya)	The sun, or its most concrete deity, as named in the *Veda*. Also regarded as one of the original vedic triad, his place being in the sky, while that of Agni is on the earth, and that of Indra is in the atmosphere.
Svabhaava	One's own nature.
Svabhaava dharma	Inclinations dictated by one's own nature.
Svayamvara	Ancient practice of a daughter choosing (by garlanding) her own bridegroom herself, usually from among a number of invited suitors.
Tapasyaa	Austere religious practice.
Toobaraka	A beardless man.
Vaishnavaastra	Weapon (missile) empowered by Vishnu.
Vaanara	Monkey. Ape.
Vana-vaasa	Living in a forest. Exile to the forest.
Vara	Boon. Gift. Reward. Blessing.

Varna	Colour. Class of men, tribe, or order, probably from contrast of colour between the dark aboriginal tribes and their fairer conquerors. Applied in the Rig-veda to indicate the difference between the Aryas and the Dasas. But more commonly applicable in the context of the four principal classes described in Manu's code, viz., Brahmanas, Kshatriyas, Vaishyas, and Shoodras.
Vedanta (Vedaanta)	Comprises the *Upanishads*, which are regarded as the culmination (end) of the *Vedas*. It is one of the great divisions of ancient Indian philosophy. Its chief doctrine (as expounded by Shankarachaarya) is that of *Advaita*, or non-dual *Brahman*, viz., that nothing really exists but the One Self or Soul of the universe, called the *Brahman* or the *Paramaatman* (Absolute Entity); that the *Jeevaatman* or the individual human soul, and all other phenomena of nature are really identical with this supreme Entity; and that their perceived existence is only the result of *ajnaana* or ignorance. The liberation of the *Jeevaatman*, its deliverance from transmigrations, and its reunion with the *Paramaatman*, is only to be effected by removal of that ignorance through a proper understanding of the *Vedanta*.
Vishaalabuddhi	One of vast intellect. An honorific of Vyasa.
Vishnu	One of the principal Hindu deities. Although he comes second in the triad as 'the preserver', he is identified with the supreme deity by his worshippers. In the vedic period, however, he was not the foremost god, although he was frequently invoked with other gods, especially with Indra (whom he assists in killing the demon Vrtra, and with whom he drinks the *Soma* juice). In the *Mahabharata* and the *Ramayana* he rises to the supreme status, which in some places he now enjoys as the most popular deity of modern Hindu pantheon.

Vrshni	Name of a Yadava tribe, often mentioned together with the Andhakas.
Yajna	Vedic sacrificial rite.
Yaksha	A class of semi-divine beings, who are attendants of Kubera, the god of wealth. A spirit or ghost appointed to guard a treasure hidden underground.
Yaksha-prashna	Name of an important episode/ chapter near the end of the *Mahabharata*'s third book (*Vana-parva*), containing a curious series of questions made by the god Dharma disguised as a *baka-yaksha* (first as a crane, then as a *yaksha*), and Yudhishthira's brilliant answers to those.
Yavana	An Ionian Greek. In later times, also any foreigner or barbarian.
Yoga (Yoga-shaastra)	Another main division of classical Indian philosophy. The *Yoga* philosophy, as taught by Patanjali, involves rigorous practice of concentration of thoughts and abstract meditation. Its chief aim is to teach the means by which the human spirit may attain complete union (*yoga*) with *Eeshvara* or the Supreme Spirit.

SUPPLEMENTARY NOTES

THE *MAHABHARATA'S PARVAS*

The *Mahabharata* consists of 18 divisions, each being called a *parva* or *parvan*. Each *parva* again contains smaller divisions, which are also called *parva*s or sub-*parva*s. The book numbers and titles of the 18 main *parvas*, and their contents, are summarised below.

Book	Title	Contents in brief
1	*Aadi-Parva* Book of the Beginning	First narrations of the *Mahabharata*. Creation of the world. Stories of gods, demigods, demons, snakes, etc. Genealogy of the Bharata dynasty, and legends of the more famous kings. Finally, the birth and early life of the Kuru princes, and the rivalry between the cousins, the Kauravas (sons of Dhrtarashtra) and the Pandavas (sons of Pandu).
2	*Sabhaa-Parva* Book of the Assembly Hall	Creation of the Pandavas' magical palace and court by the demon architect Maya. Yudhishthira's glorious *Raajasooya* sacrifice. The jealous Kauravas' inveigling of Yudhishthira to an unfair game of dice, and the eventual exile of the Pandavas.
3	*Vana-Parva / Aranya-Parva* Book of the Forest	The 12 years of exile in the forest. Contains many stories of ancient kings and queens, such as Nala-Damayanti, Rama-Sita, Savitri-Satyavan and many others. It also carries many discourses of wise seers, descriptions of the Pandavas' pilgrimage and of Arjuna's travels, as also the curious episode of Yudhishthira's cerebral replies to the questions put by the god Dharma, in his guise as a crane-guard. This is the second longest book of the *Mahabharata*.

4	*Viraata-parva* Book of Viraata	The year of living incognito in the court of King Viraata. The hardships of Draupadi and the killing of Keecaka, her tormentor. The cattle raid by the Kauravas and their defeat at the hands of Arjuna, still in his guise as a eunuch.
5	*Udyoga-parva* Book of the Effort	Preparations for war; diplomatic efforts to bring peace eventually fail.
6	*Bheeshma-parva* Book of Bheeshma	The first of the five Books on the great battle, with the patriarch Bheeshma as the Kaurava general. Includes the *Bhagavad-Gita*. Ends with the fall of Bheeshma on a bed of arrows.
7	*Drona-parva* Book of Drona	Drona, the Brahmin preceptor of warfare, takes up leadership of the Kaurava army. The battle becomes more intense, with a significant decline from Bheeshma's standards of war ethics. Most of the great warriors are killed by the end of the Book, including Drona himself being killed in a foul manner.
8	*Karna-parva* Book of Karna	Karna becomes the Commander and puts up a heroic fight against all odds. His efforts are undone by destiny, aided by Krshna's adroit strategy. He is killed by Arjuna in questionable manner.
9	*Shalya-parva* Book of Shalya	The last day of the field battle, with Shalya as Commander, who is killed in a day. Facing defeat, Duryodhana goes into hiding, but comes out when challenged by the Pandavas. Bheema kills him by smashing his thighs in violation of the rules of fighting with mace. Krshna pacifies Balarama, who is irate at the infringement of battle norms.

10	*Sauptika-parva* Book of the Sleeping Warriors	In a nocturnal mission of gory revenge, Drona's son Ashvatthama, along with Krpa and Krtavarma, kill the sleeping warriors in the Pandava camp. Only seven survive on the Pandava side and three on the Kaurava. Ashvatthama is pursued, disgraced and cursed.
11	*Stree-parva* Book of the Women	Gandhari, Kunti, and widows of the fallen heroes on both sides, lament the dead.
12	*Shaanti-parva* Book of Peace	The longest book of the *Mahabharata*. Yudhishthira, now crowned king of Hastinapura, is weighed down by the burden of fratricidal grief. Peace comes through the instructions he receives from Bheeshma, about society, economics and politics, the duties and principles of royalty, and ultimate emancipation.
13	*Anushaasana-parva* Book of Instructions	Before his self-chosen hour of death, Bheeshma gives Yudhishthira final instructions on his role as ruler.
14	*Aashvamedhika-Parva* Book of the Horse Sacrifice	On Arjuna's request, Krshna retells the *Anu-Gita*. Birth of Pareekshit. Arjuna's conquests pave the way for Yudhishthira to perform the Horse Sacrifice. Dharma visits Yudhishthira as a weirdly enigmatic mongoose with a special message.
15	*Aashramavaasika-Parva* Book of the Hermitage	Dhrtarashtra retires to the forest, along with Gandhari, Kunti, and Vidura. Vidura casts aside his mortal self, passing on to Yudhishthira the essence of his inner strength. Dhrtarashtra, Gandhari and Kunti die in a forest fire.

16	*Maushala-Parva* Book of the Iron Bolts	The curse on the Yadavas, their drunken infighting and eventual destruction. The passing away of Balarama, and the advent of *Kali-yuga* with the passing of Krshna. Rescue of survivors by a dejected Arjuna.
17	*Mahaaprasthaanika-Parva* Book of the Great Departure	The great journey of Yudhishthira, with his four brothers and Drau-padi, across India, and their ascent of the Himalayas, where all except Yudhishthira fall to their deaths.
18	*Svargaarohana-Parva* Book of Ascent to Heaven	Yudhishthira's final test and his bodily entry to heaven.

THE CONCEPT OF 'RIGHTEOUS WAR'

The *Mahabharata* offers one of the earliest expositions in organised human thoughts on the concept of 'righteous' or 'just' war, laying down many standards that would engage the world's attention in the ages to follow. The early Greeks and Romans did occasionally discuss war ethics, but neither behaved in any exemplary fashion in the actual business of war. Cicero, for example, contended that war could not be justified other than in self-defence, redemption of honour, or vengeance. His words, however, did not sway the Roman war machine, with its overweening urge for new conquests.

In the 4th century, St. Augustine pioneered the setting out of the Christian tradition on war ethics, which was later expanded and developed by St Thomas Aquinas and others. Augustine's thoughts carry echoes of what Krshna stood for. He held that war was always the result of sin, but that it could also remedy sin, in which case (only), it could be justified. There are always two strands in considering the criteria of a just war, *viz.*: (i) it should be waged for a just cause; and (ii) it should be conducted in a just manner. The latter issue again leads to its own questions of ethics: (i) whom it is ethical to fight, (ii) how much force it is ethical to use, and (iii) which weapons can or cannot be used?

The related issue of evolving rules and conventions of war has also for long been debated in the West. In 1815, the Congress of Vienna agreed that it was a crime to wage war in breach of a treaty. It made sense, but it was also the victors' judgement on the Napoleonic wars. In 1863, President Lincoln's promulgation of the Lieber Code (Instructions for the Armies of the United States in the Field), was in fact the first written code for the conduct of war, which became the precursor of the Hague Regulations of 1907, and ultimately, the Fourth Geneva Convention of 1949. Given its importance as the first official document on war ethics (notwithstanding its context of a civil war situation), it would be pertinent to cast a quick look at the provisions of the Lieber Code. It insisted on humane treatment of populations in occupied areas, expressly forbade killing of prisoners of war other than on exceptional grounds of a unit's survival, and forbade the use of poison and also of torture to extract confessions. It also detailed the rights and duties of both war prisoners and capturing forces.

The *Mahabharata*'s code of war compares quite favourably with modern Western codes. Some remarkable features of the agreement on battle ethics reached by the two sides on the eve of the war have already been discussed in the Introduction to this book. Again, in the twelfth book of the epic (*Shaanti-parva*, Chapter 98), we come across shining illustrations of the *Kshatriya* war ethics in the words with which Bheeshma answers Yudhishthira's question as to how warfare, even when waged between *Kshatriya*s, can be justified. The grand patriarch says that a peaceful settlement is always preferable to causing injury. But when inflicting injury becomes inevitable between worthy opponents, it must be moderated by certain norms. In the first place, there are the norms of *proportionality*: chariots should not attack cavalry, and one should not assail another in distress. Then, on the issue of *just means*: there should be no use of poisoned or barbed arrows. The third guideline is on *just attitude*: one should not be enraged toward an enemy who is not trying to kill him. The last set of norms, perhaps the most humane of all, is regarding *just treatment*: a wounded opponent should not be attacked, nor one whose sword is broken, or whose bow-string is cut, nor one whose horse or vehicle is destroyed. Among captives, the wounded should be given medical treatment or sent to their own homes; and the ones not wounded should be released.

BHAHMAASTRA AND BRAHMASHIRA WEAPONS

These are the two deadliest weapons described in ancient Indian epic-puranic mythology. Both were created by Brahma, for the purpose of upholding *dharma*, and were not meant to be used on ordinary men. According to ancient records, the *Brahmaastra* never missed its mark and had to be specifically invoked and released to annihilate an individual enemy or army. The weapon was believed to cause severe environmental damage, with some of the descriptions eerily matching the hazards of modern nuclear warfare. The land where it was used became barren and did not support life; both women and men became infertile. There was also severe drop in rainfall with the land developing cracks, as in a drought.

There are several instances of the use of the *Brahmaastra* in the *Ramayana* and the *Mahabharata*, but more in the former. Vishvamitra, in the *Ramayana's Aadi-kaanda*, used it against Vashishta, but the weapon was swallowed by *Brahmadanda*, the great saints' counter-measure against the *Brahmaastra*. In the final battle of the *Ramayana*, Rama killed the otherwise invincible and grossly errant Ravana with his *Brahmaastra*. But before that, the righteous Rama prevented brother Lakshmana from using the weapon against Ravana's redoubtable son, the heroic Indrajit, with the advice that its use was not justified, nor would it benefit mankind. In the *Mahabharata*, Karna planned to use the *Brahmaastra* against Arjuna, but was unable to invoke it because of Parashurama's curse.

But *Brahmashira* was the ultimate weapon, and it finds mention only in the *Mahabharata*. It had, corresponding to the four heads (*shira*) of Brahma, a destructive force equal to the exponential product of the *Brahmaastra's* force raised to the power four (as a modern analogy, one could say that if the *Brahmaastra* were a nuclear fission bomb, the *Brahmashira* would be of the thermonuclear category). Only Arjuna and Ashvatthama possessed the knowledge to summon it. Arjuna was given a variant of the *Brahmashira* by Shiva, called the *Pashupataastra*. In that episode of the *Vana-parva*, Arjuna solicited a pleased Shiva for the weapon with these words:

Bhagavan dadaasi cenmahyam kaamam preetyaa vrshadhvaja /
Kaamaye divyam-astram tad ghoram paashupatam prabho //
Yat tad brahmashiro naama raudram bheema-paraakramam /
Yugaante daarune praapte krtsnam samharate jagat //
~ Vana; 34.8-9

O Lord Vrshadhvaja (Shiva), if you are pleased enough to grant me a boon, then I would like to be blessed with the awesome and divine *Paashupata* weapon. The weapon called *Brahmashira*, which is owned only by you, which has severe power and which can destroy the entire world at the time of aeon-ending cataclysm.

Shiva conferred the boon, but cautioned Arjuna about the use of the weapon in these words:

Na tve-tat sahasaa paartha moktyabyam purushe kvacit /
Jagad vinirdahed-etat-alpatejasi paatitam //
~ Vana; 34.17)

Paartha (Arjuna), you should never throw this weapon suddenly at any person. Because, if thrown against a weak adversary, it will incinerate the world.

In addition, Dronacarya also conferred on the deserving Arjuna the secret of the *Brahmashira*, including the instructions for both its delivery and withdrawal. Also, Drona could not refuse the knowledge to his own son, Ashvatthama, but knowing his son's propensity to deviate from *dharma*, warned him against its use:

Param-aapad-gatenaapi na sma taata tvayaa rane /
Idam-astram prayoktavyam maanusheshu visheshatah //
~ Sauptika; 12.8)

My son, even if you find yourself in grave danger, never use this weapon in battle, especially against any human beings.

There was, however, a vital difference between the capabilities of the two *Mahabharata* stalwarts in the matter of using the *Brahmashira*. Arjuna, with his virtuous nature and his self-cleansing practices as a vow-abiding *Brahmacaari*, had the requisite inner power to retract the weapon, while Ashvatthama, with his relatively impure nature and conduct, could not. Ashvatthama's use of the weapon was actually an act of desperation. When, after Ashvatthama's midnight massacre of Draupadi's sons in the *Sauptika-parva*, he was pursued by a vengeful Bheema, accompanied by Yudhishthira and Arjuna, Drona's son took fright and invoked the *Brahmashira*. He did not have even his bow and arrows with him. So, he took a piece of straw, and incanting the invocatory *mantra* for destruction of the Pandavas, threw the straw, now invested with the scorching power of the *Brahmashira*, at his pursuers.

With no other counter-measure in sight, Krshna urged Arjuna to use his ultimate weapon in the manner instructed by Drona as a last resort in self-defence. Arjuna, bowing to the gods and elders, and thinking of the Pandavas and Ashvatthama's safety, and the world's welfare, released the celestial missile with the command that it should neutralise the weapon released by his enemy. The two deadly missiles turned into flaming masses of fire, causing fearsome effects on the environment:
Nirghaataa vahavash-caasan petur-ulkaah sahasrashah /
Mahad bhayanca bhootaanaam sarveshaam samajaayata //
Sashabdam-abhavad vyoma jwaalaamaalaa-kulam bhrsham /
Cacaala ca mahee krtsnaa saparvata-vana-drumaa //
~ Sauptika; 14.9-10
Then, there were horrendous roars like incessant thunders; thousands of meteors started falling from the sky, and all living beings cringed in tremendous fear. The whole atmosphere became engulfed in awesome flames of fire and terrible sound issued from there. Mountains, forests, trees, and the whole earth began shaking with tremors.

Indeed, collision of the two *Brahmashiras* would have destroyed the universe. But sages Narada and Vyasa, benefactors of all beings, with their transcendental powers, stood between the two fireballs. Arjuna then called back his *Brahmashira*. But Aswathama could not. It had to hit a Pandava as its infallible target; so Ashvatthama commanded his weapon to attack the foetus (unborn Parikshit, Arjuna's grandchild), in Uttaraa's womb. The child, the sole heir of the Kurus, was however, restored to life by Krshna, who also cursed Ashvatthama to a blighted and lonely existence.

Such then was the power of the *Brahmaastra*s. Interestingly, the vivid descriptions of their power and effect invite interpretations from modern pseudo-scientific perspectives. The accounts of quaking earth and hills are almost at par with the modern experience of atomic bomb blasts. The encounter in space of the two *Brahmashiras* is eerily reminiscent of today's reality of anti-missile warfare and the strategy of 'Mutually Assured Destruction'. But perhaps the most intriguing part is the seeming parallelism in effects. Apparently, the *Brahmashira* could kill a foetus in the womb without killing the mother herself. This seems uncannily similar to the only modern weapon that can do the same, *viz.* a nuclear weapon, with its radiation effect. The other two effects – heat and blast – are also similar in the two cases. If not anything else, one can perhaps agree that the ancient chroniclers were blessed with either the power of prophetic clairvoyance or at least, of awesome imagination.

WESTERN INTERPRETATIONS OF THE *MAHABHARATA*
In Chapter 7 of this book, under the heading 'Legends Interpreted', we discussed the works of many Western orientalists, linguists and historians of the 19th and early 20th century, in the field of the historicity and evolution of the *Mahabharata*. Many of these analysts were not from English-speaking lands but hailed from countries like Germany, Denmark and the Netherlands, which had developed a rich tradition of oriental scholarship during the 19th century. Hence their works are in languages other than English, which constrains the scope of quoting primary references of English sources. In partial recompense for this gap in information, a brief write-up on some of these Western scholars is appended below

| **Franz Bopp**
1791-1867 | German linguist, who taught himself Sanskrit in Paris. Among his *Mahabharata* works are the edited Sanskrit texts of the slaying of Hidimba, the *Nalopaakhyaana*, the story of Savitri and of Arjuna's journey to heaven.

The English scholar Russell Martineau, who had studied under Bopp, paid him this tribute: 'Bopp's Sanskrit studies and Sanskrit publications are the solid foundations upon |

Franz Bopp
1791-1867

which his system of comparative grammar was erected, and without which that could not have been perfect. For that purpose, far more than a mere dictionary knowledge of Sanskrit was required. The resemblances which he detected between Sanskrit and the Western cognate tongues existed in the syntax, the combination of words in the sentence and the various devices which only actual reading of the literature could disclose, far more than in the mere vocabulary. As a comparative grammarian he was much more than as a Sanskrit scholar.'

Christian
Lassen
1800-1876

Norwegian-German orientalist. His *magnum opus*, *Indische Altertumskunde*, was published in four volumes, in 1847 (2nd edition, 1867), 1849 (2nd edition, 1874), 1858 and 1861 respectively. These works, the outcome of high scholarship and intense industry, constitute a great landmark in Indological studies, threading together a whole world of critical information, gathered from Indian and foreign sources, relating to the political, social and intellectual developments in ancient India.

As mentioned, Lassen's was the first systematic Western study of the Indian epics, and he pioneered the Western approach of analysing the historical development of the *Mahabharata* poem through three major recensions spread across pre-Buddhist and post-Buddhist periods. His 'three recension' theory also bears some concordance with the Indian tradition, recorded in the *Mahabharata* itself, of three ancient versions: *Jaya*, *Bharata*, and *Mahabharata*, representing short and long forms of the epic.

Adolf
Holtzmann Sr.
1810-1870

German professor and philologist. He (and later his nephew, Adolph), first studied the seeming 'inconsistencies' in the epic and suggested that many of these are ascribable to a reversal in the projection of righteousness or otherwise of the two warring sides in the battle of Kurukshetra, by contending forces of the denominational sects of Shaivism, Buddhism and Vaishnavism over the ages. This approach, which was later called the 'inversion theory' by EW Hopkins, suggested that the original story had Duryodhana and the Kauravas as the righteous side, and the subsequent glorification of Krshna and the Pandavas was the work of proponents of the 'new' divinity – Vishnu.

Albrecht Friedrich Weber 1825-1901

German scholar of literature and Sanskrit archaeology. In 1867 he became the senior professor of language and literature of ancient India at the University of Berlin. Author of many books and papers on classical subjects, he was a close friend of Max Muller. As mentioned in Chapter 7, Weber propounded two major concepts relating to the *Mahabharata's* history. One was a perceived parallelism between the Krshna and the Christ stories. The other was tracing the roots of the story to the literature of the Vedic period.

Sören Sörensen 1848-1902

Danish orientalist. He wrote in Danish. But his doctoral thesis on the place of the *Mahabharata* in Indian literature, incorporated in *An Index to the Names in the Mahabharata and a Concordance to the Bombay and Calcutta Editions and PC Roy's translation*, Williams & Norgate, London, 1904-1925; reprinted by Motilal Banarsidass, Delhi, 1963, is a valuable source for scholastic reference.

Sörensen's working hypothesis of the Mahabharata's original form as a warrior story by one author and its subsequent enlargement by grafting of other sections found support from Western scholars, but his drastic pruning of the epic to just 8000 stanzas has been a matter of debate.

FE Pargiter 1852-1927

British scholar and member of the Indian Civil Service. He became the Vice President of the Asiatic Society, London. His book, *Ancient Indian Historical Tradition*, London 1922, Reprint

Motilal Banarsidass, 1997, is an important document, especially for its effort in tracing the history of ancient genealogies, which, however, has been questioned by some as ignoring traditional records and applying an arithmetic thumbrule in assuming lengths of generations/reigns. In particular, some of its sweeping conclusions, such as discounting all historicity in Vedic records and suggesting that the *Puranas* were originally in Prakrit (local) language, have been controversial, to say the least. There have also been suggestions that he held a colonialist brief of belittling Vedic and post-Vedic Sanskrit scholarship, but that may not be wholly fair to his substantial contribution in the field of Indology.

Hermann Oldenberg 1854-1920

German scholar of Indology, and professor at Kiel (1898) and Gottingen (1908). His 1881 study of Buddhism, based on Pali texts, is an important resource for scholars. With TW Rhys Davids he edited and translated into English *Thervada Vinaya* texts, *Grhya sutra*s (*Grhya-sootra*s) and Vedic hymns, in the monumental 'Sacred Books of the East' series edited by Max Muller. As mentioned, Oldenberg's posthumously published (1922) work on the Vedic origin of the *Mahabharata*, the importance of Pareekshit and Janamejaya in Vedic history, and on evolving grammatical usages and rhetoric/prosodic styles in the epic, is an important contribution to its historical study.

EW Hopkins 1857-1932

Noted American Sanskrit scholar. He became professor of Sanskrit and Comparative Philology in Yale University in 1895. He was also secretary of the American Oriental Society and editor of its journal. His output of books and papers on early Sanskrit literature was quite prolific. We have already made many references to his very important 1901 book on the *Mahabharata*, titled *The Great Epic of India*.

Gerrit Jan Held
1906-1955

Dutch anthropologist and Indologist. His book, *The Mahabharata: an ethnological study*, Kegan Paul & Co., London/Amsterdam, 1935, has been the source of some valuable ethnological concepts mentioned at Chapter 7, especially the importance of tribal 'potlatch' (community feast) rituals and gambling tournaments in the socio-economic life of the period of the *Mahabharata*, and their impact on the epic story.

Acknowledgements

Newton, in a letter to Robert Hooke, famously observed: *If I have seen further, it is by standing on the shoulders of giants*. What was modesty for Newton is maxim for lesser mortals. Hence, in this ambitious mission of re-interpreting the Mahabharata, I have tried to drink deep from the 'Pierian spring' of India's and the World's wisdom.

In my eclectic search for interpretive insights, I am indebted to the works of many Indian stalwarts, particularly those of Rajshekhar Basu, Buddhadev Basu (Bose), and Irawati Karve, as also several Western authors, especially EW Hopkins and John Brockington. To the extent possible, I have cited copious references of all source materials along with the chapter end-notes. Any error or omission is entirely attributable to my inadvertence.

I must also acknowledge my debt to Bhagwan Govind Joshi; in the course of my myriad interactions with him, I came across nuggets of shining wisdom about India's classical past seen through the prism of modernity, with which I have tried to embellish the narrative. I have also gained from my fruitful interactions with my brother, Gautam Basu, in the matter of bringing out several inter-cultural comparisons relating to certain thematic and historical aspects of the *Mahabharata*.

I also owe a debt of gratitude to Chandralekha Maitra, Executive Director, Leadstart Publishing, for her several suggestions which have enriched the book in the best traditions of editorial value addition. It was, thanks to her gentle persuasion, that the crucially relevant chapter on Draupadi, as also the Introduction, Overview and Appendix on Names and Places, was added. I further convey my thanks to Suchita Vemuri, for her meticulous editing.

Finally, I must acknowledge the value of all the sustained moral support of my nearest ones, to whom this work is dedicated, in enabling me to pursue my work, at times in blissful freedom from other daily chores.

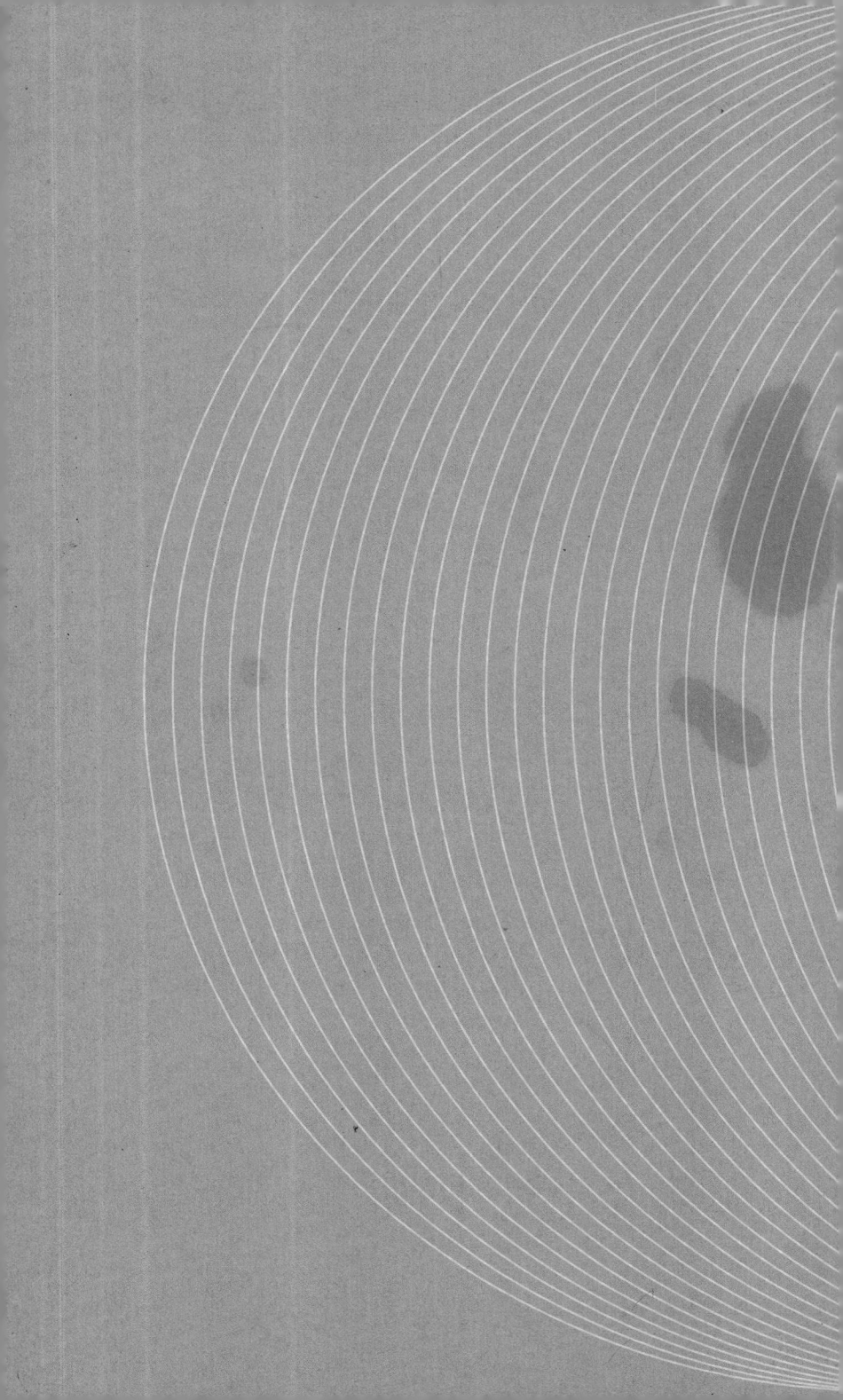